STIEGEL GLASS

BY

FREDERICK WILLIAM HUNTER, A.M.

INTRODUCTION AND NOTES BY HELEN MCKEARIN
WITH ONE HUNDRED AND SIXTY-NINE ILLUSTRATIONS
INCLUDING SIXTEEN IN COLOR

DOVER PUBLICATIONS, INC.
NEW YORK

Published in Canada by General Publishing Company, Ltd., 30 Lesmill Road, Don Mills, Toronto, Ontario.
Published in the United Kingdom by Constable and Company, Ltd., 10 Orange Street, London WC 2.

This Dover edition, first published in 1950, is an unabridged and corrected republication of the work originally published by Houghton Mifflin Company in 1914. This edition also contains the following new material by Helen McKearin: Introduction and Notes (at ends of chapters).

International Standard Book Number: 0-486-20128-7
Library of Congress Catalog Card Number: 67-4311

Manufactured in the United States of America
Dover Publications, Inc.
180 Varick Street
New York, N. Y. 10014

THIS BOOK
WHICH COULD NOT HAVE EXISTED
IN ITS PRESENT FORM WITHOUT HIS ASSISTANCE
IS DEDICATED TO MY BROTHER-IN-LAW
J. B. KERFOOT

INTRODUCTION

COLLECTING, as instinctive with man as with the magpie, is often practiced by veritable human magpies but more frequently it has orderly direction, and above all, demands communication between those it fascinates. Its ecstatic heights can be realized only by communion in the spoken or printed word. The published lore amasses as collectors in the field multiply, for the things man finds collectable inevitably inspire their own literature.

As the 19th century turned into the 20th a monk's cell could have held the group concerned with American glass; today not even Madison Square Garden or the Rose Bowl could hold it. The American Hobby Federation estimates there are 250,000 collectors of our old and modern glasswares. The small group in 1900 could have discussed only one book devoted to American glass. It was Edwin Atlee Barber's just published *American Glass Wares Old and New*—the new being glass with "modern political designs" (1896), recent Libby cut glass, and Tiffany Favrille; the old, mainly bottles and flasks. For many years this little volume of one hundred eleven short pages has itself been a collector's item, not an important reference book: it contains nothing which is not amended or amplified in later writings. This cannot be said of *Stiegel Glass,* the second book devoted to American glass: it contains material not easily found elsewhere and nowhere in so usable a form: for instance, the descriptive lists of engraved and enameled wares and the data on Manheim glass and workers. *Stiegel Glass* was limited to four hundred twenty copies, their publication costs, I have been told, paid by the author because, in 1914, its launching seemed too great a financial risk for any publisher. Today there is a many-branched glass literature, all but a fraction written since 1920. Many of the books and magazine articles on all kinds of American glass depended on material mainly from secondary sources but many resulted, as did *Stiegel Glass,* from patient delving, chiefly in documentary and other primary sources, and from studies of the glass itself.

For a few years *Stiegel Glass* was the Bible of the few collectors of American glass, especially those concentrating on free-blown glass and pieces molded either for form and pattern or for pattern only. Bottles such as Barber listed were in a class, a rather lower class, apart. Pressed glass, just catching collector's eyes, was comfortably assigned to a place called Sandwich. Fine cut and engraved glass was, as a matter of course, foreign. "Wistarberg" and "Stiegel" covered the remainder, for *Stiegel Glass* seemed to prove it so. For most collectors, it determined and labeled the supposed types made by the Wistars and by Stiegel; in fact, for years to come, it froze their conceptions of typical American blown or molded glass as one or the other. By report and extension of application its influence spread far beyond the limited circle of readers. The significance of its very faint hints of other and later glassmakers usually met unseeing eyes and deaf ears.

However, before many years, Mr. Hunter's prediction that "after being all but forgotten for a century" Stiegel's glassworks would "put antiquarians at loggerheads and set collectors by the ears" was fulfilled, but not perhaps exactly as he anticipated. It was mainly his own conclusions and attributions which, provoking disagreement with him, became criticism's target. The perfect faith of some insatiably curious and inquiring collectors cracked as their own studies uncovered evidence invalidating the Stiegel-Wistarberg coverage. They did not doubt that household articles of most types described by Mr. Hunter were made at the Wistars'. But they did learn that the "Wistarberg" types not only were made in other New Jersey and in New York and New England glasshouses but that they were also fashioned from the glass used for bottles and windowpanes, *not* from flint or lead glass, not even at Wistarberg.

As studies of American and foreign glass expanded these collectors were convinced that, *although Mr. Hunter's methods were sound,* most of his categorical conclusions on distinguishing characteristics and infallible signs of origin were based on too small a body of glass; that, as John B. Kerfoot his companion-investigator later admitted, enthusiasm sometimes curbed logic before a refutation of a Stiegel or Wistarberg premise could be reached. The dissenters did not doubt that engraved and enameled wares like Figs. 113-138 and 145-157 were made at Manheim; such glass doubtless being more familiar would have been more tempting than any other to Pennsylvania-German hausfraus. But, while believing that continued comparative studies might eventually establish a standard guide, they found and still find engraved and enameled glasses too similar to permit unqualified attributions. Also, excepting a few patterns, such as those of the bottles, Figs. 105 and 108, having no known exact foreign prototypes, they found this true of the "Bristol" types. They learned, moreover, that certain features placed some pieces outside and beyond the Stiegel pale. For example, a galleried rim like that of the sugar bowl, Fig. 29, was a sure sign of the 19th century fabrication. The new lights on the subject led to the terms "Stiegel type" and "South Jersey type," so familiar today and in use among informed collectors even before 1925. When he comes to Part II: *Stiegel Glass* the reader should mentally add "type" to "Stiegel" and substitute "South Jersey type" for "Wistarberg." He will then find one of the clearest pictures of American glass in these categories.

As George S. McKearin, my father, was among the dissenters, I heard many debates in which passages of *Stiegel Glass* were relegated to an apocrypha. Consequently when I read the book it was with a prepared, even prejudiced, mind but also with more information about American glasshouses and glass than Mr. Hunter and Mr. Kerfoot had in 1913. Nevertheless, I believe it still fills a great need and also that in all American glass literature *Stiegel Glass* alone approaches belles-lettres. The writing is no frigger of a green apprentice: it is the work of a master craftsman with words. Its fiction quality of arresting attention companions a convincing sincerity. Its style is warm and vibrant, informal and intimate. Even the dry dusty fabrics of law and court records are shaken out and cut with style in an interesting fashion. And that appreciation of old documents and advertisements which led to the inclusion of the Lazarus Isaacs agreement because it has "a flavor of its own" resulted in one of the most engaging and valuable aspects of *Stiegel Glass*. Throughout the book one is aware of a nice blend of sound historical sense, understanding of human behavior, proper appreciation of tradition, and a deep respect for documentary data. The character and biographical sketch of Henry William Stiegel stands unequalled as a penetrating and sympathetic study of the man in his setting. Stiegel and his glass-making appear as realities in their social and historical context, not as isolated phenomena in a vacuum environment. And the drama of his life and times is present. Without ever descending to melodrama, Mr. Hunter accents the romance and flashing highlights of Stiegel's career. The colorfulness of the legends is preserved but only under the searchlight of documented facts.

In the glass section it is obvious that the intent was to follow the same research methods and objective consideration of the material available—advertisements, account books, and ledgers, fragments unearthed on the glasshouse sites, contemporary wares and locally owned pieces attributed to Stiegel. Earlier glassmaking ventures were surveyed and in few instances additional information about the houses has been discovered since that survey. Also, realizing the ultimate in appreciative enjoyment of glass is attained only in a full knowledge of its nature and fabrication, Mr. Hunter included a valuable, graphic chapter on glassmaking in general and descriptions of techniques used at Manheim, or at least in its period. But, when he judged pieces to be or not to be Stiegel, the emotional attachment of the collector to the things he collects took precedence over his lawyerlike detachment in weighing evidence. It is doubtful if Mr. Hunter, the lawyer, wary of the pitfalls of circumstantial evidence and family tradition, would have accepted one small blue fragment bearing a segment of some sort of panel as proof that Stiegel made paneled vases, like Fig. 85, and all their cousins too, but the fact looked to the collector's eye "as the eye like the look." Today these vases are believed to be 19th century New England forms and many of the other articles are known to be of Pittsburgh production. While we should be eternally thankful that his intuition was a "most effective spur to investigation," we can but wish he had allowed himself to ponder on the possible significance of "imitating" in his own statement that the Stiegel houses were "destined within a few years to be imitating the output of the chief centers of Europe," and of "equal" in Mr. Bartram's that the glass was "equal to any he saw from Great Britain." However it must be said in Mr. Hunter's defense that he did not have all the information about American and foreign glass of either the 18th or the 19th century uncovered by his followers.

The necessary warning against blind acceptance of all data on Stiegel and "Wistarberg" glass is not without parallel. I know of no book on American glass which is without error; for the literature in this field is still a young, growing body continually nourished by research and new findings which often overturn established beliefs. No one worker in the field can hope to garner all possible data or to avoid completely mistaken deductions. If it were not for students like Mr. Hunter, neither too selfish to share their information nor too vain to risk almost inevitable errors, knowledge of American glass would remain static. Mr. Hunter's preface and final paragraph on page 184 show that he was not afflicted with delusions of infallibility. If he had had the information which challenges many of his conclusions, he doubtless would have hastened to revise them. I hope he would have approved of the notes which I have added to his chapters on glass.

Stiegel Glass, in my opinion, remains a vital member of American glass literature, definitely a valuable source book to which writers, as they have since 1914, will always turn. In fact the serious student *must* read it for himself. He certainly cannot accept my critical opinion or that of anyone else without checking it against the original.

Helen McKearin
New York City, April 1950

PREFACE

URING the summer of 1911, while automobiling in Berks and Lancaster Counties, Pennyslvania, I repeatedly had offered to me for purchase unimpressive specimens of glassware, the would-be sellers always informing me (and always with something of the solemn manner of acolytes serving the altar) that they were authentic pieces of STIEGEL GLASS. But as it happened that I had for some years been a collector of Chinese glasswork of the Yung-Chêng and Ch'ien-lung periods, these rather crude-looking "sherry" glasses and plain undecorated and uncolored "flips" (many of them not even Stiegel as I now know) made not the slightest appeal to me.

But the occurrences did, as occurrences even more trifling will, bring up from the submerged depths of my memory certain childish recollections and thereby awakened in me a certain — although by no means a collector's — interest. It chanced that my family on both sides had been long associated with this section of Pennsylvania; my father's people having been ironmasters in Berks County and some of my mother's ancestors having been Lutheran clergymen in the same region. And I suddenly saw myself, a small boy in dresses, standing open-mouthed at my grandfather's knee while he told me the story of the eccentric nobleman and romantic figure who, in the old days, rode post behind eight white horses across central Pennsylvania, with horns blowing and bands playing and cannon booming; and who had made — but the glass which he made interested me little in comparison with the white horses and the cannon. And later on, when it fell to my lot to move the accumulations of years from the house where I had spent a good share of my life, I still felt much of the same mind toward some pieces of old glassware (a plain blue cream pitcher and a tumbler enameled in colors among other pieces) which my mother had carefully packed away and which I recalled her having told me were Stiegel pieces, given to her mother by *her* mother-in-law whose parents were contemporaries of Stiegel's. I sent them, I know, to the auction rooms, together with much other discarded material, where they brought, if I remember rightly, twenty cents the lot. And as, in 1911, I examined and disdainfully rejected the pieces then offered me, I felt that I had not erred in my disposal of these family heirlooms.

Yet my grandfather's story, thus recalled to my memory, roused my curiosity; so that I took to making casual inquiries about "the Baron," as well as about the glass that he had made. And I soon found that as to the man himself, while there appeared to be a well-coördinated and generally followed body of tradition, it was almost impossible to find any solid bottom when one probed into the spongy material of these legends; and as to the identification of the glass, beyond an almost universally expressed conviction that any piece that rang when you struck it with a lead pencil was Stiegel, it appeared to be a well-established custom of the country that every player made his own rules.

And then, one day, I stumbled upon a piece of glass that changed my attitude instantly toward Stiegel and all his works. It was a toilet bottle some five and a quarter inches high; blown from a light amethyst glass of beautiful color; extremely individual and graceful in shape and lightly covered with an impressed, reticulated design which enhanced without obscuring the form of the piece. Moreover, the hand-blown bit had about it the unmistakable personality of handiwork done with love. And although the very moderate price asked for it then seemed exorbitant, I bought it; feeling in my bones, as the saying is, that it was of Stiegel make and being glad to own it even if it proved not to be. And from that moment there was born in me a desire which soon ripened into a decision. I was going to do what lay in my power toward clearing up this double haziness — the haziness of history as regarded the man and the haziness of identification as regarded the glass of his making.

The pursuit has proved an engrossing one. And it has constantly been productive of those alternate extremes of discouragement and elation — doubtless familiar to all explorers — due to seeing the most promising leads come suddenly to nought; and of stumbling, at the end of apparently hopeless quests, upon treasure trove of unhoped-for richness. In the course of it I have met with much kindness; and while, wherever possible, I have acknowledged this in appropriate places, I wish here to bear grateful witness to the fact and to thank all of my actual or would-be helpers whom I have not elsewhere mentioned.

What I found and what I failed to find are both set forth in the following pages. I have by no means succeeded in banishing haziness from either branch of my subject. Yet I trust that I have at least laid down a foundation of certainty upon which those who follow me may build.

CONTENTS

PART I. HENRY WILLIAM STIEGEL

PART II. STIEGEL GLASS

ILLUSTRATIONS

1. Green Glass Bottle. $11\frac{3}{4}''$ ($\frac{1}{4}$ size).
2. Olive Glass Bottle. $14''$ ($\frac{1}{4}$ size).
3. Nile Green Glass Bottle. $10\frac{1}{2}''$ ($\frac{1}{4}$ size).
4. Dark Red-brown Glass Bottle. $11''$ ($\frac{1}{4}$ size).
5. Light Green Glass Bottle. $7\frac{3}{4}''$ ($\frac{1}{3}$ size).
6. Light Green Glass Bottle. $8\frac{3}{4}''$ ($\frac{1}{3}$ size).
7. Green Glass Jug Stand. $1\frac{5}{8}''$ ($\frac{1}{2}$ size).
8. Green Glass Jug Stand. $2''$ ($\frac{1}{2}$ size).
9. Light Green Glass Mustard Jar. $2\frac{1}{2}''$ ($\frac{1}{2}$ size).
10. Light Green Glass Mug. $6\frac{7}{8}''$ ($\frac{1}{2}$ size).
11. Light Green Glass Mug. $4\frac{5}{8}''$ ($\frac{1}{2}$ size).
12. Light Green Glass Chemical Vessel. $7\frac{3}{4}''$ ($\frac{1}{2}$ size).
13. Light Green Glass Bowl. $3''$ ($\frac{1}{2}$ size).
14. Light Green Glass Molasses Jug. $7''$ ($\frac{1}{2}$ size).
15. White Glass Sweetmeat Jar. $7''$ ($\frac{1}{2}$ size).
16. White Glass Pocket Bottle. $6\frac{1}{2}''$ ($\frac{1}{2}$ size).
17. White Flint Measure Glass. $5\frac{3}{4}''$ ($\frac{1}{2}$ size).
18. White Flint Flip with Flaring Foot. $5\frac{3}{8}''$($\frac{1}{2}$ size).
19. White Flint Carafe. $7\frac{3}{4}''$ ($\frac{1}{2}$ size).
20. White Flint Funnel. $4''$ ($\frac{1}{2}$ size).
21. White Flint Child's Decanter. $3''$ ($\frac{1}{2}$ size).
22. White Flint Toy Cow. $8\frac{1}{2}''$ ($\frac{1}{2}$ size).
23. White Flint Lamp Reflector. $6\frac{1}{2}''$ ($\frac{1}{2}$ size).
24. Blue Flint Egg Glass. $3\frac{1}{2}''$ ($\frac{1}{2}$ size).
25. Blue Flint Mug. $5''$ ($\frac{1}{2}$ size).
26. Blue Flint Creamer. $4\frac{3}{4}''$ ($\frac{1}{2}$ size).
27. Blue Flint Sugar Bowl. $6''$ ($\frac{1}{2}$ size).
28. Blue Flint Sugar Bowl. $6\frac{1}{2}''$ ($\frac{1}{2}$ size).
29. Blue Flint Sugar Bowl. $6\frac{1}{2}''$ ($\frac{1}{2}$ size).
30. Blue Flint Vase. $8''$ ($\frac{1}{2}$ size).
31. Amethyst Flint Pocket Bottle. $7\frac{1}{4}''$ ($\frac{1}{2}$ size).
32. White Flint Wine Glass. $4''$ ($\frac{1}{2}$ size).
33. White Flint Wine Glass. $4''$ ($\frac{1}{2}$ size).
34. White Flint Wine Glass. $8''$ ($\frac{1}{2}$ size).
35. White Flint Wine Glass. $4\frac{1}{4}''$ ($\frac{1}{2}$ size).
36. White Flint Wine Glass. $6''$ ($\frac{1}{2}$ size).
37. White Flint Wine Glass. $4''$ ($\frac{1}{2}$ size).
38. White Flint Champagne Glass. $4''$ ($\frac{1}{2}$ size).
39. White Flint Sillabub Glass. $4''$ ($\frac{1}{2}$ size).
40. White Flint Measure. $3\frac{3}{4}''$ ($\frac{1}{2}$ size).
41. White Flint Wine Glass. $3\frac{3}{4}''$ ($\frac{1}{2}$ size).
42. White Flint Wine Glass. $4''$ ($\frac{1}{2}$ size).
43. White Flint Wine Glass. $3\frac{3}{4}''$ ($\frac{1}{2}$ size).
44. White Flint Cordial Glass. $3\frac{1}{4}''$ ($\frac{1}{2}$ size).
45. White Flint Straight Sided Glass. $6\frac{1}{2}''$ ($\frac{1}{2}$ size).
46. White Flint "Cotton Stem" Champagne Glass. $5''$ ($\frac{1}{2}$ size).
47. White Flint Champagne Glass. $4\frac{3}{4}''$ ($\frac{1}{2}$ size).
48. White Flint Champagne Glass. $5\frac{3}{4}''$ ($\frac{1}{2}$ size).

✱ COLOR PLATES FOLLOW PAGE 124

PART I
HENRY WILLIAM STIEGEL

STIEGEL GLASS

PART I: HENRY WILLIAM STIEGEL

CHAPTER I

STIEGEL'S START IN LIFE

HERO worship is sometimes magnificent, but it is never biography.

On the other hand, I once heard a poor-spirited pastor preach a funeral sermon for one of his flock from the text, "She hath done what she could." And this I take to be equally far removed from the proper spirit of the historian.

Yet it sometimes happens that circumstances force one, or the other, or even both, of these forms of presentation upon the memory of a dead man who, in his lifetime, deserved neither of them. And this is what has happened in the case of Henry William Stiegel. Nor, now that the time is ripe, is this difficult to explain.

Viewed from the early years of the twentieth century, Stiegel is instantly seen as making a living claim upon our interest and attention by reason of two contributions which he has made to the current consciousness of our time. One of these is the surviving glass of his manufacture, which, as we are just beginning to realize, deserves and is soon to have an honored place among the historic vestiges of our early national life. The other contribution is less tangible, but more potent. It is a legend — the glowing mirage of a picturesque personality.

But the cult for "Americana" is even yet in swaddling bands and was not only unborn, but undreamed of, in Stiegel's day.

And legends root in graves.

At the time of his death and in the eyes of those contemporaries who survived him, Stiegel was merely a discredited ironmaster who had had too many irons in the fire.

What he had actually accomplished toward the development of Pennsylvania had long been lost sight of in the fact that he had accomplished nothing for himself.

His glass was as little thought of as any other local product claiming as its proudest boast to be "as good as imported."

His legend was n't sprouted.

For nearly sixty years his very memory survived only as a pensioner in old wives' tales; and it was 1844 before a historian of Lancaster County embalmed the oral tradition of him in print like a fly in amber.

Time went on and other local historians retold the curious tale — adding, here a bit of flotsam folklore, there a bit of chance-found documentary evidence of fact. The seed, as seeds must, was germinating in the dark. And the glass, as glass will, was patiently biding its time in corner cupboards and farmhouse attics.

And then, in our own time, the legend suddenly came to blossom and the glass began to take on its antiquarian interest. And what more natural than that the sanguine, at this sight, should mistake Stiegel for a hero of romance by the simple error of crediting the unearned increment of the years to the account of the man himself; or that the conservative should try to restore the balance of the scales by voicing a dissent that sounded very like disparagement?

But the time has come to go a little deeper. And it is the object of the following sketch, in so far as that is now possible, to brush aside the haze of the years and discover what manner of personality it actually was that is thus glowingly reflected on the clouds of tradition.

Henry William Stiegel was born at Cologne, on the Rhine, on May 13th, 1729. His parents were John Frederick and Dorothea Elizabeth Stiegel, and he was the eldest of six children.

Nothing is really known of his antecedents. Indeed, the names of his parents, the number of his brothers and sisters, the true place of his birth and the correct date of that event and of his death were all either unknown or mistakenly given until the discovery a few years since of a family record kept on the blank leaves of a religious manual. Tradition, and every writer who dealt with Stiegel previous to 1911, had it that he had been born in Mannheim, in Germany; the Palatine city so ruthlessly razed by the French in 1689, and said, in consequence, to have been kept so tenderly in remembrance by her exiled sons. Considering Stiegel's proprietary connection with Manheim, Pennsylvania, and the absence of all authentic information, this assumption was sufficiently natural. But it is an excellent example, at once of the way in which traditions grow, and of the danger of accepting even their most plausible details too confidingly at their face value. In this case tradition was not content with the mere staging of Stiegel's birth at Mannheim. It shows him to us arriving in this country with the plans of that ill-fated city in his pocket, and assures us that he gave to the Lancaster County village of Manheim (in those days an "n" was easily lost in transportation) not only the name, but the outlines of his native town. Tradition — and the historians prior to 1911 — also had the date of his birth as 1730.

The Reverend Thompson P. Ege, in his "History and Genealogy of the Ege Family," published in 1911, was the first to give the correct facts. The joint authors of the excellent little article on "Baron Henry Wilhelm Stiegel," published in the "Souvenir Book of Manheim Old Home Week" (June 30th to July 5th, 1912), followed his lead. And Mr. A. S. Brendle in his paper on "Henry William Stiegel," read before the Lebanon County Historical Society on August 16th of the same year, also follows suit. None of these writers give their authority for the new information. But it was evidently the same as my own.

This is nothing less than the equivalent of the Stiegel family Bible. And I am indebted to the courtesy of Mr. Luther R. Kelker, of Steelton, Pennsylvania, Custodian of the Pennsylvania State Library at Harrisburg, for the opportunity to examine and the permission to describe this interesting relic. It is a tooled leather volume containing a German treatise on the elements of religion. It is divided, internally, into two parts; and between these there are several blank leaves, a new title-page, and so forth. The title-page and several pages of text are missing from the first part; but the title-page of the second part is intact and reads, "Das Under Buch Vom Wahren Christenthumb [The Elementary Book of True Christianity], by Johannem Armat, Frankfort-am-Mayn, 1664." On the front fly-leaf of the volume the name of Anthony Stiegel, the younger brother of the "Baron," is written; and on the blank pages at the front and back of the volume are entered the records of the births and deaths of Anthony's children by his two wives, Maria Elizabeth Glessner and Christina Neip, as well as later records in the Glessner-Neip-Stiegel-Aschey connection. And on two blank leaves between the first and second parts of the book the following entries are written in a faded German script that is so nearly illegible as to be difficult to make out even with the aid of a strong glass: —

John Frederick Stiegel died June 22nd 1741 aged 44 years 6 months and
   five days. His wife Dorothea Elizabeth died January 11th 1781 aged
   76 years and 8 months.
CHILDREN.
   Henry William Stiegel, born May 13th 1729 Cologne. Sponsor Henry
      Minnich et al. Died January 10th 1785.
   Catharine Elizabeth, born November 25th 1730. Died January 30th
      1733.
   Catharine Maria, born April 4th 1733. Died June 27th 1739.
   Matthew Frederick, born September 12th 1735. Died February 26th
      1736.
   Joanna Sophia, born December 10th 1736. Died June 6th 1741.
   Anthony, born September 2nd 1739. Died January 9th 1785.

Many of the later entries in this record are in the handwriting of Christina Neip Stiegel, Anthony's second wife, who lived in Schaefferstown, Lebanon County, Pennsylvania, and died in 1824. And there seems to be no question that, in the absence of any other evidence bearing upon these points, and in view of the nature and source of this record, it must be accepted as authoritative. The name of John Frederick Stiegel's wife is very hard to make out. "Dorothea Elizabeth" is the only thing that I could make of the entry; and it is evident that Dr. Ege and Mr. Brendle deciphered it in agreement with me. Moreover, the eldest child of Anthony Stiegel, born May 3rd, 1765 (and died November 26th, 1768), was named Dorothea Elizabeth, and Dorothea Elizabeth Stiegel was sponsor at the christening. No record has ever been found of this Dorothea Elizabeth's maiden name. But Mr. Brendle, in the paper already referred to, says that she was born in Enkirchen on the Moselle. He does not, however, give the

source of this information. His further statement that she
was born on May 11th, 1704, is evidently arrived at by sub-
tracting "76 years and 8 months" from the date of her death.

The discovery of this family document is, however, interesting for another reason than that it clears up the matter of
Stiegel's birthplace, his exact age, the names of his parents,
of his brothers and sisters, and the dates of their respective
deaths. An equal interest attaches to it because it practically
closes the discussion and casts the deciding vote in the mooted
matter of the validity of Stiegel's baronetcy.

No family historian with German blood in his or her veins
can possibly be conceived as omitting any official title from any
formal record. No scribe belonging to a race so appreciative
of distinctive tags; so punctilious in giving his due to each
holder of such designations at every occasion of written address; so scrupulous in gathering up the very fragments of
title — so that nothing be lost — that it sees no touch of the
grotesque in referring to "Frau Geheimraetin Professor Doctor
Schmidt," — no scribe reared in these traditions could conceivably write "John Frederick Stiegel" when "John Frederick
von Stiegel" was allowable.

It is high time, moreover, that this tempest in a biographic
teapot was stilled. It has raged in its Lilliputian way for something like three-quarters of a century. But the force has gone
out of it. The fly-leaves of "Das Under Buch Vom Wahren
Christenthumb," held out as a weather gauge, don't even flut-
ter in a remaining breeze. But as the question as to whether
Stiegel was or was not of noble blood has been given so prominent a place in all writings about him, it is advisable to go into
the matter with some thoroughness. And as this is as good a
place to do so as any other, we'll thrash the matter out now and
dispose of it.

And first let me put down, in all the impressiveness of their isolation, the only authenticable facts that a most exhaustive search has enabled me to adduce on the affirmative side of this debate: —

(1) Stiegel was habitually spoken of by the provincial population of his day as "Baron."

(2) He himself acquiesced in this designation by one overt act now provable. He had the following inscription cast on the front plate of some of the stoves made at Elizabeth Furnace:

"Baron Stiegel ist der Mann
Der die Oefen giessen kann."

Beyond these two facts everything that has ever been advanced to uphold the official character of his title resolves itself on examination into rumor, tradition, hearsay and inferences drawn from these. Tradition has it that he kept by him the accredited habiliments and full regalia of his rank, and that "whenever he went abroad" he always took this baronial costume with him. But Tradition, as we have already seen, has a lively imagination and a facile faith. It was only necessary for some Lancaster County Mennonite to clap eyes on the satin small-clothes and lace ruffles of the dinner costume that so luxury-loving a young blood would be sure to have brought back with him from abroad (where he does appear to have gone once during his American career) in order to set Rumor embroidering coronets on the sleeves of her report.

Again one of the best-informed of the writers on the subject of the Stiegel traditions, Dr. J. H. Sieling, writing in 1896, asserts that he signed the constitution of the Brickerville Church as "Henry William von Stiegel." But the Rev. F. J. F. Schantz, D.D., in an exhaustive and careful study of the "History of the Brickerville Congregation" read before the Lancaster

County Historical Society in 1898, shows that this constitution, which was adopted by the congregation after some internal dissensions and which dealt elaborately with the government of the congregation and with the rights and duties of its members, was signed on December 24th, 1769, at Warwick and that the signatures in their order were Daniel Kuhn, P.F.P., Heinrich Wm. Stiegel, Michael Huber, etc., etc.

Again, the venerable patriarch, Henry Melchior Muhlenberg, who was associated with Stiegel in the affairs of the Brickerville Church and was wont to stay the night with him at Elizabeth Furnace when he preached there, as well as his son Dr. Frederick A. C. Muhlenberg, who was for a time pastor of the congregation, while they frequently mention Stiegel in their letters, invariably refer to him either as "Mr. Stiegel" or as "Mr. Henry William Stiegel."

Governor Pennypacker, in an address to the Pennsylvania-German Society, is recorded as remarking that he knew "Two noblemen whose lineage was known for hundreds of years, Count Zinzendorf of Bethlehem and Baron Stiegel of Lancaster." In the case of Count Zinzendorf the orator happened to be on safe ground, but it is quite obvious that in the case of Stiegel and his centuries of known lineage he was, let us say, speaking with rhetorical license. There are numerous such statements as that of Governor Pennypacker, but while they are doubtless all made in as good faith as this, they are equally founded on nothing.

By the bye, Count Zinzendorf is found visiting Stiegel's father-in-law at Brickerville soon after Stiegel's marriage to Miss Huber, and it is within the bounds of possibility that the picturesqueness of his title may have been one of the factors that inclined Stiegel to accept, when it was conferred upon him, the rank of "Baron by acclamation."

C. E. Huch, in his study of Stiegel printed (in German) in 1907, states that the name is not found in the register of the German nobility. He adds that Stiegel's true name may have been Stengel, as there was a family of that name and of baronial rank living in the early eighteenth century at their ancestral home of Stengelhof, near Mannheim, in Baden. This fact, if accurately reported, might have been important and was certainly interesting so long as the Mannheim tradition survived. It is now become irrelevant.

The Rev. Thompson P. Ege, under the heading of "A Modern Coincidence," says that in a suburb of St. Petersburg there is one of the largest iron plants in the world called Stiegel and named after its founder and head, a German Baron Stiegel who, in 1911, was still alive. There are iron works and a man at the head of them that answer this description near St. Petersburg, but they belong to and are run by a Baron Stieglitz.

Stiegel, when he landed in Philadelphia, signed the declaration required of all German immigrants as "Heinrich Wil. Stiegel." He was naturalized sixteen years later as "Henry William Steigel." I have seen over fifty letters and documents signed by him and in no single case does the "von" or any equivalent of it appear.

It has been argued that there was a strong prejudice in democratic America at that time against any assumption of monarchical caste or distinctions, and that Stiegel, like other immigrants entitled to a title, simply dropped it in deference to popular prejudice and preference. The only trouble with the argument is that, instead of dropping a title at the popular behest, Stiegel seems to have assumed one at the instigation of the populace.

But there is not the slightest evidence that he assumed the title with any intent to deceive or to play the impostor. He

was doubtless given the title first by his naïve and admiring
Mennonite neighbors, who thought that so splendid a creature
deserved a title whether he had one or not. He was, as it were,
brevetted on the field for magnificence. He may have been
called "Baron Stiegel" as a boy at school will be called "Fatty
Tompkins." And this brevet, this nickname, not only stuck to
him, but flattered him. It expressed both his own quality and
his people's appreciation. He liked it, he answered to it, but he
never claimed it. On the face of the locally celebrated "Baron
Stiegel stoves" he placed with good-natured boastfulness the
statement that

> "Baron Stiegel is the cove
> That can cast your iron stove."

But he signed his correspondence, his deeds, his agreements,
and his state papers with the handleless name to which he was
born.

But it is not the whole duty of a biographer to satisfy his
own reason. In a matter of this kind it is incumbent upon the
investigator to exhaust the sources of evidence, and I have
therefore not only ransacked the records of heraldry, but had
searches made both in this country and abroad that covered not
only all the States of Germany, but Austria, England, France,
Holland and Russia. It is, of course, impossible to prove a
negative, but it at least makes an affirmative look peaked when
all the recognized authorities declare with one voice that no
Stiegel family ever existed in Europe with a claim to noble
blood.

I then tried to get some local information about the Stiegel
family by investigation at Cologne. Hoping to get a starting-
point for inquiry by finding the registered record of John
Frederick and Dorothea Elizabeth's marriage. I found, however, that the Cologne Archive marriage records only run back

some forty years, previous to which time each parish kept its own data. Mr. Louis Vandory, of Cologne, then undertook the search for me, and with the extremely courteous counsel of Professor Doctor Keussen, the director of the Cologne Archives, searched the records of all the Lutheran Churches of the early eighteenth-century city. This examination having failed to reveal any trace of the Stiegel family, Mr. Vandory extended his search to the cities near Cologne on the west bank of the Rhine. He reports that neither at Bonn, Remagen, Andernach, Godesberg, Weissenthurm, Coblenz, Boppard, St. Goar, Bingen or Mainz are there any records of a Stiegle or Stiegel family; nor is any such name known at the present time nor preserved by tradition.

"I then," Mr. Vandory writes me, "looked up a register of persons who had any kind of legal process before the Cologne Imperial Court, as it is evident that families of some wealth would have had in the course of so many hundreds of years some legal matter or controversies. I only found the name of a man of Nuremberg by the name of Hans de Stieger, who had a process here in 1597."

Again Mr. Vandory writes me that he has searched the registers of publications of several historical societies—Aachen, Wupper-valley, Lower Rhine, etc.—and found a few similar names like J. E. A. Stiegler, a merchant of Burtscheid, Franz Stickle, Henry and Andreas Sticker, Quirin Stieger, but no trace of any Stiegel family, and he adds, "As you state that the family might have been of noble origin, I have thoroughly read, page by page, the excellent work of A. Fahne on the 'History of Families of Cologne and in the Duchies Juelich and Berg.' I did not find anything about a Stiegel family, nor even about a family with nearly similar name."

There is, it seems to me, nothing more to be said.

Your true democrat dearly loves a lord; and for the better part of a century the democratic historians of this allegedly noble American pioneer have, as it were, stood round the death-bed of his supposed Baronetcy administering biographical oxygen to that moribund pretension. But the title has at last passed beyond the aid of therapeutics. Let us close its eyes kindlily, give it decent burial, and pass on to more vital matters. But first, as we fill the grave, let us speak a word of comfort; the Stiegel legend has, indeed, lost an earthly gaud, but it gains a spiritual asset. Henceforth it will have the picturesque distinction of being haunted by the ghost of a Baronetcy that never existed.

CHAPTER II

STIEGEL'S START IN AMERICA

IN Philadelphia in the middle of the eighteenth century such formalities of inspection and qualification as were imposed upon emigrants from abroad were usually gone through with at the Court-House, and all male persons above the age of sixteen were required to repeat the following declaration and then to subscribe their names thereto or — by no means an infrequent alternative in those days — to make their mark: —

"We subscribers, natives and late inhabitants of the Palatine upon the Rhine and places adjacent, having transported ourselves and families into this province of Pennsylvania, a colony subject to the Crown of Great Britain, in hopes and expectation of finding a retreat and peaceful settlement therein, do solemnly promise and engage that we will be faithful and bear true allegiance to His Present Majesty King George the Second and his successors, Kings of Great Britain and will be faithful to the proprietor of this province and that we will demean ourselves peaceably to all His said Majesty's subjects and strictly observe and conform to the laws of England and of this province to the utmost of our power and the best of our understanding."

On August 31st, 1750, there arrived at Philadelphia from Rotterdam, via the port of Cowes, Isle of Wight, the ship Nancy, Thomas Coatam, Master, which landed at Samuel McCall's wharf with two hundred and seventy immigrants on board. Stiegel, his widowed mother and his eleven-year-old brother Anthony were of this company and among the names of the male passengers over the age of sixteen signed to the required declaration above quoted, appears his signature; it reads: Heinrich Wil. Stiegel.

Tradition had it that this young immigrant, the supposed eldest son of a noble and wealthy house, had upon coming of age taken his share of the family fortune and, stopping for a time in England where he moved in the most select circles, had come to the land of opportunity and promise to carve out a career for himself with the snug sum of forty thousand pounds sterling (equal, say, to a million in our money at the present time) as a carving tool.

We shall presently see from evidence which, while circumstantial, is practically incontrovertible, that no such sum as this — no very great sum of any kind indeed — could have been in the possession of the Stiegels when they landed. We shall indeed see more than this, — namely, that no great sum of ready money, not borrowed, was ever in H. W. Stiegel's possession, then or later. And these two facts, once grasped and well established in our minds in contradistinction to the flamboyant claims of legend and tradition, explain a number of facts otherwise difficult to understand, and throw a steady, clear, illuminative light upon the man's career and upon the supposed contradictions of his character.

To begin with, it explains his coming to America.

The eldest sons of noble families, with forty thousand pounds sterling to their individual fortunes and with no black mark opposite their names on the police books, are very little given, in 1750 or any other time, to seeking opportunities for their talents and their ambitions in the back woods of the world. But that a young man just turned twenty-one, whose father had been dead nine years and of whose immediate family only his mother (a doubtless sturdy woman of forty-six) and one young brother remained alive, should elect to gather together his modest resources and, taking his family with him, should seek a chance for his doubtless very consciously possessed talents and abilities, as well as for the investment of his capital, in a new world — this is quite the most comprehensible thing on earth. And this, I make no doubt whatever, was actually the state of his affairs and the state of his mind when, on that August day in 1750, he signed, in the German manner, that so English declaration.

Where he had embarked we do not know. Whether or not he had "spent some time in England" we do not know either. The ship by which he came had come direct to Philadelphia from an English port and this may quite conceivably have lain at the root of the report that he had come from England. On the other hand, the glass-maker of later years was manifestly familiar with the English glass methods and there is nothing inherently improbable in his having stopped for a while in England on his way to settle in an English colony. Nor, for that matter, is it anything but what we would expect to find that such a stop (or even the report of such a stop) had been expanded into a period of "shining in the selectest social circles" by the same Jack-and-the-Bean-Stalk process of gossip-growing that turned his modest patrimony into a fortune and his courtesy title into an inherited one.

Indeed, at this period the ascertainable facts about young Stiegel are of the most meager. He comes, practically out of the unknown, to that Philadelphia wharf of Samuel McCall's. We see him for a moment, upstanding, doubtless fair-haired and blue-eyed, of a confident and resourceful bearing, setting foot on the land of his hopes and dreams. We see him, with those other new-comers destined to obscurer but often happier lives, repeating, and subscribing to, that declaration of good intentions in the Court-House, and then, for a period of two years, we see him no more.

This is by no means odd. If he had, in sober earnest, been

Baron Stiegel with forty thousand pounds in pocket, why then it would have been amazing. Even to-day, with its million and a half of population, Philadelphia does not allow real barons with their pockets full of investable cash to disappear from view with this instantaneous thoroughness. It was not, we may be sure, as unworldly as that even in its Quaker days. But that no record remains of the doings of a young stranger of excellent parts, but of, as yet, no performance, during the time when he was orienting himself in a new land and hunting for the opportunity he had come to seek, — this is only what we would expect.

There are numerous rumors, but they have even less weight than the ordinary "It is said's" of tradition, that he went to New York, and that he went as far west as the Alleghenies in his search for what he wanted. But as the strongest sort of emigrational tide was running at the time of his arrival and for those of his race, from the port of Philadelphia to the Counties of Berks and Lancaster (between 1736 and 1756 more than half of the original Scotch-Irish population of Lancaster County were bought out and replaced by German-Swiss immigrants); and as we lose sight of him in Philadelphia and find him again only two years later already enough at home in Lancaster County to be contracting an advantageous marriage with the daughter of one of the pioneer Ironmasters of the State, it seems to be fairly evident that with no very great delay he followed the procession of his countrymen to the region they had chosen to appropriate and make their own.

Albert Bernhardt Faust, in his "German Element in the United States" (Houghton Mifflin Co., 1909), says that he journeyed to Lancaster and from there drifted to Ephrata where Miller and Beissel received him kindly, and finding that he was interested in iron advised him to go to the neighborhood of Shuferstadtel where ore had been found. He adds that Stiegel, "accompanied by his faithful servant Jacob of Ettenheim," found the place and then returned to Philadelphia for more capital and laborers.

There can be no question of his having gone to Lancaster. And that so interested and intelligent a young investigator, so predisposed, moreover, to an interest in religious matters, should have visited the fifteen-mile distant town of Ephrata or Dunkertown, founded in 1733 by the German religious society of Seventh-Day Baptists, and should have visited and possibly been entertained at the monastic institution called the Cloister, started two years later, in 1735, by John Conrad Beissell, who was later joined by Peter Miller, a one-time pastor of the Reformed Congregation at Tulpehocken — all this is more than likely to have happened. And it may, indeed, have been upon the advice of these excellent men that he directed his steps toward Schaefferstown and so discovered, not, indeed, any virgin deposits of iron, but the virgin daughter of the man who was already busy exploiting those deposits. At any rate, on November 7th, 1752, he married Elizabeth Huber, daughter of Jacob Huber, the owner and operator of one of the oldest iron furnaces in the province; a furnace destined to play an all-important part in the subsequent career of the young man who thus gained his first connection with it, and situated seven miles south of Schaefferstown and a mile north of where the Village of Brickerville now stretches along the Horseshoe Pike, or Paxton Road as it was then called.

As a matter of fact, it was some years before he "returned to Philadelphia for more capital," or at least before he began his active career of industry promoting and land speculation in partnership with Philadelphia capitalists. And as for that feudal retainer of his, himself apparently of gentle if not noble extraction — as for "his faithful servant, Jacob of Ettenheim" — this reference is, so far as I know, that worthy's only emergence from the oblivion into which he immediately vanishes again.

Jacob Huber's iron furnace stood on the eastern slope of that northern spur of the Blue Ridge that divides the Lebanon and the Lancaster valleys, deep sunk among the hills on the bank of a little tributary of Middle Creek called Furnace Run. Something like four hundred acres of land were, at this time, held by Huber in connection with his furnace; much of it covered with oak and chestnut, from which in winter time charcoal was made for the ore-smelting. Rich beds of limestone lay a couple of miles east of the property and much iron ore was found in the neighboring hills. In the chimney stack of the old Huber furnace there is said to have been a large stone with the following couplet carved on its face: —

"Johann Huber der erste Deutsche Mann
Der das Eissen werk follfurren kann."

There has been a certain amount of confusion arising from the fact that this inscription was said to have read "Johann Huber," while it was known that Stiegel's father-in-law was named Jacob. Some of the historians compromised the difficulty by giving the old gentleman both names and calling him "John Jacob." On the tax-rolls of the time, however, he is down as "Jacob Huber," and so figures and signs himself in the deed of the furnace to Stiegel in 1758: "Jacob Huber, Ironmaster of Lancaster County and Magdelena his wife." Moreover, in 1774, in a letter to John Dickinson, Stiegel refers to a copy of "Jacob Huber's last will" and also to a "John Huber," who, from the context, would appear to be his son. So both names were used in the family, but Stiegel's father-in-law was Jacob. The "Johann" of the chimney-stack may have been the old man's brother or the name may have been another of Tradition's misprints. But be that as it may, we seem to see in the naïvely self-assertive rhyming of this Huber couplet, — which one may perhaps venture to translate

"Johan Huber, the first German man
To turn out iron work thus spick and span," —

the impregnating example which later bore fruit in that similar couplet which Stiegel is sometimes said to have carved upon the stack of his own new furnace and which we know that he had cast on the face of some of his stoves.

And now, having seen young Stiegel married to Jacob Huber's daughter Elizabeth, in that deep cleft in the hills that to this day is so beautiful and picturesque a spot, we once more — and this time for a period of nearly five years — all but lose sight of him among the mists. We know that on November 5th, 1756, his daughter Barbara was born. We know, too, thanks to a series of daybooks, journals and ledgers relating to Elizabeth Furnace, Charming Forge and the Manheim Works, many of the entries in which are in Stiegel's own handwriting, and the whole collection of which was found among the papers of John Dickinson and is now in the possession of the Pennsylvania Historical Society, that on September 22nd, 1756, he and his Philadelphia partners began a joint operation of the Huber furnace. But with these exceptions there emerges from the files and records of the period no single hint of his existence, and this, I once more pause to point out, is quite what one would expect once it is recognized that he was a young fellow of ability, energy, and some means, working hard to place himself in a new land,— and not a man of large wealth and social distinction condescending to a struggling community.

Stiegel was undoubtedly hustling during those years between 1752 and 1756. This is made evident by the fact that when, at last, he does come to the surface, it is with the energy and forceful suddenness of a virile swimmer after a dive. He evidently, during these years, kept in close touch with the affairs of the Huber furnace, and he also during that time made close connections with some of the Philadelphia business men. His first visible activity after the eclipse is the bringing of these two — the Philadelphians and the furnace — together. So much it is safe to assume, but it is also a safe assumption that during this period he engaged in no very extensive or extended operations, for as soon as he did start on his active business career he is traceable at almost every point; whereas in the period under discussion he has left no least track to indicate that he was active.

Tradition, indeed, has it that he had a home in Philadelphia and divided his time between that city and the furnace — a most likely arrangement. And the family tradition (I had this from Miss Annie L. Boyer, of Harrisburg, who tells me she had it from her mother Mrs. Rebecca Boyer, a great granddaughter of Stiegel's) asserts that after his marriage he built a house at Fort St. David, Falls of the Schuylkill, five miles north of Philadelphia, where he continued to spend part of his time until 1765. I have, however, been unable to find the record of any conveyance to H. W. Stiegel of any property in this region. Indeed I have only found one piece of Philadelphia real estate ever standing in Stiegel's name; and this consisted of two lots, thirty feet by one hundred, on the north side of Mulberry (now Arch) Street, the fourth street from the Delaware River. This passed from "Henry Keppele, of the City of Philadelphia, merchant, and Catharine his wife," to "Henry William Stiegel of Elizabeth Township, in the County of Lancaster, Iron Master," by deed poll dated March 15th, 1765, and recorded in Philadelphia August 23rd, 1794 (Liber D–47, page 15). The consideration was £450. This was a fashionable residence quarter at that time, but in 1774 and presumably earlier Stiegel used the place as a store from which to sell and distribute his Manheim glass. Moreover Dr. Charles R. Mills of Philadelphia who has made the history of the region immediately surrounding the Falls of the Schuylkill his specialized hobby, writes me: "I have considerable knowledge of the Falls of the Schuylkill and vicinity and have published some historical memoranda regarding the same. I do not, however, recall and I have not been able to find in my notes any reference to Baron Stiegel or any one of this name residing in or near the village."

On the other hand John Dickinson, Stiegel's friend and advisor later on, was president of a fishing-club at the Falls of the Schuylkill.

On the whole however it seems probable that, at this time at any rate, Stiegel resided during such periods as he spent in Philadelphia in some other quarters than in a residence of his own.

CHAPTER III

THE CARVING OUT OF A CAREER

IT will be recalled that Stiegel arrived in Philadelphia on the 31st of August, 1750, on board the ship Nancy. In the "Pennsylvania Gazette" of September 6th, 1750, appeared the following advertisement: —

"Ship Nancy, Thomas Coatam, from Cowes. For London and Rotterdam will sail by the middle of October. For freight or passage apply to Charles and Alex Stedman or said commander on board at Mr. Samuel McCall's Wharf."

And now six years later we find, by the daybook already referred to, that this same Charles and Alexander Stedman and H. W. Stiegel are beginning a joint operation of the Huber furnace. It seems at least possible that the foundations of the connection that led to this partnership were laid in some intercourse between the agents of the ship Nancy and the energetic young passenger who then crossed on her. They might well have taken to each other, for they were evidently of similar temperaments; sanguine, impulsive, little given to counting costs till these fell due or to looking before they leaped. And later on, when these traits had gotten them both into business difficulties and they fell out in trying each to save his own financial skin, they turned out to be equally litigious and equally ready, each of them, to blame the other for their joint mistakes. But these things were some years off, and for the present these partners, once fairly launched on their campaign of promotion and speculation, let no Lancaster or Lebanon County grass grow under their feet.

Stiegel's wife Elizabeth, however, died on February 3rd, 1758, before this campaign of her husband's was much more than begun. She died either in childbirth or very shortly after the birth of their second daughter, Elizabeth, and is buried in the graveyard of the Brickerville Lutheran Church. Her grave is marked by a large, oblong, horizontal stone upon which (in a mixture of old German and hybrid Latin) the following lengthy inscription, said to have been composed by Stiegel himself, is carved:—

"HIER RUHT — ELISABETH ENT SELT DEN WÜRMEN ÜBERG EBEN SOLANG BIS IEHOVA SIE RUFFT ZU EINEM ANDERN LIBEN GOTT IST DIE SEEL IN JESU GLUTH UND WUNDEN BEREITS DUCH KLUFT U HÖHL DER SUNDEN WERCK ENT BUNDEN UND DIES ESIST DER RUHM DEN HR DIE NACH WELT GIBT

"DEFUNCTA A PATRE ELISAB IAC HUBERS FILIA NATA 1734 D 27 MAARTZ NUPTA HENRI GUILHELMO STIEGEL 1752 D 7 NOV DENATA A 1758 D 13 FEB RW"

This, allowances being made for some difficulties and ambiguities, reads in a literal translation,—

"Here rests Elizabeth lifeless given over to worms so long until Jehovah shall call her to another life. God's is the soul in Jesus' love and wounds already through the grave and cavern freed from the works of sin. And this is the praise given her by the afterworld

"Elizabeth the daughter of Jacob Huber died at her father's house. She was born the 27th day of March 1734. She married Henry William Stiegel the 7th day of November 1752. She died the 13th day of February 1758."

There is a curious bit of later history connected with this stone. Soon after the revival of the local interest in the Stiegel legend and the establishment of the Feast of the Roses, a

company of Manheim enthusiasts, having obtained the informal sanction of one or two of the trustees of the Brickerville
Church, removed the monument, intending to set it up in
Manheim as a Stiegel relic. Strenuous objection, however,
developed on the part of the Stiegel heirs, and the stone was
duly returned to its original place.

The death of his wife left Stiegel, a young man of twenty-
nine, just in sight of the busiest years of his life, and with the
possibilities and demands of a vastly ambitious career just opening out before him, with two young daughters on his hands;
and it is small wonder that he did not long delay in marrying
a second time. On October 24th, 1758, eight months after
Elizabeth Huber's death, he married Elizabeth Hölz, sister of
Anna Catharine Hölz, the wife of George Michael Ege, a man
of means and of prominence in the province, a member of the
Independent Troop of Horse of Philadelphia, and a veteran
of the French and Indian War. The ceremony was performed
at the Hölz home in Roxborough, a resort near Philadelphia,
and the record of the marriage is preserved in the archives of
St. Michael's Lutheran Church, Germantown. George Michael
Ege was a witness. Tradition has it that the second Mrs. Stiegel
had kept house for her husband in Philadelphia; this probably
meaning that she was permanently in charge of the establishment, whatever and wherever it was, that the Stiegels had
maintained in that city. Their marriage ring, with the inscription "H. V. Stiegel and Elizabeth Hölz — in" is still in the
possession of the descendants of their only child, Jacob Stiegel,
who is believed to have been born in 1760.

Shortly after this marriage, on January 18th, 1759, George
Michael Ege died and at the urgent solicitation of the Stiegels
his widow and her two sons (George, aged eleven, and Michael,
aged six) came to make their home at Elizabeth Furnace; the

two families being from that time on bound together by the closest ties.

Meanwhile, as already hinted, the management of the Huber furnace has been passed over, either by lease or deed — the instrument is not of record — to a partnership consisting of Henry W. Stiegel, Charles and Alexander Stedman, and John Barr. The Stiegel account-books show them to have begun partnership operations at the furnace on September 22nd, 1756. And a bill of sale, dated May 1st, 1758, acknowledged June 30th, 1758, and recorded January 28th, 1768, in Philadelphia, in Liber I–4, page 111, conveys to these partners, for the sum of £500, "the messuages, buildings, improvements, ways, waters, water-courses" belonging to Jacob Huber and "now actually in the possession of Chas. Stedman, Alex. Stedman, John Barr and Henry W. Stiegel." Stiegel, as we shall see elsewhere, described this purchase as consisting of four hundred acres of land with the furnace and buildings.

How long John Barr remained in this business alliance is not disclosed by any documents that I have seen. But that, some time before the middle of 1766, he had disposed of his holdings to the other partners jointly, is evidenced by the fact that on July 1st of that year, Alexander Stedman mortgaged a one-third undivided interest in the furnace to Daniel Wister, of Philadelphia, and by the further fact that all subsequent records and transactions show the Stedmans and Stiegel to have been each seized of a one-third share in the several properties in which John Barr had originally had an interest. We will, therefore, dismiss Mr. Barr from further consideration. He figures, as one of the purchasers, in the deeds to several of the tracts bought by the "Company" in the first year or so of its activity, but, having so figured, he concerns us no longer.

The acquirement of the Huber furnace was the beginning,

and the operation of it and of Charming Forge were the most remunerative accomplishments of this Stedman-Stiegel activity. But their ambitions grew so rapidly by what they fed upon, and the scope of their undertakings widened so rapidly, that it is likely enough that they came to look upon this first joint undertaking as a mere sample of what all their enterprises were to become and expected some day to point to it as the humble beginnings of a great power.

The management of the furnace was, from the first, evidently entrusted to Stiegel or possibly to Stiegel and Barr for a time. Some of the deeds to the numerous parcels of land acquired by the partners — as fast and as far as they could get hold of it, apparently — in the neighborhood of the furnace read to "Henry W. Stiegel and John Barr of Elizabeth Township, Iron Masters." Others read to "Henry W. Stiegel and Company of Elizabeth Furnace, Iron Masters." Others to "Henry William Stiegel on behalf of himself and Company of Elizabeth, Iron Masters." And during 1758 and 1759 alone, these purchases, together with applications for warrants for unpatented lands, amounted to some thousands of acres. Stiegel's own inventory of the partnership lands adjoining the furnace, made a few years later and in his own handwriting, shows a total of $6559\frac{1}{2}$ acres, besides other partnership lands in Elizabeth Township amounting to $3894\frac{1}{2}$ acres additional.

This, even for so sanguine and headlong a trio as were now operating together, would appear to have been a pretty fast pace, but, as we shall see, neither the initiative nor the acquisitiveness of either party to their joint partnership was exhausted by their joint undertakings. First Stiegel and then the Stedmans made extensive independent investments on their own initiative and later let their Elizabeth Furnace partners in on the new ventures.

Stiegel's independent investment was the purchase of another iron property some miles distant from Elizabeth Furnace, across the hills on the eastern slope of which this first bought property lay and on the side of the Lebanon Valley. This was the property subsequently known as Charming Forge, a valuable asset, and, like Elizabeth Furnace, a most picturesquely located plant. It lay a few miles north of the Village of Middleton (now Wolmansdorf), in Heidelberg Township, in a narrow gorge-like valley on the bank of Tulpehocken Creek, and in later years, together with Elizabeth Furnace, was the chief source from which Stiegel drew the funds for his Manheim undertakings. The works had been erected in 1749 by a hammersmith named George Nikoll and one Michael Miller, and had already passed through several hands. Stiegel's initial purchase here (made in partnership with Michael Gross, a merchant, of Lancaster) consisted of 88 acres with the forge plant, bought from Michael Rice on April 2, 1760. They paid £1450 for it, and immediately started adding to the holding until by 1763 they had something like 3100 acres. Gross, by an unrecorded deed dated February 5th, 1763, transferred his interest to Stiegel, and Stiegel, on February 12th of the same year, sold to Charles and Alexander Stedman an undivided one-half interest in the property for £3132, they remaining his debtors for £1028–4–6.

The Stedmans' independent purchase consisted of the land in Manheim Township upon which the village of Manheim grew up later under the fostering influence of Stiegel's enterprises there. They purchased, on February 17th, 1762, from Isaac Norris and his daughter Mary Norris, a tract of 729 acres, the residue of a 1400-acre tract which had belonged to James Logan, Mary Norris's grandfather, and out of which he had, in his lifetime, sold 621 acres. And on September 20th, of the same year of 1762, Stiegel purchased an undivided one-third interest in this 729-acre tract for the sum of £1000 lawful money of Pennsylvania.

Here, then, laid down as it were on a map before us, we have the outlines of the Stiegel-Stedman joint interests: First, Elizabeth Furnace, with its between 6000 and 7000 acres of adjoining lands and the scattered holdings in the same township amounting to nearly 4000 acres more. Second, about twenty miles distant, across the Blue Ridge spur and across the Lebanon Valley, Charming Forge with its 3000 acres of adjacent land. Third, the Manheim tract.

It would be superfluous here to list the component parcels of land and to enumerate the several purchases from which these tracts were made up. We are here concerned with the broad facts of these threefold holdings upon which, as upon a tripod support, all the subsequent relations of Stiegel and the Stedmans, and all the subsequent career of Stiegel himself rest. Having this before us we will look in turn at the activities connected with each of them and will then be in a position to appreciate the later and more complex interdependences of these respective enterprises and to understand the vortex of financial embarrassment and personal discord in which the partners were engulfed.

The foundation of them all was laid by the successful operation of Elizabeth Furnace under Stiegel's management. Here, for the first time, as far as we can now see, he had a suitable opportunity to exercise the energy and initiative and versatility of his mercurial abilities. There can, I think, when one comes to examine his career in the light of definite knowledge, be no question but that H. W. Stiegel had the rocket temperament. He went up with all the confidence, celerity, and spectacular effect of one of these sky-scaling devices, and he not

SCULL MAPS OF THE PROVINCE OF PENNSYLVANIA 1759 AND 1770, SHOWING THE CHANGES MADE BY HENRY WILLIAM STIEGEL'S ACTIVITIES

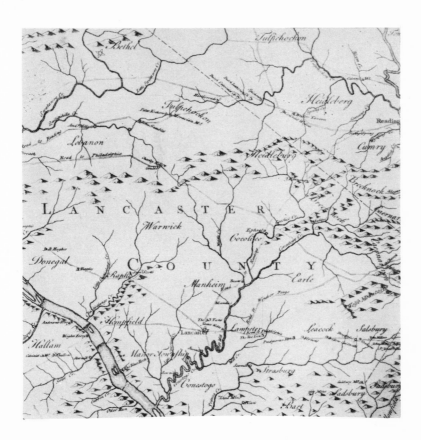

January 1, 1759. Scull's Map of the Province of Pennsylvania (showing a portion of Lancaster County). Philadelphia: Engraved by Jos. Turney and printed by John Davis for Nicholas Scull, January 1, 1759.

By Courtesy Robert Fridenberg.

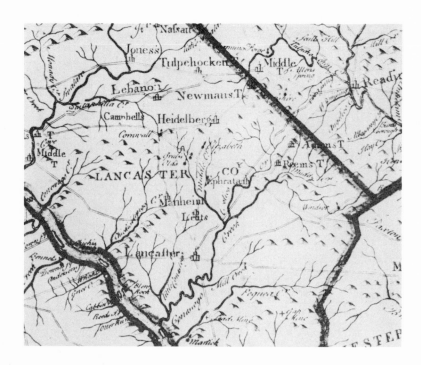

April 4, 1770. Scull's Map of the Province of Pennsylvania (showing a portion of Lancaster County). Printed by James Nevil for the author.

To the Honorable Thomas Penn and Richard Penn Esquires True and Absolute Proprietors and Governors of the Province of Pennsylvania and the Territories thereto belonging and to the Honorable John Penn Esquire Lieutenant Governor of the same THIS MAP of the Province of Pennsylvania is humbly dedicated by their Most Obedient humble Servant W. Scull.

By Courtesy New York Public Library.

only came to a pause as far short of his apparent goal as they, and came as definitely and disastrously to earth as one of their sticks, but he showed the same utter lack of recuperative ability once his bolt had been shot. For the moment, however, we are concerned with the time when the match of a free hand and a congenial task had just been applied to the powder of his ambitions, and the immediate result was that the Elizabeth Township furnace sprang into a hitherto unparalleled prominence in the industries of the province.

It has always been assumed, by the way, that Stiegel gave to this plant the name of "Elizabeth Furnace" in honor of his wife, but the matter is, to say the least, open to doubt. The enterprise is first officially and of record referred to as "Elizabeth Furnace" in a deed to "Henry William Stiegel and Company of Elizabeth Furnace, Iron Masters," bearing the date of December 21st, 1758; previous deeds referring to him as of "Elizabeth Township" and "of Elizabeth." His first wife had then been dead more than ten months and he had already married another Elizabeth. Moreover, the wife of Alexander Stedman, one of his partners in the original purchase of the plant, was also named Elizabeth. Finally, the furnace was situated in that division of Lancaster County already known as Elizabeth Township. The matter is of no great importance, but it seems well to state the facts. We can, then, each after his personal preference, select the source of this celebrated appellation.

The furnace, by any other name, would doubtless have prospered equally well, for the new manager was not only energetic, but had imagination. He soon began to specialize, and that in a line that particularly appealed to the needs of the time and the neighborhood. He began to improve the crude heating devices of the country and gradually evolved a type of stove that made his name known far and wide throughout the section. His first achievement is said to have been the improvement of the Benjamin Franklin open hearth, which was intended for insertion in the huge fireplaces of colonial construction, thus economizing fuel and bringing the source of radiation nearer to the room to be heated. Stiegel is said to have so altered the Franklin hearth that it would stand out in the room itself. He then began building an iron jamb stove intended to be imbedded in the wall with its hinder end projecting into a second room and furnishing a sort of Dutch oven, so called, for baking purposes. Finally he devised a "six-plate" and eventually the triumphant "ten-plate" stove which later maintained for many years its standing as the finest achievement of its kind.

One of these stoves is still preserved in the Mansion at the old Elizabeth Furnace site. It bears the inscription, "H. W. Stiegel, Elizabeth Furnace 1769." Others bear in relief a profile of George III, the forehead adorned with a wreath of laurel, and in the corners of these, and of some other plates, decorations appear in which callipers, rules, and try-squares figure; and upon this an hypothesis has been based assuming that Stiegel was a Mason. I have caused searches to be made in both Pennsylvania and New York, and it appears that in no lodge in either state is there any record of Stiegel's having been either an original or an affiliated member.

Stiegel tore down the old furnace of his father-in-law's time, erected a more modern and capable plant, put up a number (tradition says twenty-five) tenant houses for his employees, and finally built for his own occupancy a really fine house with offices and stores and other buildings adjoining; and had, if one may judge by the fine dignity and ample proportions of the mansion which is still standing, and by the solid construction of the other buildings which have survived, a property that may well have ministered to his pride and have given him confidence in his ability for greater things. Later on, when he had let this confidence in his ability smother his judgment, had gotten into inextricably ramified difficulties, and had developed a habit of occupying spare moments by making calculations of his resources on sheets of paper or on blank leaves of his haphazard account-books, we get a very detailed and definite account of what assets were in evidence both at Elizabeth Furnace and at Charming Forge. Likewise, as we shall see, of what had been done and was being done at his Manheim Glass House. But during those early years of prosperous enlargement and plain sailing, we can only see the general outlines of his success.

Some idea of the extent and diversity of the business finally worked up by Stiegel at Elizabeth Furnace may be gained from the following portion of one of his advertisements printed in the "Pennsylvania Chronicle and Universal Advertiser" of March 27th, 1769, and in the "Pennsylvania Gazette" of March 23rd, and of May 4th of the same year, —

IRON CASTINGS

"Of all dimensions and sizes, such as kettles or boilers for pot-ash works, soap boilers pans, pots, from a barrel to 300 gallons, ship cabooses, kachels, and sugar house stoves, with cast funnels of any height for refining sugars, weights of all sizes, grate bars and other castings for sugar works in the West Indies, &c. are all carefully done by HENRY WILLIAM STIEGEL, iron-master, at Elizabeth Furnace in Lancaster County, on the most reasonable terms. Orders and applications made to Michael Hilligas in Second Street, Philadelphia, will be carefully forwarded. . . ."

Nor was this catering to the sugar planters' needs in the West Indian Islands, with which at this time the colonies had considerable trade, an empty reaching-out after a desired connection. In a statement of accounts in Stiegel's own handwriting, which is in my possession and which is indorsed on the back —

"ACCOUNTS TOTAL

Ch. & Alex. Stedman H.W. S. the Iron Works and Manheim estates taken from the Company's Ledgers signed and sealed every Year by each of the parties " —

I find entered under date of 1766 the sum of £418–4–4 as received on account of West Indian orders. In another document, also in my possession and indorsed on the back in Stiegel's own hand, "Total account of a ten year partnership with Ch. & A. Stedman," the total receipts of Elizabeth Furnace are put down at £10,636–10–7 and the disbursements at £7717–4–3½.

At Charming Forge a similarly sound business seems to have been developed and carried on, although here the output was for the most part bar-iron — marketed, by the way, at prices calculated to make any present-day iron-smelter rub his eyes in an incredulous envy. In the second of the Stiegel-Stedman trial-balances referred to above, the sum of £1859–4–5 is entered as received from a shipment of 69½ tons of bar-iron to London. This was in 1765, and this brings us, by a connection that will appear shortly, to the question of Stiegel's alleged trips to Europe, to the beginnings of his dabbling in the manufacture of glass and to the possible bearings that the only trip abroad of which there is any discoverable evidence may be deemed to have had upon this foreign branch of his iron business and upon the rapid development of his glass industry.

Tradition has been fond of crediting him with repeated trips to the old country — dealing in characteristically broad generalizations and implying, without committing itself, a sort of princely habit of frequent travel. "Whenever he went abroad he took his baronial costume with him" — that sort of thing.

As a matter of fact, unless he made repeated trips during the years preceding his emergence from obscurity as one of the purchasers of the Huber furnace, or again unless he traveled after his reduction to complete poverty caused him once more to disappear into invisibility, there was but a single period when he could have gone, and when he apparently did go, to Europe and return between the records we possess of his presence in this country. At any other time than that between October 22nd, 1763, and January 27th, 1764, it would, I think, be possible to prove an alibi for him if he were accused of having been out of this country for three months running.

The account-books of Charming Forge show the following sums as having, on the dates specified, been drawn for "H.W.S. trip to London": —

```
1763
Sept. 26........................£120
Oct.   8........................  60
Oct.  15........................  60
Oct.  22........................  60

1764
Jan.  27........................ 120
Feb.   3........................  60
Mar.   2........................ 120
```

And as I find no trace of his presence here during the interval between these entries, I take it that he must have drawn the first £300 before starting on his trip and the last £300 after his return, either to recoup himself for moneys there expended or to meet drafts negotiated during his absence. It seems altogether possible that the shipments of bar-iron sent to London a year after his return may have been a result of connections made by him during his visit. And when we turn, as we will now do, to the experiments in glass-making which he had been carrying on at Elizabeth Furnace during the months preceding his voyage and then study the definite and sophisticated course adopted by him in developing his Manheim undertaking, I think that we will see not only why he was anxious to visit England at this time, but what came of his having done so.

Meanwhile Stiegel was in various ways identifying himself with the country and the community of his adoption.

On April 10th, 1760, he had become a naturalized citizen of Pennsylvania and (as the Act of Parliament quaintly puts it) a "natural born" subject of Great Britain. He could have taken this step some three years sooner, but it is likely that he was only now brought to consider it important because of his increasing wealth and of his just developing ambitions of becoming an extensive landowner.

By an Act of Parliament, enacted in 1740 for "the naturalizing of such Foreign Protestants and others herein mentioned as are settled or shall settle in any of His Majesty's Colonies in America," it was provided that such applicants for naturalization, "having inhabited and resided the space of seven years and upwards and not having been absent out of said Colonies for a longer space than two months out of the said seven years, and having produced to the Court a Certificate of their having taken the Sacrament of the Lord's Supper in some Protestant or Reformed Congregation in this Province within three months," and having taken and subscribed the oaths and made and repeated the declaration prescribed, should be "certified by the officers of the Court as natural born citizens of Great Britain." The original documents connected with Stiegel's naturalization are no longer, I believe, in existence. The pre-Revolutionary records of the Court of Common Pleas in Lancaster are still preserved, but no files of naturalization papers connected with the Supreme Court at Philadelphia, before which tribunal Stiegel appeared in perfecting his citizenship, are known to exist prior to 1797. It is supposed that they were destroyed, or, at any rate, that they disappeared, during the British occupancy of that city.

However, in the second volume of the second series of the Pennsylvania Archives, on pages 402–4, there appears a list of 130 men who, on April 10th, 1760, took the prescribed oath of allegiance in accordance with this Act of Parliament; and also a list of 21 persons who, being Quakers or having conscientious scruples against taking the oath, made affirmation in compliance with the terms of the act. The name of Henry William *Stiegle* appears as the 128th among the jurors. This spelling is doubtless an error of transcription, for, while some of the earlier writers on his history adopt this spelling as the normal one, I have never seen a single signature of his or a single instance in which he has entered his own name on the journals and ledgers of Elizabeth Furnace, Charming Forge or Manheim, in which he has varied from the spelling commonly followed. His naturalization papers were signed by William Allen, Esq., Chief Justice of the Supreme Court, and certified to by William Allen.

He was also interesting himself in the religious and educational activities of his neighborhood. His books show numerous sums paid for the salary of the local schoolmaster, as, for instance, — £78 in 1762 for the salary of John Matthias Cramer, presumably at Brickerville.

In June of this year, too, the Lutheran Ministerium of Pennsylvania and adjacent states assembled at the Brickerville Church, and Stiegel was among the lay delegates and his prominence in Church circles even at this period is attested by an entry in Henry Melchior Muhlenberg's memoirs showing that on February 27th, 1762, he rode four miles to Mr. Stiegel's iron works, preached from Psalm 22, verses 26 and 27, and stayed the night.

Some idea, too, of Stiegel's personal prosperity at this time

and of the establishment that he was maintaining at the Furnace Mansion is given us by one of those estimates he was so
fond of making (at this time of his resources, but later on, alas,
of his debts), and which, in his own handwriting, is preserved
among the Stiegel papers by the Historical Society of Pennsylvania.   It runs as follows: —

Servants Retinue	£208. 7.6
Musical instruments	375.12.2
Household Furniture	483. 0.5
Clothing	206.16.3
Negro Cyrus	80.
Debts due me	2028.4 .4

This estimate of his "Personal Property," as it is headed, not
only disposes (since we know the extent and the approximate
cost of his real estate holdings) of the tradition of his £40,000
fortune, but shows how even at the beginning of his career he
indulged his tastes for art, for comfort, and for display in a
manner out of all proportion to his resources.

The Negro Cyrus, mentioned in this inventory, must have
been quite a character and was doubtless much valued by his
master. He worked for Stiegel at Elizabeth Furnace and later
made himself a master workman in the glass-making technique,
acting as teaser and blower at Manheim. Stiegel owned him
until 1779.

CHAPTER IV

STIEGEL'S BEGINNINGS AS A GLASS-MAKER

STIEGEL had three glass houses, first and last; but it is only the final one — the one that broke him — that has found a place in the Stiegel tradition.

And even here — true to the obsessional bias, the *idée fixe* of this splendor-mongering legend — the emphasis of history has all been laid upon the size of the ultimate dome-shaped building at Manheim; upon the fact that this was built of bricks imported from England and carted the weary miles from Philadelphia, and upon the reputed possibility of turning a six-horse team around inside of it. Little has been said about the glass that was made there, and as for the concrete beginnings of this historically important industry, they have been so long lost sight of that their very existence has been forgotten. No single chronicler of Stiegel's activities has hinted, and as far as I know no single person living in the summer of 1913 suspected, that for two years previous to the opening of the Manheim factory, and possibly for a year after that event, Stiegel had had a glass house in operation at Elizabeth Furnace in conjunction with the other industries of that busy place. This is not, however, the first instance in which the spectators of a rocket's flight have recalled, afterwards, only the pyrotechnics that accompanied its end.

I stumbled upon the first clue to the existence of this Elizabeth Furnace glass house by the merest chance, and for a long time I had nothing but one of those instinctive convictions — one of those deep-sprung *flairs* of undefendable certainty that we speak of as "feeling a thing in our bones"—with which to bolster my belief. There were times when my conviction that such a glass house had existed almost answered to the small boy's definition of Faith—"a belief in what you know is n't so." But intuition is often the most effective spur to investigation, and I not only left (literally) no stone unturned, but to the best of my ability no file unfumbled, in the hope of finding some substantial confirmation of my idea. And when Mr. Ernest Spofford, Assistant Librarian of the Historical Society of Pennsylvania, seeing my persistent interest in matters pertaining to Stiegel, one day brought out to me from the as yet uncatalogued possessions of the Society a pile of books and papers that proved to be daybooks, journals, ledgers, and miscellaneous letters and memoranda of Stiegel himself, I think the thing that gave me most pleasure in the whole treasure trove was the incontrovertible and illuminating information these books supplied as to the existence, the scope, and the operation of this glass house.

Several times during the summer of 1913 it had been suggested to me that I might see some fine specimens of authenticated Stiegel glass at the "Baron's" old mansion at Elizabeth Furnace, the present summer home of the Coleman family. Finally, in August, I made my way over there from Manheim, and just as my car crossed the little bridge over Furnace Run and approached the beautifully situated old house, my eye (by that time automatically acting on the principle that everything that glitters may be glass) was caught by a sparkle at the edge of the road and I stopped the car and got out to investigate. The road was made of slag from the old furnace and among the cinders I picked up and put in my pocket several bits of dark emerald and smoky blackish glass. Later on, having got permission to see the house from the overseer who happened to be present, and having gone through the very beautiful and interesting old place under the guidance of Mrs. Miller, the wife of the farmer resident on the estate, Mr. Miller volunteered to show me over the furnace site and, as I had asked him numerous questions about the glass bits I had found, took a pick over his shoulder. He told me that for some years the roads around Brickerville had been top-dressed with the slag from the old plant and led me to a place some hundreds of yards southeast of the house and on the other side of Furnace Run, where the tree-grown and vegetation-covered slag-heaps had been laid open by the quarrying road-menders. And here, digging into the edges of the heap, we uncovered pocket after pocket of black vitreous material, in which, now and again, we found chunks of green glass. And in one spot I uncovered and pocketed a small fragment of thin, light-green glass, open pot, that appeared to be a piece of some finished vessel — the piece later on commented upon in the chapter on the decay of glass.

Unfortunately, however, this piece completely disintegrated before I reached home, and when I laid my find before my brother-in-law, Mr. J. B. Kerfoot, with whom I was in the habit of thrashing out most points connected with my investigations, and told him of the theory I had conceived in explanation of the presence of these fragments among the furnace refuse, he threw critical cold water on my enthusiasm, suggested that I was dealing with a mere by-product of early smelting methods, and challenged me to produce a piece of some recognizable glass factory output before setting up a theory that had nothing tangible to back it.

On Sunday, the 14th September, I again visited the Elizabeth Furnace site, and this time Mr. Kerfoot accompanied me. Once more we dug well into the old slag-piles, and this time I found a large piece of emerald glass now in the Metropolitan Museum, beside a number of other pieces of glass which, while they did not convince either of us of the exact nature of the activities that had produced them, did make me more certain than ever that I was on the track of a really significant discovery and determined me to pay one more visit to the site and extend my search to other parts of the grounds.

This last visit was paid on Saturday, October 18th, and this time we went supplied with a grubbing hoe and a spade, and after a careful canvassing of the slag-piles we uncovered, in pockets nearer the surface than the scene of my earlier search, a fluted fragment of a white transparent flint flip glass or tumbler, pieces of bottles in green and olive glass, and pieces of what appeared to be window glass, but these pieces were so small that it was impossible to be sure that they were not bits of large bottles. We also unearthed several bullets, a wagon axle, a hub rim, and a cannon ball about two and three-quarters inches in diameter. In the rear of one of the old tenant houses to the northeast of the road and opposite the mansion, in what is now a ploughed field, we also found a fairly plentiful scattering of glass fragments, many of them showing the scaly, iridescent surface indicative of long interment. But as these were found on or near the surface, I discarded them. Specimens of the emerald green, of the olive, and of the open pot green glass found on these strips are now in the Metropolitan Museum, New York, and are here reproduced in color in Plate VIII.

Whether Stiegel, having been born in Cologne, one of the oldest centers of glass manufacture in northern Europe, brought with him a predisposition to the establishment of that industry in his adopted country, or whether, seeing the local need as another opportunity, he was merely exercising his characteristic versatility of enterprise in engaging in glass-making, there is unhappily no way for us to discover. The one thing that inclines the student of his career to feel that he may, from the very start, have had a waiting niche in the hall of his ambitions for this special undertaking is the fact that when it came to the pinch he sacrificed everything else for it. He was willing, as we shall see, to make a single bundle of all he possessed in the way of lands, furnaces, and investments and sell them at what he looked upon as a bargain price in order that, with the proceeds, he might complete his final Manheim plant. But of course this may simply indicate that the thing which he had started as a side issue gradually, as it developed, came to stand to him for the main one, — that an experiment lightly undertaken had grown to be an engrossing hobby.

It was probably early in 1763 that — urged to it by either a long cherished desire or by the promptings of local needs — Stiegel began building his Elizabeth Furnace Glass House. The particular volume that would contain the expense charges of this building operation is one of those that are missing in the series preserved by the Historical Society of Pennsylvania, but luckily enough the next book begins in time for us to catch the entry under date of September 18th, 1763, showing that they that day began glass-blowing with Christian Nasel, Martin Grenier and Benjamin Misky as blowers.

Stiegel's bookkeeping was always of a chaotic order. It seems to have been indulged in more or less intermittently and with a fine free disregard for uniformity of method; and as often as not the entries are suggestive more of a diary than of a business account. I can imagine that an expert accountant, trying to unravel the hopeless tangle of Stiegel's finances during the years preceding his failure, would find no language lurid enough to express his opinion of these books. But with us it is different. The fact that they are full of confusion is as nothing compared with the fact that they are full of intimate details. The fact that they are financially unenlightening is as nothing compared with the fact that they are aglow with local color. And while it is true that Charming Forge matters, the various activities of the Elizabeth Furnace industries, the Manheim Glass House and store accounts, and even the affairs of Stiegel's King of Prussia Tavern at Manheim, appear and disappear from their pages with a verbal rather than with a proper bookkeeping differentiation, the very naïveté of these records often adds to the vividness of their revelations.

Look, for instance, at the sheer deliciousness of the coexistence on one page of the records of the following two entries: —

"September 17th, 1771; Henry Sharman to one bottle of rhum..................1s
"September 17th, 1771 Henry Sharman fined 5s for getting drunk and Leaving an Arch Empty about three hours."

And it is from this series of books, incurably informal, haphazard and go-as-you-please from an accountant's point of view, but gratifyingly although intermittently illuminating from the point of view of the historian, that the following facts about the Elizabeth Furnace Glass House and much of the information about the first and second Manheim Glass Houses have been gleaned.

It appears from these accounts that Stiegel had, at Elizabeth Furnace, in addition to the original iron business of the plant, a glass house, a store, a second store called familiarly the "cellar store," which appears to have handled the output of the glass house, a mill and a malt house; the latter presumably connected with a brewery which he owned at Heidelberg (now Schaefferstown), and which was operated by Lorenze Keller. Actual glass-blowing began in the glass house on September 18th, 1763. Bottles and window glass made up the chief, if not the entire output of this glass house. These, indeed, being

the prime need of the community, were what all the early glass
plants in this country gave their first if not their entire attention
to, and the earlier activities of the first Manheim factory were
preponderantly of a similar character.

The workmen at the Elizabeth Glass House were paid by the
piece, and in addition to the blowers already named Daniel
M. Daniel and Michael Griesbach were also employed in that
capacity, while George Glass, Mathias Hoffart, Michael Miller
and Anton Walder were paid various sums for making glass
there. Anthony Stiegel was also employed by the glass house
and seems to have been at Elizabeth Furnace from 1762
till March 15th, 1765, when a final payment of £ 9–9–10 was
made to him for supervising work in the glass house. From
September 20th, 1764, to January 7th, 1765 (another entry gives
these dates as September 15th, 1764, and February 20th, 1765,
and the double statement and included discrepancy is thoroughly characteristic of Stiegel's accounts), the glass house is
put down as having sold glass to the amount of £ 128–19.
They made sales to one Isaac Young and to Mayer Josephson,
of Reading; and not only did the furnace supply all the castings,
stoves and other hardware required in the building and out-
fitting of the Manheim plant, but the Elizabeth Furnace Glass
House sold the Manheim plant the window glass for its windows,
and either continued to manufacture window glass which it
sold to the Manheim glass store for distribution, or continued
for some time after the opening of the Manheim store to sell
its accumulated surplus of window glass to the latter establishment. On October 7th, 1765, a month before the Manheim glass
house started work, the Elizabeth Furnace Company sold the
Manheim plant a bill of castings and potware, one large and
one small six-plate stove and two middling five-plate stoves,
and on the same date the Elizabeth Furnace store sold the

Manheim plant 5 dozen 6-quart bottles, 5 dozen of 7x9 window glass, 10 dozen of 6x8 glass and 7 dozen of 4x6 glass.

On December 4th, 1765, the Manheim store sold window glass purchased from the Elizabeth Glass House for £7–13 and on the 20th bought more window glass to the amount of £4–5–6. Finally, on November 24th, 1766, the Elizabeth Furnace store appears to have sold to the Manheim store glass to the amount of £252–16–4. This probably represents a final clearing-out of the remaining product of the Elizabeth Furnace glass pots. It is interesting and possibly significant to note that the fragments of glass found at the Elizabeth Furnace site, with the exception of the emerald green already referred to, are apparently of the same colors and general character as the common glass made in the neighborhood of Cologne as described in Edward Dillon's work on "Glass" (Minthurn, London, 1907), while in the later manufacturing developments at Manheim, the English, the finer German, and even the Venetian methods were employed and their output approximated to.

Stiegel drew the first £120 for his contemplated trip to London three days after the Elizabeth Furnace Glass House began glass-blowing — September 26th, 1763. A month later, on October 22nd, he drew the last £60 of the £300 he appears to have taken with him on the trip. He drew the second £300 which we suppose him to have drawn after his return between January 27th and March 2nd, 1764; and he began the ledger marked "Ledger A. No. 1 for the Manheim Glass House," and which contains the accounts of the building operations connected with that enterprise, on October 6th, 1764. It would, therefore, seem to be a fair inference that this presumed trip abroad was suggested to him by his desire for information in regard to more skillful and technically developed processes of glass-making than that which he or his Elizabeth Furnace force

had brought with them from the shores of the Rhine; and that
at least some of the ambitious ideas which he later put into
practice in Manheim, and the foreign connections that enabled
him to import skilled workmen from England, Germany, and
Italy, are to be credited for their beginnings to that adventure.

CHAPTER V

THE BEGINNINGS OF MANHEIM

ON September 30th, 1734, a patent was issued by John Penn, Thomas Penn and Richard Penn for 1400 acres of land (including the site of the present town of Manheim) to James Logan, of Stenton, in the province of Pennsylvania. Logan sold 671 acres of this land during his life, and when he died he left to his daughter Sarah (by his will dated November 25th, 1749) "700 acres" of this land, meaning and intending thereby (as subsequent deeds are careful to explain and claim) the unsold portion of his original 1400 acres. Sarah Logan married Isaac Norris and died, leaving a daughter Mary, and on February 17th, 1762, Mary Norris then being over twenty-one years of age and a spinster, she and her father sold the 729-acre tract to Charles and Alexander Stedman, who, as we have seen, sold William Henry Stiegel an undivided one-third interest in the property on September 20th of the same year.

It is evident that the partners, soon after this transaction, determined upon the laying-out and promoting of a town on this new tract of land, for on the Elizabeth Furnace books and on the Ledger A. No. 1 of the Manheim accounts various sums are entered during 1763, 1764, and 1765 as paid to Thomas Lincoln for work done at Manheim; and certain partition deeds, dated March 14th, 1765, in which the Stedmans convey a series of Manheim lots to Stiegel, describe the lots so conveyed as "shown on a certain draft or plan of the Town of Manheim and lots adjacent lately drawn by Thomas Lincoln, surveyor."

Poor Lincoln, however, got little permanent benefit, although he doubtless derived much enjoyment, from these rewards of his labor; for the account-books of Stiegel's King of Prussia Tavern at Manheim show that all of this money and a good deal more beside found its way into the till of that house of entertainment.

It is also evident from various entries and memoranda that the sale of Manheim lots was begun early in this period, some being sold in fee, some for a part payment for the land plus a yearly ground rent, and some for no initial payment, but for an annual ground rent; and the confusion that early crept into this somewhat complex system was made the worse confounded by the deferred and defaulted payments of some of the purchasers and by the decamping of others.

Stiegel himself was also soon deep in his plans for the new town. I have found no clews to the actual dates of construction or to the actual cost of his Manheim residence, but tradition says that he began building the Mansion in 1763 and completed it in 1765 — which would mean that he began it a year before he began his Manheim glass plant and finished it about the same time. It stood on what is now the northeast corner of North Prussian and East High Streets, where part of its original walls are still visible in the three-story store now occupying the site; and it was not only for the time and place a residence which exceeded the local dreams of magnificence, but, apparently, a dignified and handsome home, though of moderate size. It is said to have been built of imported English brick, was forty feet square, was two stories high and had a broad flat railed platform surmounting the gabled roof — the bandstand where his famous workman band is said to have made music for Manheim on summer evenings and to have assembled to welcome their arriving employer and patron when he dashed into town from Philadelphia or Charming Forge or Elizabeth Furnace in his coach and four.

Each of the two floors is described as having been divided by halls into three rooms. The wainscotings, cornices and other architectural decorations of the interior are said to have been very fine. The fireplaces were adorned with tiles, samples of which are still preserved by the Historical Society of Pennsylvania. The parlor walls were painted with scenes of falconry; handsome tapestries were hung there, some of which are to be seen to-day in the Manheim museum of Mr. George H. Danner; and in addition to the roomy dining-hall and a kitchen fitted out with English china and the ample conveniences necessary to so hospitable an entertainer, the second floor contained a private chapel with arched ceiling, pews and a pulpit, where, when no clergyman was available, Stiegel himself conducted services for his neighbors and workmen. The plans, as tradition has handed them down to us, do not seem to provide for many sleeping-rooms, and if Stiegel's far-famed hospitality did not always limit itself to the hospitality of the table, he must have been frequently driven to bedding his guests in the chapel pews. But doubtless the more humble aspects of this Manheim establishment have been lost sight of in the glare of its more public glories.

It was about the same time also that he built the brick office on the northwest corner of North Charlotte and West High Streets which was not torn down till a few years ago. The glass house itself was begun in October, 1764, and occupied over a year in building. Its total cost is difficult to disentangle from the books, where no sort of differentiation is maintained between amounts properly chargeable to construction and the various expenditures connected with Stiegel's other activities. In summing up one series of accounts, running from December 28th,

1764, to August, 1765, however, £573–14–8½ is set down to "Building Glass House." But something like £1600 seems to have been expended first and last upon the building and equipment of this first plant.

On October 29th, 1765, I find the entry, "This day the glass ovens being finished the fire was put in."

On November 5th, again, "paid 16/ for 4 gallons of rum, treating the workmen. Charged to building account."

And on November 11th, "This day in the afternoon the glass makers began to work." This must, indeed, have been a red-letter day to the ambitious and energetic patron of the new town who thus saw his dreams taking concrete form.

Martin Grenier, Christian Nassel, Christian Gratinger, Conrad Waltz and Jacob Halder were the first blowers.

George Ege and Philip Wisenand were the first customers, the former paying 5–6d. for a dozen pocket bottles and the latter 6d. for one pocket bottle on November 12th.

On December 21st, something over £60 were paid to four of the above-named blowers for making 328 dozen various-sized panes of window glass.

On December 23rd, the minister at York bought two cream jugs and one sugar for 3s.

Such were the humble beginnings of the great Stiegel Glass Works, destined within a few years to be imitating the output of the chief glass centers of Europe, to be desperately competing with them for the American market, to have stores in Philadelphia and New York and agents in a score of Colonial towns, and alas to ruin its founder, and, after being all but forgotten for a century, to put antiquarians at loggerheads and set collectors by the ears.

For the first year or so, however, the Manheim plant, like that of Elizabeth Furnace and like all other early American glass houses, devoted most of its time to the making of bottles and window glass. 1766 was started with five blowers, Martin Grenier, Christian Nassel, Conrad Waltz, Christian Gratlinger and Jacob Halder, and the factory turned out for the most part gallon, half-gallon, quart and pint bottles, and pieces of small glass. This product was sold to merchants in Reading, Lancaster, York, and other neighboring towns, and was delivered by wagons and packed for shipment in hogsheads. The books contain long lists of such consignments, each hogshead being numbered and a list of its contents being noted, as, for example —

```
No. 5
     3 doz half Gallons @  12 /..............£1.16
    11 doz Quarts        @   6/..............  3. 6.
     3 doz Pints         @  4/6............. 0.13.6
        The Hogshead        .................    3.6
                                             £5.19.
```

On April 14th, 1766, the books show that "This evening the Glass House ended the season the workmen being worn out." And the fires under its glass pots were not started again until November 15th. Business, however, appears to have been good in the interim and glass to the amount of £601. 1. 15 was sold during the year. Immediately upon the resumption of work, Stiegel began taking on additional workmen, and such entries as the following appear on the books: —

"November 29th. Agreement made with Martin Betz to work in the glass house for 1 year at £1 per month. N.B. He is to have ten pounds of nails in Bargain."

"December 13th. Agreement made with Andrew Holder to drive ox team for 1 year at £33, and in Bargain a pair of shoes."

Quart, pint, and half-gallon "tumblers" appear at this time among the goods sold, also, "Electer glasses." Several boys were also employed to help the blowers and shearers. Business on these lines seems to have been brisk up to about the first of May, 1767, but to have then fallen off and the balance of 1767 and all of 1768 to have been dull times.

It has nothing to do with the stringencies we are considering, but it is interesting and a bit amusing to note that in the "Pennsylvania Gazette" of September 29th, 1768, Stiegel offers a reward of two pistoles for the return of a servant, Nicholas Moyse, who had run away from Elizabeth Furnace with his wife, "a chunky woman of a fresh complexion and very talkative." Most runaways leave that sort of wife behind.

But to return to our bottles; the total sales from January 1st, 1767, to May 1st, 1768, seem to have amounted to £660. 3. 9, most of this business having been done in the spring of 1767. And there are ample reasons visible for this. The Colonies were then going through the period of economic stress that was soon to lead to the Revolution; and the English Parliament was busy playing fast and loose with its policy toward American commerce and manufacture. The famous Stamp Act of 1765 went into effect just ten days before the first Manheim Glass House started active work and whatever the true onus of this tax may have been upon the actual business transacted in the Colonies, there can be no question as to the psychologically depressing effect that it had on the colonial business community. Two of the Philadelphia weeklies, — "The Philadelphia Journal and Weekley Advertiser" published by William Bradford, and the "Pennsylvania Journal," — ceased publication; Bradford explaining that his paper is "Expiring in Hopes of a Resurrection to life again" because it is unable to bear the burden of the tax, and the "Pennsylvania Journal" publishing its own epitaph thus: "The Last Remains of the Pennsylvania Journal which departed this life the 31st of October, 1765, of a stamp in her vitals, aged 23 years." The act was repealed in the following year, but the Townshend Act of 1767, levying duties on colonial imports, had an effect quite as widespread and depressing. Meetings were held in protest and non-importation resolutions passed, and as glass was one of the taxed commodities (the Townshend Act taxed crown plate, flint and white glass 4*s.* 8*d.* per hundredweight avoirdupois and green glass at $\frac{1}{2}d.$ it was one of the articles selected for non-importation. At a large meeting held in Boston on October 28th, 1767, for instance, one of the resolutions adopted was to the effect "That the town will by all prudent ways and means encourage the use and consumption of glass and paper made by any of the British American Colonies; and more especially of this province."

In other words everything in the local business conditions made for stagnant trade and shrinking credits, while the hopes held out by such declarations as the Boston one above quoted were quite enough to set a sanguine plunger like Stiegel to dreaming dreams about supplying all America with glassware and to considering mortgaging everything he owned in order to do so.

And this, in the event, is exactly what happened. Stiegel's Manheim business, apparently a fairly prosperous one during the 1765–6 and 1766–7 seasons, fell off most markedly in the latter part of 1767 and was probably less than self-supporting in 1768 and during the spring of 1769. Yet there is reason to believe that as early as May, 1767, Stiegel had formed the project of erecting a much larger and more ambitiously equipped plant and everything that he did from that time on shows that he clung to this project, and to the hope of financial salvation that he doubtless came to see in it, with a faith that gradually took on the semblance of foolhardiness and that at last hardened into fanaticism. In the end, as we shall see, he put all his financial eggs into this glass basket. And the nearer he drew to bankruptcy the more he acted as though the Manheim plant had made him a millionaire.

It was doubtless in connection with some of the inquiries relative to these enactments of Parliament that Governor John Penn, in a letter to the Lords of Trade and Plantations, dated from Philadelphia on the 21st January, 1767, refers to the "glass manufactury which was erected about four years ago in Lancaster County 70 miles from this city, by a private person. It is still carried on, tho' to a very inconsiderable extent, there being no other vent for their ware, which is of very ordinary variety, but to supply the small demands of the villages and farmers in the adjacent inland country." This is the letter which Benjamin Franklin quoted in 1768 in writing to his natural son, William Franklin, then Governor of the Province of New Jersey. This reference is evidently to the Elizabeth Furnace plant, and while the description is not flattering, it is doubtless sufficiently accurate from a London standpoint.

Moreover, it was exactly the "small demands of the villages and farmers in the adjacent country" that, at the time we are considering — that is to say 1766 and 1767 — more than offset for Stiegel the depressed conditions of the general colonial trade. The glass plant was prosperous in a quiet way, whereas the Stedmans were evidently pinched by the depression, since in 1765 they mortgaged their Manheim interests to Isaac Cox for £2700 and Alexander Stedman, on July 1st, 1766, mortgaged his third interest in Elizabeth Furnace to Daniel Wister, Merchant, of Philadelphia, for £720 and on September 4th of the same year a writ of Fieri Facias was issued by the Sheriff of Philadelphia against him at Wister's instance.

Stiegel's plans at this time are inferred from a most interesting document — an inventory, in his own handwriting, of the acreage of his various holdings exclusive of Manheim and a statement of his desire to sell out his share of the Elizabeth Furnace and Charming Forge properties for the sum of

£8000 ready cash in Pennsylvania currency. It is in the possession of the Historical Society of Pennsylvania and is reproduced in full in the appendix. It indicates, I think, that he was already contemplating the concentration of all his resources upon the Manheim manufacturing enterprise and had begun to dream of supplying the American market with a product to which the British import taxes promised to supply a sort of protective tariff. But he never seems to have published this statement as an advertisement, if such had been his intention; and it is certain that he found no purchaser for his share of the properties on these terms.

Indeed these properties, as one would expect in such uncertain times, do not seem to have proved saleable at all. For the Stedmans, who were now deep in financial difficulties, advertised their Manheim interests for sale in the " Pennsylvania Gazette " of March 24th, 1768, without results. And on March 9th, 1768, Stiegel himself, evidently seeing no prospects of a sale, mortgaged his Elizabeth Furnace and Charming Forge interests, as well as his Manheim holdings and his scattered lands in Lancaster and Berks counties, to Daniel Bennezet of Philadelphia for the sum of £3000.

The good feeling that had characterized the early years of the partnership between Stiegel and the Stedmans had evidently before this given way to dissensions. It is probable that the difficulties in which these Philadelphia merchants found themselves involved as the business of the colonies declined, made them more exacting in their demands upon their partner's management of their iron investments, and it is quite possible that Stiegel's increasing attention to the Manheim glass house, in which they were not joined with him, together perhaps with the probable reports of his undoubted extravagance, may have helped to disturb relations that had begun so amicably.

Indeed the Stedmans would seem, first and last, to have gotten but little return for their joint investments with Stiegel. Not only were they induced to invest in Charming Forge with him on the basis of a liberally watered valuation, — a favor which they returned in kind in the case of the Manheim property, — but a careful examination of the carelessly kept accounts of the various enterprises in which he was the working director of the partnership, inevitably raises the question in the mind of the examiner as to whether, in the long run, any actual money benefit ever accrued to the Stedmans from the business.

At any rate it is evident from the advertisement already referred to as published in the "Pennsylvania Gazette" of March. 24th, 1768, that a none too friendly dissolution of their relations was under contemplation. After offering the Manheim interest of the Stedmans for sale, the advertisement goes on to state that all persons having claims against either Elizabeth Furnace or Charming Forge are notified to deliver copies of their accounts to William Atlee in Lancaster in order that they may be settled and adjusted, adding that, "as a final settlement will be made of all the Company's Accounts of said iron works in March next, it is absolutely necessary that every person's demand should be made known to each partner."

Moreover, a lease (the original is in my possession) made in *September*, 1768, and leasing Charles Stedman's ⅓ interest in Elizabeth Furnace and his ¼ interest in Charming Forge to Stiegel from *April* 1st, 1768, to April 1st, 1769, for £300, and endorsed under date of October 1st with a receipt for the first half of the rent money, looks like a temporary settlement of, or an attempted escape from, some of these interpartnership disagreements. I own a somewhat similar document by the terms of which Alexander Stedman, on April 1st, 1769, leases his interests in these two properties to Stiegel for a year for a con-

sideration of one ton of bar iron per month; and another agreement between them, dated the 24th January, 1770, which recites
that on the approaching 1st of January 3 tons of this iron will
be due, and that Stedman does "hereby certify that upon Mr.
Stiegel's paying me the said 3 tons of bar iron or giving me an
order for the same, he, the said Henry William Stiegel, shall
retain in his hands so much of the stock belonging to me as
shall be sufficient to pay and satisfy him for my part and share
of the expense and cost laid out by him for repairing the said
works during the continuance of the 1st lease."

Moreover, a document, also in my possession, labelled "State
of the Case; A. Stedman vs. Henry Wm. Stiegel," recites at
some length and in legal language that "Henry W. Stiegel held
against the will and Consent of Alexander Stedman a certain
Iron Work Estate in the County of Lancaster with sundry
tracts of land and plantations containing 10,000 acres, ⅓ of
which is the property of the plaintiff." Also that in 1769 Stedman had brought a partition suit against Stiegel, but that the
latter had refused to grant judgment, and that, the case being
tried in the Supreme Court at Lancaster, the Jury had, "without leaving the Barr," found for Alexander Stedman, and that
"the declaration of Judgment went accordingly." It then goes
on to set forth that Stedman holds himself injured in the sum
of £1250, saying that "the Plaintiff does apprehend that it is
not material whether the defendant lost or gained by the said
estate during this period. He, the Plaintiff, holds it is sufficient
to say that he has been unjustly held out of his estate by the
Defendant and that therefore he ought, in justice, to make full
satisfaction to the Plaintiff by paying him at the rate of and
agreeable to the profits made in former years." It also sets forth
the claim that Stiegel "let several of the Plantations belonging
to said estate for considerable sums of money annually, and

that he has used the wood, ore and Implements and did likewise use a large quantity of Cynder;" for all of which Stedman demands as his share the sum of £250.

This document dates from 1772. But I quote it here since it gives the best obtainable idea of the bickerings and dissensions into which the Stedman-Stiegel partnership was falling at the time when Stiegel was contemplating his ultimate Manheim effort. It was in the very midst of these thickening difficulties, in the spring of 1769, that, on April 20th, the Stiegel books show that he closed the doors of the first Manheim glass house for the season and put all his available workmen and teams, as well as hired masons, carpenters and others, to work on the building of the new factory. And surely a man who, amid such discouraging conditions and faced by such a political and financial outlook, will gallantly tackle an enterprise of that magnitude and uncertainty, must believe that it offers him a sure escape from his entangling difficulties. If not, we can only fall back upon the Greek proverb and own that whom the gods would destroy they first make mad.

CHAPTER VI

THE CAREER CULMINATES

PERHAPS, after all, the Greek proverb will be thought to offer the more satisfactory explanation of Stiegel's conduct at this time. He did, it is true, spare neither energy nor — I was about to say "money," but "indebtedness" would be a juster term — in bringing his new glass factory to perfection. But at the same time he not only redoubled his extravagance, but seems to have taken to spending sums which he did n't have, very much as some men take to drink, — to have tried, as it were, to drown his worries in a sea of debt.

It will be remembered that in 1768 he borrowed £3000 from Daniel Bennezet on his various properties, and we have supposed that with this money he intended to develop his new plant. But in the same year in which he was building the new glass house he also built the tower (said to have been 50 feet square at the base, 75 feet high, and to have had a 10-foot square platform on top where a cannon was mounted) on the hill back of Elizabeth Furnace, and "The Castle," another tower-like structure, on top of another hill on the borders of Schaefferstown. Here also he is said to have had a cannon mounted on the tower top, and to have used the first floor of both structures as banquet halls where he entertained lavishly. A third cannon was placed on the band platform on top of the Manheim house, and Stiegel's arrivals are said to have been celebrated and his departures announced by the burning of powder.

It was no doubt also at this time that he developed, or at least brought to their most spectacular completeness, those habits and accessories of travel that have never — even in these days of private cars and six-cylinder Limousines — been forgotten in the Pennsylvania countryside. It is said that he used to start out from Philadelphia, to go either to the Furnace or to Manheim, with a coach and either four or eight horses, that this equipage was preceded through the country roads by outriders and a pack of hounds, and that watchers were stationed on the towers at Elizabeth and Schaefferstown and on the Mansion at Manheim who gave notice of the approach of this cavalcade so that its arrival might be met with music and the salute of guns.

Something, however, must be allowed here for the compound interest which Tradition pays on all investments of reality. The eight horses, for example, plus the outriders, is obviously an exaggeration. For on the Elizabeth Township assessment rolls for 1771, Stiegel is taxed £12 on 4040 acres of land, 10 horses and 3 cattle, and the following year he is assessed on 4100 acres, 8 horses and 3 cattle. He doubtless had other horses at Manheim, but what with the work on the estate, the riding necessary for all errands and messages, and the hauling connected with the iron works, 10 horses scarcely offers a chance of relay to a coach and eight. But there is no question that at this time he added to the luxurious comfort and lavish hospitality of his home life a deliberate sensationalism of public display.

Nothing madder or more futile can be conceived than this squandering of money obtained at the risk of his entire fortune. Moreover, either the multiplicity of his preoccupations, or the defiant mood born of desperate straits, was beginning to make him careless; for there is a paper in the Harrisburg State Library showing that in April of this same year of 1769, in a suit brought by Christopher Koocher, a judgment for £5–18 was entered against him, which attorney's fees of £3, a sheriff's fee of

16*s*., and a crier's fee of 1*s*.6*d*. brought up to a total of £9. 15. 6. This was destined to be the first of many judgments and indeed, like the tiny hole in the dyke which a splash of mud would have filled, the final undermining of Stiegel's solid achievements and superficial magnificence was decreed when that small entry was made on the court records.

Yet, as often happens, the onlookers at this desperate game seem to have thought Stiegel's position most secure at the very moment when it had finally become desperate. On October 1st, 1769, he was elected a Trustee of the Brickerville Congregation, and when in the same year the troubles in the Church were finally adjusted by the adoption of the Constitution, he was thought the most fitting guardian of the records of the dissension. The Church Books note that "In the presence of the Congregation and by a majority vote, the papers in the contest were given to Mr. Stiegel for safe keeping" (In Gegenwort der Gemeinde und der meisten Stime; die Kauf Briefe sind dem Herr Stiegel zur sorgfaeltigen Verwarung gegeben wurden).

But if he proved a bad general in his fight, now starting, against failure, he made indeed a gallant figure in the field until defeat actually overtook him. His one objective now became the achievement of an intercolonial recognition for his glass, and for the next few years he not only fought valiantly for the business connections and the advertising publicity which would secure this, but did wonders in developing his new factory to a point where it would sustain the reputation he strove to give it. His new glass house must have been a really fine affair and its equipment can not but have been measurably complete for its products remain to bear witness to its possibilities. Moreover he enlarged his force from its original small numbers to something like a hundred hands, and changed the exclusively German make-up of its original personnel to a cosmopolitan one in which English, German, Irish and Italian laborers of skilled training coöperated in the production of wares that were well fitted to rival in the American markets the imported glass products of Bristol and Germany. Even the Venetian decoration was, in a few cases, crudely approximated to—doubtless by the work of William and John Rago.

The Merchants of Boston and Philadelphia signed a non-importation agreement as to tea, glass, paper and painters' colors for the year 1769, and they were soon joined in this by New York, Salem, Massachusetts, and the province of Connecticut; and shortly after this Stiegel fired the first gun in his campaign for colonial recognition. This was an advertisement the first part of which dealt with the Elizabeth Furnace iron products and has already been given in connection with the description of that enterprise. The advertisement then continued —

> "The said Stiegel begs leave further to inform the public, that his Glass Manufactory in Manheim town, in the county aforesaid, is again at work, where are made all sorts of bottles, window glass and sheet glass; also retorts and other glasses for doctors and chymists. Orders, with proper directions, made to the said Michael Hillegas, will likewise be forwarded by him to said manufactory with despatch."

This appeared in the "Pennsylvania Chronicle and Universal Advertiser" of March 27th, and in the "Pennsylvania Gazette" of March 23rd and of May 4th, 1769, and as the Stiegel account books show that the works shut down on April 20th and the entire force turned in to help build the new factory, the advertisement would seem to have been largely a statement of intention and an attempt to create a market for a large surplus that the old glass house had on hand. The books indicate that he sold glass to the amount of £287. 12. 1 during this year and had on hand unsold at its close bottles to the value of £99. 17. 11

and sundry ware to the value of £6. 7. 9. This gives us an excellent idea of the ratio in which the old factory had run to bottles and window glass.

And nothing could better mark the ambitious change of the factory's policy and the broadening of its scope than the next advertisement to appear. This was printed in the "Pennsylvania Journal and Weekly Advertiser" of July 5th and of August 9th and 23rd, and ran as follows, —

AMERICAN GLASS WARE

consisting of a very necessary, useful and curious variety of white and blue FLINT, manufactured at MANHEIM GLASS WORKS, in Lancaster county, Pennsylvania, TO BE SOLD by BROOKS and SHARP, at the house of Nicholas Brooks in Front Street near Lombard Street, Philadelphia, where, merchants for exportation, retailers in Philadelphia, country storekeepers &c may be supplied with any quantity for cash or short credit and where all orders from the country &c shall be punctually complied with.

As the proprietors have been at an immense expense in erecting said works, and engaging some of the most ingenious artists in said manufacture, which is now arrived at great perfection, and above all, as at this crisis it is the indispensible duty, as well as interest of every real well wisher of America, to promote and encourage manufactures among ourselves, they hope from the glorious spirit of patriotism at present voluntarily and virtuously existing here, to receive the approbation and encouragement of the public, which they expect to merit a continuance of, by selling their goods on much lower terms, than such imported from Europe are usually sold.

N.B. Those Families who formerly sent orders to the Works, which were not complied with, may be immediately supplied, by applying as above.

The note at the end, encouraging disappointed customers to hope for better luck in getting their orders filled, bears out the idea that the Hillegas advertisement of 1769 was more in the nature of a prospectus than of a statement of facts.

In the Day Book of the Manheim Glass Works, under date of December 18th, 1770, I find an entry reading "This day fire was put in the Furnace and Glass making began," and at first I thought that this marked the first opening of the new works. But it is evident from the list of the new output, entered on two pages of the Ledger at the end of 1770 and headed "Statement of Glass sold, consigned and at glass store. For the year 1769 to April 1st, 1770," as well as from the advertisement just quoted and other internal evidence in the accounts, that this must refer to the fall season of 1770 and not to the first work done in the new building. The list just mentioned, a most interesting and instructive summary of the various shapes made at the factory and of the numbers manufactured, is printed in full in the chapter on the nature of the factory's output.

Stiegel was indeed making a splendid bid for the support of his fellow colonials, and from now on until his irretrievable ruin in 1774 he emerges from the musty records of his business and from the crackly advertisements in the old weeklies as for once the heroic figure legend has loved to picture him. Like a football player, ducking down the slippery field with the ball tucked tightly under one arm and the other extended to ward off the tacklers of the opposing side, he carried his glass project desperately forward, ducking and dodging amid judgments, foreclosures and sheriff's sales, with an effective although unavailing mixture of desperate courage and naïve effrontery.

In February, 1769, Isaac Cox foreclosed his mortgage upon the Stedmans' $\frac{2}{3}$ interest in Manheim, and on August 4th of that year he took title to this part of the property under a sheriff's deed. And thereupon Stiegel (it illustrates the splendid temper of the man's self-confidence) actually induced Daniel Bennezet to release his own Manheim interests from the blanket mortgage on his lands which Bennezet held (the consideration for the release named in the endorsement dated January 29th, 1770, is 5s.), and on February 1st, 1770, purchased the Stedmans' shares from Cox for £3000 and gave him a mortgage for £2500 covering all his Manheim holdings except the glass house, and another mortgage for £560 on the latter. This was football tactics of a decidedly spectacular order. He had gotten rid of interference by shouldering it and carrying it with him. He now owed Bennezet £3000 less five shillings on his holdings outside of Manheim, and owed Cox £3060 on his Manheim estate. And, by another record in the Harrisburg State Library, it appears that on April 23rd, 1771, a fee was paid to revive a judgment in the suit of Henry Keppele (from whom he had in 1765 bought his Philadelphia lots) against H. W. Stiegel, and that on October 5th a judgment was rendered against him for £297. 11. 5.

But he only broadened his advertising campaign, extending his notices from the Philadelphia to the New York papers. In the "Pennsylvania Gazette" of June 20th, 1771, and in the "Pennsylvania Journal and Weekly Advertiser" of June 20th and 27th, 1771, the following advertisement appeared, —

AMERICAN FLINT GLASS

Is now made at the Factory in Manheim, in Lancaster County EQUAL in quality with any imported from Europe where all merchants, storekeepers, and others, may be supplied on very reasonable terms; and as the Proprietor of those works well knows the patriotic spirit of the Americans, he flatters himself they will encourage the manufactories of their own country and hopes to be favored with their orders for Flint Glass; and begs leave further to assure them, that whatever commands he may receive, shall, with great punctuality and dispatch, be executed. Wholesale dealers may expect proper allowance or abatement on buying large quantities. — Patterns and orders will be received (and forwarded to the Manufactory) at Philadelphia, at the London Coffee house, and by Mr. Isaac Melcher, in Second Street; at

AMERICAN FLINT GLASS.

Henry William Stiegel,

PROPRIETOR of the firſt American flint-glaſs manufactory, in Pennſylvania, is juſt arrived in this city,
and opened a warehouſe near the Exchange, the corner op-
poſite to Mr. WALDRON's ; where he hopes for the encouragement of thoſe who wiſh well to the eſtabliſhment of
manufacturers on this continent ; and that the glaſs he offers to the public, will be found to rival that which is imported and ſold at lower prices.

Quart, pint, and half pint decanters ; pint crafts ; double flint pint, half pint and jill tumblers ; ſyllabub and
jelly glaſſes ; three feeted ſalts and creams ; wine and water glaſſes ; vinegar and muſtard crewets ; phials and other
bottles, for Chymiſts and Apothecaries, &c.

As his ſtay in town will be very ſhort, he begs the favour
of an early application to him from thoſe, who want a
ſupply of glaſs-ware.   6† 7⊙

a. New York Journal or the General Advertiser.
     Jan. 14 1773
      " 21
      " 28
     Feb. 4

American Flint Glaſs Store,

REMOVED from the ſtore kept by Mr. Henry Wm. Stiegel, near the Exchange, to the ſtore of JAMES and ARTHUR JARVIS, between Burling and Beekman's Slips, in the Fly ; who have for ſale of the American manufacture, quart, pint, and half pint decanters ; pint, half pint, gill, and half gill, flint and common tumblers ; carrofts, enamel'd, mafon, and common wine glaſſes ; jelly and cillabub glaſſes, with and without handles ; muſtard and cream pots, flint and common ; ſalts, ſalt linings, and crewets, wide-mouth bottles for ſweetmeats, rounds and phyals for doctors, wine and water glaſſes, ink and pocket bottles.---Orders taken for all kind of glaſſes for chymical or other uſes, agreeable to patterns. It is expected that all friends to American manufactures will do their utmoſt in promoting this. They have likewiſe for ſale as uſual, a very large and general aſſortment of earthen, delf, &c. Alſo a variety of Engliſh garden ſeeds of the laſt year's growth, viz. Early charlton, marrowfat, badmansdwarf, and golden hotſpur peas ; winſor, ſcarlet runners, and large white kidney beans ; lettice and cabbage of various kinds, carrot, parſnip, radiſh, turnip, &c. &c. Pepper, coffee, redwood, logwood, &c. &c.

*** Ready money given for broken FLINT GLASS.

b. New York Gazette and Weekly Mercury.
Feb. 8 1773
" 15
" 22
March 1

Lancaster, by Mr. Paul Zantzinger; at York Town, by Mr. George Stake; and at Baltimore, by Mr. John Little.

N.B. A GLASS CUTTER and FLOWERER, on application, will meet with good encouragement, at said Manufactory

HENRY WILLIAM STIEGEL

On July 25th and September 26th the same advertisement appeared with, however, a changed "N.B." stating that "Four boys are wanted as apprentices at the above Glass Works about 13 or 14 years of age." It is therefore supposable that the glass cutter and flowerer had applied and met with the promised "encouragement."

And the "New York Gazette and Weekly Mercury" in its issues of July 9th, August 5th and August 19th, 1771, displays the following notice, —

AMERICAN FLINT GLASS

Is now made at the factory in Manheim, in Lancaster county, in the province of PENNSYLVANIA, equal in quality with any imported from Europe, where all merchants, store-keepers and others, may be supplied on very reasonable terms; and as the proprietor of those works well knows the patriotic spirit of the Americans, he flatters himself they will encourage the manufactories of their own country and hopes to be favoured with their orders for FLINT GLASS, and begs leave further to assure them, that whatever commands he may receive, shall, with great punctuality and dispatch, be executed. Wholesale dealers may expect proper allowance or abatement, on buying large quantities. Patterns and orders will be received (and forwarded to the manufactory) at Philadelphia at the London Coffee House, and by Mr. ISAAC MELCHOR, in Second Street, at Lancaster by Mr. PAUL ZANTZINGER, at York Town by Mr. GEORGE STAKE and at Baltimore by Mr. JOHN LITTLE.

A Glass cutter and flowerer, on application will meet with good encouragement at said manufactory.

N.B. Said Melchor acquaints the publick, that he has lately received from the factory, a large and compleat assortment of

glass, which he is now opening and disposing of. Many gentlemen having already supplied themselves from him, renders it
needless to say that it is equal to most imported from Europe in
quality or cheapness. Patterns sent, will, with orders, be exactly
executed.

HENRY WILLIAM STIEGEL

And this active advertising evidently brought good results. On
July 1st, 1772, a new name, "The American Flint Glass Manufactory," was adopted for the Manheim glass houses. And taken
as a whole 1772 was the factory's most prosperous year. David
Rittenhouse mentions it repeatedly in his correspondence. On
February 4th, 1770, writing to Mr. Barton, he says "I have
seen a little curiosity with which you would be pleased; I mean
the glass described by Dr. Franklin, wherein water may be kept
in a boiling state by the heat of the hand alone and that for
hours together. The first time I shall be in Lancaster where I
hope to be next June, I expect to prevail on you to accompany
me to the Glass House where we may have some of them made,
as well as some other things I want."

These "pulse glasses" — small vials partly filled with water
and having the air exhausted from them and the mouth sealed
— were brought by Dr. Franklin from Germany and introduced
into England with some improvements of his own. The heat
of the hand was sufficient to make the water boil under the low
pressure prevailing in the vaccuum.

Later in same year David Rittenhouse again writes, "I am
much obliged for the glass tube, it will make a pretty barometer
though the bore is somewhat too small. I have compared it
with an English tube and do not think the preference can be
given to the latter. Please procure from the Glass House some
tubes of a size fit for spirit levels. The bore must be half an
inch in diameter and from 4" to 8" in length, as straight as
possible and open at one end only."

Again on June 20th, 1771, Stiegel himself, in a letter written from Elizabeth Furnace to John Dickinson, his friend, advisor and attorney, says that, "Mr. Bartram says the glass is equal to any he saw from Great Britain and agreed with me for a large quantity with a resolution to stop his importation and take all from me." He adds, "Concerning the works, they are too High and nobody at present times will give near the price for them, if you can sell them I have no objection," — the first intimation that reaches us of a desire to extricate himself from his difficulties by disposing of his factory which he later made every effort to put into execution.

The number and the distribution of his agencies was also greatly increased during these months of rapid expansion and determined effort. In Lancaster, Paul Zantzinger, to whom he was later to sell his Charming Forge interest when making his final efforts to keep financially afloat, was one of his large distributors; and he had many other customers there. In York, first and last, he had five agents. In Carlisle, the same number; in Philadelphia, Michael Hillegas, the London Coffee House, Isaac Melchor and Brooks and Sharp all handled his goods and took orders for his executing. Boston was one of his good markets, but here, oddly enough, local predilections seem to have made it impossible to sell his glass under its true colors, and I have found no single instance in which the dealers of that city, even those who like Mr. Cushing, his agent, and James Perkins and later Elizabeth Perkins, were large customers of the Manheim works, offered the glass in any way except as "imported."

Nor did he neglect either the more homely advertising possibilities nearer home, nor the chances of increasing trade by ministering to the vanities as well as to the material needs of his customers. On July 18th, 1771, the books show that Martin Gratz was paid for hauling glass to the "York Fair Glass

Home," and on September 18th of the same year it appears from the same records that Martin Grenier was reprimanded for neglecting a day's work; that the teams were busy hauling glass to Lancaster, and that "the Looking Glass Factory purchased Lead."

Stiegel, probably, therefore, is the first man who induced the Pennsylvania Menonnites to see themselves as others saw them.

In November, 1771, Garret Rapelje of New York, whose place of business was opposite the Fly Market, ordered 4 hogsheads of Stiegel glass from Michael Hillegas, and the success of the glass there was doubtless sufficiently great to induce Stiegel to take personal steps to capture the New York Market. In January, 1773, he went on to that city himself and rented a store, or warehouse, on Broad Street near the exchange and opposite the house of Mr. Waldron; the following advertisement appears in the "New York Journal or the General Advertiser" on January 14th, 21st, 28th and February 4th, 1773:—

AMERICAN FLINT GLASS.

HENRY WILLIAM STIEGEL,

Proprietor of the first American flint-glass manufactory, in Pennsylvania, is just arrived in this city, and opened a warehouse near the Exchange, the corner opposite to Mr. WALDRON'S, where he hopes for the encouragement of those who wish well to the establishment of manufacturers on this continent: and that the glass he offers to the public, will be found to rival that which is imported and sold at lower prices.

Quart, pint, and half pint decanters; pint crafts; double flint pint, half pint and jill tumblers; syllabub and jelly glasses; three feeted salts and creams; wine and water glasses; vinegar and mustard crewets; phials and other bottles; for Chymists and Apothecaries, &c.

As his stay in town will be very short, he begs the favour of an early application to him from those, who want a supply of glassware.

His stay in town was not only short, but the special warehouse for the display and sale of his glass was not retained. Perhaps it was only his intention to make a special display for a short time as a means of introducing his goods to the New York public. At any rate, the " New York Gazette and Weekly Mercury " of February 8th, 15th and 22nd, and of March 1st, 1773, contains the following, —

AMERICAN FLINT GLASS STORE

REMOVED from the store kept by Mr. Henry William Stiegel, near the Exchange, to the store of JAMES and Arthur JARVIS, between Burling and Beekman's Slips, in the Fly; who have for sale of the American manufacture, quart, pint, and half pint decanters; pint, half pint, gill, and half gill, flint and common tumblers; carrofts, enamel'd, mason, and common wine glasses; jelly and cillabub glasses, with and without handles; mustard and cream pots, flint and common; salts, salt linings, and crewets, wide-mouthed bottles for sweetmeats, rounds and phyals for doctors, wine and water glasses, ink and pocket bottles. — Orders taken for all kinds of glasses for chymical or other uses, agreeable to patterns. It is expected that all friends to American manufactures will do their utmost in promoting this. They have likewise for sale as usual, a very large and general assortment of earthen, delf, &c. Also a variety of English garden seeds of the last year's growth, viz.; Early charlton, marrowfat, badmans dwarf and golden hotspur peas; winsor scarlet runners, and large white kidney beans; lettice and cabbage of various kinds, carrot, parsnip, radish, turnip, &c. &c. Pepper, coffee, redwood, logwood, &c. &c.

Ready money given for broken FLINT GLASS

James and Arthur Jarvis remained his New York agents until, in 1774, his affairs there seem to have been closed out at the time of his failure by Templeton and Steward, auctioneers.

John Little and later Melchor Keener were his agents in Baltimore; a Mr. Harze in Hagerstown, Maryland, and Conrad Geork in Frederick in the same province. And he had numerous other agents throughout Pennsylvania; a complete list of whom, together with a list of customers to whom glass was sold, is printed in the appendix.

I have also printed in the appendix a full list of all of Stiegel's employees, both at Elizabeth Furnace and at Manheim, with the nature of their employment where that was discoverable from the records. The list may be of interest to the many descendants of the men thus shown to have been connected with an enterprise so prominent in Pennsylvania traditions; and as I was myself anxious to discover the nationalities of the new workmen and to identify if possible the men to whose hands the various and markedly individual decorations on the enameled pieces are attributable, and had compiled the list for that purpose, it seemed worth preserving.

It is of course perfectly evident to any student of early glass that Stiegel had expert help trained in the Bristol technique. Also that he had German workmen whose knowledge of the use of vitrifiable enamels was a professional one. And not only were the blowers and decorators employed in the last glass house thus specially trained, but the pot men and foremen who mixed and made the delicately colored glasses of the later period of the factory were evidently experts.

The conclusion is therefore warranted that Stiegel brought men over from Europe especially for the manning of his last factory. But the direct evidence of this that I have been able to obtain is so slight, that the fact of his having, in June 5th, 1772, taken on three indentured servants — Archibald Jackson for 4 years at £15; Patrick Flanigan for 5 years at £15; and John Williams for 7 years at £15 — is about the extent of it.

One of his experts we know that he did not obtain by importation, since the original contract between them is still in existence and may be seen in Mr. George A. Danner's museum in

Memorandum of an Agreement made this 4th Day of June 1773, between Henry William Stiegel Owner the American Flint Glass Manufactor of the one Side, and Lazarus Isaac Glass Cutter of Philadelphia of the other Side Witnesseth, that the Said H Willm Stiegel agrees to employ the Said Lazarus Isaac, at his Glasshouse in Lancaster County, as a Cutter and flowerer. And in each Branch of that Business, he the Said Lazarus Isaac promises, to do all in his Power and Capacity, to Serve the Said H. W. Stiegel for the Term of one Year from the date hereof According to the orders and Directions, he shall from Time to Time recieve from him the Said H. W. Stiegel at the Premisses, or from his Deputy And further to Contribute every thing in his Power for the Interest of the Work he is employed in. In Consideration of all which well and Truely done and performed, the Said H. W. Stiegel Promises and Covenants hereby to pay the Said Lazarus Isaac the Sum of Five Pounds Ten Shillings monthly, and every month, during the Said Year. And further to find him a House to live in, and also a Piece of Land for a Garden. As to fire Wood he is to be Suplied like the other Workmen, at five Shilling per Cord, hauled to his Door For the Rest of the Materials belonging to the Work Said H. W. Stiegel is to find them Except his own Tools and Utensils belonging to his Work.

For the true performens of all Promisses and Covenants the parties Bind themselves to each other in the penal Sum of One Tousond Pounds Larofull Money of Pensylvania, to bee paid by the Party making Default In Witness whereof they have here unto Set their Hand and Seal

Sealed and delivered in the presence of us.

Henry Wm Stiegel

Lazarus   his

Mark.

Bissmer

Jacob Frank

STIEGEL-LAZARUS CONTRACT, JUNE 4, 1773

Manheim. Mr. Danner kindly consenting to the reproducing of this document, a facsimile of it is here printed. And as the text throws considerable light on the customs of the time between employers and employed, and has a flavor of its own, it is here printed in full. It runs as follows, —

CONTRACT LAZARUS ISAACS

June 4, 1773. Memorandum of an Agreement made this 4th day of June 1773, between Henry William Stiegel owner of the Ameriican Flint Glass Manufactor of the one side, and Lazarus Isaacs Glass Cutter of Philadelphia of the other side.

WITNESSETH, that the said H. Will Stiegel agrees to employ the said Lazarus Isaacs, at his Glass House in Lancaster County, as a Cutter and flowerer. And in each Branch of that Business, he the said Lazarus Isaacs promises, to do all in his Power and Capacity, to serve the said H. Willm Stiegel for the Term of one Year from the date hereof according to the Orders and Directions, he shall from Time to Time receive from him the said H. W. Stiegelet the Premises, or from his Deputy. And fourther to Contribute every Thing in his Power for the Interest of the Work he is employed in. In Consideration of all which well Truely done and performed, the said H. W. Stiegel Promises and Covenants hereby to pay the said Lazarus Isaacs the sum of Five Pounds Ten Shillings monthly, and every month, during the said Year. And fourther to find him a House to live in, and also a Piece of Land for a Garden. As to fire wood he is to be supplied like the other workmen, at five shillings per Cord, hawld to his Door. For the Rest of the materials belonging to the Work, Said H. W. Stiegel is to find them. Except his own Tools and utensils belonging to his work. For the true performance of all Promises and Covenants the parties Bind themselves to each other in the penal Sum of One Thousand Pounds Lawful money of Pennsylvania, to be paid by the Party making Defauld. In Witness whereof they have hereunto Set their Hands and Seal

Sealed and delivered in the   HENRY WM STIEGEL   (LS)
presence of us   his
RUDOLZU BRÜNNER   LAZARUS [Name in Hebrew] ISAACS (LS)
JACOB FRANK   mark

Thus, to all outward appearances, the glass factory affairs were running smoothly and promisingly. The number of workmen was being increased, their pay was changed (December 15th, 1770) from a piece-work basis to that of monthly salaries. The factory was organized in a more formal fashion, and stricter rules enforced for the guidance of the men. For instance, on September 18, 1771, there is an entry in the books showing that "Felix Farrell was reprimanded for making glass for strangers without leave according to the 1st article in the rules of the factory." Yet, beneath the surface, Stiegel's affairs were steadily growing more hopeless and desperate. It is easy to understand that he must have been hard put to it to supply himself with the ready money necessary for these activities, even though he pushed his credit to the utmost and paid no bill of whatsoever kind that he could in any wise manage to leave outstanding. And when we come to consider the extent of his debts at the time of his final failure and the number of judgments that were out against him, we will see that he did not hesitate to take full advantage of these tactics.

He even let the management of Charming Forge pass out of his hands, doubtless finding himself unequal to making that venture profitable while his whole time was given to his Manheim venture. An unrecorded lease, now in my possession, shows that he leased his half of that property to Paul Zantzinger on May 26th, 1772, for a term of four years at an annual rental of £150; the lessor to have the right of cutting 500 cords of wood a year, and binding himself to keep the forge in repair at his own expense. And he had for some time been entertaining the idea of organizing a lottery, the proceeds of which he hoped would extricate him from his difficulties, and the history of which we will take up in the next chapter. But, meanwhile, the straits to which he was being reduced are indicated by a letter written by him from Manheim on February 15th, 1773, to John Dickinson, in which he says, "My glass house is making money fast and is in fine order and the last addition thereto finished;" but in which he also says, "Was informed by Mrs. Stiegel that the Sheriff of Lancaster County in persuance to Isaac Cox's execution levied all my effects and taken an inventory of all my household furniture."

CHAPTER VII

THE STIEGEL LOTTERY

ON February 27th, 1770, at a meeting of the German Society of Pennsylvania, Stiegel, who is thought to have been one of the original members of the society, offered them £100 if they would designate a man to run a lottery. His plan was not accepted, but the society did conduct a lottery on plans of their own, and raised £808 toward their new building by it; and the success of their venture very probably played its part in inducing Stiegel, later on, to try to avail himself of the same devise for extricating himself from his difficulties. At any rate, we find him on June 15th, 1772, writing to John Dickinson, "Thank you for the hint given me concerning lottery. Messrs. Willing and Morris and others have proceeded against me, which makes me and my family very uneasy and distressed and as the sale of the produce of the factory is slow for cash, though I have £1200 value on hand, I am not able to raise the necessary money to discharge my debts."

Again, on the 22nd of the same month, he writes to the same correspondent: "Messrs. Stedman at our last court obtained a verdict for partition. Think it would be your interest to buy Glass Works and then either rent or sell them. Think the legislature ought to have done things for Encouragement to make up for my loss sustained in bringing the factory to Perfection. I have been advised by many gentlemen in this and neighboring Provinces as well wishers to this Beneficial Manufactory in this country to put a Lottery on foot for that purpose to give them an opportunity to show their Zeal."

An ELEGANT ASSORTMENT of

HENRY WILLIAM STIEGEL's
G L A S S

Is to be SOLD by

WILLIAM SMITH, Broker;

At his store in Front-street, near the London Coffee-house.

THE friends and well-wishers to America have, on all laudable occasions, with an ardent zeal, shewed a spirit of patriotism worthy of themselves, and made it their particular study to encourage their own manufactures in preference to all others. It is therefore hoped, that so noble a resolution will induce them at this time, to purchase these wares, especially as they will be sold on as good terms, (and as neat in their kinds) as any imported from Europe, which on inspection (by impartial judges) it is no ways doubted will be acknowledged.

N. B. At the same place Two Pence per lb. will be given for all broken FLINT GLASS.　　　　3 m.

THE Proprietor of the American FLINT GLASS Manufactory, at Manheim, in Lancaster county, with the advice of many gentlemen in this city, his friends, has offered a Scheme of a LOTTERY to the patronage of the public, to enable him to carry on a Manufactory of public advantage, and to raise a sum of money for that and other beneficent purposes in the scheme mentioned.

This Lottery is calculated as much to the advantage of the Adventurers as any that hath as yet appeared. The encouragement he has already met with in the sale of a large number of the Tickets, though but just published, persuades himself the first Class will be ready for drawing at the short time appointed: Therefore those Gentlemen who incline to become Adventurers, are desired to be speedy in applying for Tickets, which by enquiring of the following Gentlemen, they may be informed where Tickets may be had, viz:

Mr. *Charles Stedman*, in Second-street; Mr. *William Smith*, Mr. *Michael Shubart*, Mr. *Leonard Melchor*, Messrs. *William* and *Thomas Bradford*, Messrs. *Hall* and *Sellers*, Mr. *John Dunlap*, Mr. *Henry Miller*; *Dieterich Reese*, at the sign of the King of Prussia; *Peter Wiltberger*, at the sign of the Butcher's Arms; *Henry Funck*, at the sign of the Black Bear; *Tobias Rudolph*, at the sign of the Three Kings, in Market-street; *Lewis Farmer*, at the sign of the Buck; *George Button*, at the sign of the Red Lion, in Second street; *Martin Kreider*, at the sign of the Swan, in Third-street; *Jacob Ehrenzeller*, at the sign of the Bay Horse, in Fourth-street; *Rudolph Bunner*, at the sign of the Prince of Orange, in Race street.

N. B. The Prizes will be published immediately after the drawing of the first Class, and paid by the Treasurer, with the greatest punctuality.　　　　4 w.

LOTTERY ADVERTISEMENT, IN PENNSYLVANIA JOURNAL AND WEEKLY ADVERTISER, MARCH 10, 1773

We know nothing of the development of the plan; who undertook the management for him; or indeed any of the preliminary details. But that Stiegel's idea took definite form within a few months after these letters were written is shown by the following advertisement, that appeared in the "Pennsylvania Journal and Weekly Advertiser" on March 10th, 1773:—

AN ELEGANT ASSORTMENT OF
HENRY WILLIAM STIEGEL'S

GLASS

is to be sold by

WILLIAM SMITH, Broker; at his store in Front-Street near the London Coffee-house.

The friends and well-wishers to America have, on all laudable occasions, with an ardent zeal, shewed a spirit of patriotism worthy of themselves, and made it their particular study to encourage their own manufactures in preference to all others. It is therefore hoped, that so noble a resolution will induce them at this time, to purchase these wares, especially as they will be sold on as good terms, (and as neat in their kinds) as any imported from Europe, which on inspection (by impartial judges) it is no ways doubted will be acknowledged.

N.B. At the same place Two Pence per lb. will be given for all broken FLINT GLASS.

The Proprietor of the American FLINT GLASS Manufactory at Manheim, in Lancaster County, with the advice of many gentlemen in this city, his friends, has offered a Scheme of a LOTTERY to the patronage of the public, to enable him to carry on a Manufactory of public advantage, and to raise a sum of money for that and other beneficent purposes in the scheme mentioned.

This Lottery is calculated as much to the advantage of the Adventurers as any that hath as yet appeared. The encouragement he has already met with in the sale of a large number of Tickets, though but just published, persuades himself the first Class will be ready for drawing at the short time appointed; Therefore those Gentlemen who incline to become Adventurers, are desired to be speedy in applying for Tickets, which by enquiring of the following Gentlemen, they may be informed where Tickets may be had, viz.

Mr. Charles Stedman, in Second-street; Mr. William Smith, Mr. Michael Shubart, Mr. Leonard Melchor, Messrs. William and Thomas Bradford, Messrs. Hall and Sellers, Mr. John Dunlap, Mr. Henry Miller; Dieterich Heese, at the sign of the King of Prussia; Peter Wiltberger, at the sign of the Butcher's Arms; Henry Funck, at the sign of the Black Bear; Tobias Rudolph, at the sign of the Three Kings, in Market Street; Lewis Farmer, at the sign of the Buck; George Button, at the sign of the Red Lion, in Second Street; Martin Kreider, at the sign of the Swan, in Third Street; Jacob Ebrenzeller, at the sign of the Bay Horse, in Fourth Street; Rudolph Bunner at the sign of the Prince of Orange, in Race Street.

N.B. The Prizes will be published immediately after the drawing of the first Class and paid by the Treasurer with the greatest punctuality.

The early date appointed for the drawing of the first class is not here given, but on June 9th, 1773, the " Pennsylvania Journal and Weekly Advertiser " published a full page of the successful numbers. The page is headed:—

A LIST of the Numbers which were Drawn PRIZES in the First Class of the AMERICAN FLINT GLASS MANUFACTORY LOTTERY. Those NUMBERS that have no Sums affixed to them are PRIZES of TEN SHILLINGS and those which have not £ affixed are computed in shillings.

Notes at the side of the page indicate that Number 2907, being the first number drawn, got a special prize of £5 in addition to the 10s. it was entitled to; and that Number 2510, being the last number drawn, got a special prize of £10 in addition to its original 10s. prize. No. 2098 drew the largest prize, drawing £100. The lowest and highest numbers to win prizes were No. 1 and No. 4997.

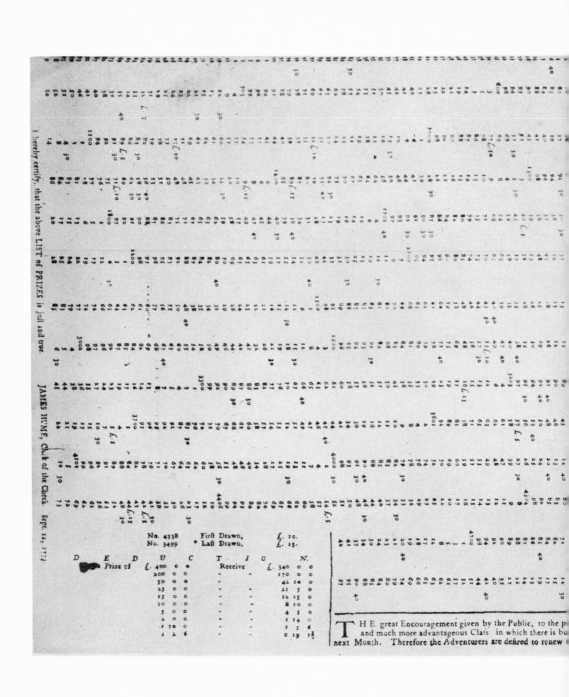

| | No. 4338 | First Drawn, | £. 10. |
| | No. 3499 | Laſt Drawn, | £. 15. |

D	E	D	U	C	T	I	O	N.
Prize of	£. 400	0	0	Receive	£. 340	0	0
	200	0	0		170	0	0
	50	0	0		42	10	0
	25	0	0		21	5	0
	15	0	0		12	15	0
	10	0	0		8	10	0
	5	0	0		4	5	0
	2	0	0		1	14	0
	1	10	0		1	5	6
	1	1	6		0	19	1½

THE great Encouragement given by the Public, to the p[...]
and much more advantageous Claſs in which there is bu[...]
next Month. Therefore the Adventurers are deſired to renew [...]

☞ *Those Numbers that have no Sums opposite to them, are Prizes of THREE DOLLARS each; and those which have not £. affixed, are computed in* SHILLINGS.

No. Priz.	No. Priz.	No. Priz.	No. Priz.	No. Priz.	No. Priz.	No. Priz.	No. Priz.	No. Priz.	No. Priz.	No. Priz.

Classes of this Lottery, enables the Promoters of it to inform the generous Adventurers, that the Third and Last, very rich, ... more than one Blank to a Prize, and the Prizes very valuable, is expected to begin drawing on Monday, the 18th of ... ts by Monday, the 4th of October, timely for the Drawing.

The following scale of REDUCTION is also provided for:

Prize of	£400. 0.0 receive		£340. 0.0
" "	200. 0.0	"	170. 0.0
" "	50. 0.0	"	42.10.0
" "	25. 0.0	"	21. 5.0
" "	15. 0.0	"	12.15.0
" "	10. 0.0	"	8.10.0
" "	5. 0.0	"	4. 5.0
" "	2. 0.0	"	1.14.0
" "	1.10.0	"	1. 5.6
" "	1. 2.6	"	0.19.1½

And at the foot of the page appears the following notice:

"The first class of the above LOTTERY having met with unexpected success, and a great Part of the Tickets in the Second Class being already engaged, it is proposed to draw the said Second Class, on Pettie's Island, on Monday the 12th of July next, or sooner if the necessary Preparations can be accomplished. Those persons therefore, who desire to become Adventurers, are requested to be speedy in their Application."

The stream of Adventurers seems, however, to have flowed less swiftly than was anticipated, as the second drawing did not take place till September 12th, and the announcement of the winning numbers (this time occupying full pages in both the " Pennsylvania Journal " and in the " Pennsylvania Gazette") did not appear until the issues of September 15th, 1773. This time the heading reads:

A List of the NUMBERS that came out PRIZES in the Second Class of the American Flint Glass Manufactory, Pettie's Island CASH LOTTERY
Those Numbers that have no sums opposite to them, are Prizes of THREE DOLLARS each; and those which have not £ affixed are computed in SHILLINGS.

The same list of reductions is given. Number 4338 is declared to have been the first number drawn and to be entitled to a special prize of £10 on that account; and number 3499 to have been the last number drawn and to be entitled to a special prize on that account of £15. No. 1892 (the date of the inauguration of the annual Stiegel festival, The Feast of Roses) drew the largest prize of the drawing, namely £200. It appears from this that the inducements to "Adventure" in the second class drawing had been made greater than in the first. Oddly enough, the lowest and highest numbers to draw prizes (and hence the first and last numbers to appear on the printed list) are the same in the second as in the first drawing — namely Number 1 and Number 4997.

At the foot of the page is printed, "I hereby certify that the above LIST of PRIZES is just and true. James Hume, Clerk of the Check. Sept. 12th, 1773."

And on the right hand side, parallel with the columns of winning numbers, one reads:

> "The great Encouragement given by the Public to the preceding Classes of this Lottery, enables the Promoters of it to inform the generous Adventurers, that the Third and Last, very rich, and much more advantageous Class in which there is but something more than one Blank to a Prize, and the Prizes very valuable, is expected to begin drawing on Monday, the 18th of next Month. Therefore the Adventurers are desired to renew their tickets by Monday, the 4th of October, timely for the drawing."

This drawing, however, seems never to have taken place; presumably because it proved impossible to sell enough tickets. Ledger No. 3 Manheim Glass House, one of the Stiegel account books, shows that 35 tickets for the third drawing were sold to John Phillips — one of the generous supporters of the lottery. And in a letter to F. A. C. Muhlenberg, dated November 24th, 1773, we read that, "On the twenty-first Sunday after Trinity, 1773, Mr. Henry William Stiegel presented to the Evangelical Lutheran Church of this place 12 tickets of the third class of his lottery, with the stipulation however that if they draw any prize it is to be used in each case for the benefit of the congre-

gation, but in such a manner as Mr. Stiegel with the consent of
the consistory of the church determine and direct. The following are the numbers 4748, 4758, 4184, 3238, 3399, 4233, 4385,
4747, 4386, 4417, 4546, 4647. Mr. Stiegel also adds the following condition: that if any of the affiliated congregations which
have been presented with tickets, should win a big prize, the
money is to be divided among them in a brotherly manner,
according to the number of tickets held by them. The tickets
have been returned to Mr. Stiegel in whose care they are to
remain until after the drawing."

This selection of tickets seems to me to be rather interesting,
as showing that Stiegel was by no means free from the picturesque weakness of the gambler's superstitions. 4546, 4647,
4748, 3399, 4386 and 4747 are manifestly chosen either for their
Abracadabrish suggestions, or for the implications of luck in
their internal geometric progressions. And his careful choice
of these promising numbers is no less eloquent of his interest
in the Church than is his providing for the spending of the proceeds in keeping with that incurable faith in the week-after-
next which lay at the root of his ruin. For in more ways than
in merely being a good Lutheran, he was of the company of
those who "trust to God." The world, to his eyes, was so full
of a multiplicity of splendid chances, that he (being he) could
afford to take any number of them. And when these began, in
outward appearance, to go against him, he persistently refused
to believe that Fate really meant it. To the very last he looked,
like Micawber, for something to turn up. And it was far more
the loss of this confidence in his own star, than the mere loss of
his accumulated property, that broke his spirit and prevented
his ever rising from the misfortunes that were now about to
overwhelm him.

At the end of November, then, this drawing, advertised to

take place on October 18th, was still hanging fire; and no announcement of winning numbers drawn in it, such as was published after each of the other two drawings, seems ever to have appeared. The lottery entries on the Stiegel books (like most other accounts thereon) are very hard to get any summarizable information from. It seems to have remained until September 30th, 1774. The total sums paid out seem to have aggregated £638. 12. 11, and the American Flint Glass Company seems to have made, as a result of all this advertising and excitement, the miserable sum of £83. 3. 10. John Dickinson, John Philips and Thomas Murgatroyd seem to have been the most generous supporters of the lottery — or else its most lucky beneficiaries. Dickinson seems to have drawn £282. 8. 7$\frac{1}{2}$, Philips £230. 4. 6 and Murgatroyd £157. 14. 7.

But it is quite evident that there were disputes, if not deficiencies due to diverted funds. In a statement of profits and losses on his holdings, made out on November 14th, 1774, by Stiegel in his own hand, we find the entries "Henry Miller Printer Lottery Ads. paid £39. 15" and again "Lottery Creditors account paid £168. 17 from sale of glass by William Smith."

This last entry may refer to the Pettie's Island lottery which we have been discussing, or it may refer to another matter upon which we have only so much knowledge as is afforded by the following hints, gleaned from the Manheim books and from another one of Stiegel's memoranda of his financial condition.

On August 15th the Manheim Ledger No. 3 shows an entry as follows, "Profit Heidelberg Lottery. Daniel Schman £426. 9. 8."

On September 1st another entry reads, "Cost general expenses lottery £43. 4. 10."

And in the second memorandum, just referred to, and which we will examine in detail later on, there stands entered under the head of "Actions in suit" and figured in as part of his total indebtedness the item, — "Heidelberg Lottery £390." But whether these entries refer to troubles arising from the non-payment of prizes to Heidelberg subscribers to the Pettie's Island drawings, or whether they have reference to another lottery managed from Heidelberg by Daniel Schman, and sufficiently supported to have left sums of this size in dispute, there is no way of determining. It seems likely, however, that Schman was his selling agent in Heidelberg (Schaefferstown), for the sale of tickets to his Pettie's Island drawings among the inhabitants of that region where Stiegel was so prominent a figure; and that the suit for £390, and the £168. 17 paid to Heidelberg Lottery creditors from the proceeds of the auction subsequently held by William Smith in Philadelphia, refer to prize money not paid over to the winners.

On the Manheim books on February 14th, 1774, is the entry of a settlement of accounts with Lazarus Isaacs, the "Cutter and Flowerer" whose agreement with Stiegel we examined in the last chapter. He is charged, among other items, £3 for 2 lottery tickets. The price of tickets, then, seems to have been the very respectable sum of £1. 10, and it is evident that if John Dickinson and men of that caliber were among the most generous of Stiegel's patrons, his own workmen were also to the fore in combining (after the Church Fair method) a chance of personal profit if they won, with the certainty of contributing to a worthy cause if they lost.

CHAPTER VIII

THE FAILURE

THE lottery seems to have been Stiegel's last active effort to retrieve his fortunes.

He had, of course, hoped that the proceeds from it would enable him to continue his boldly conceived and lavishly conducted campaign looking to the permanent establishment of his glass factory as a paying institution of intercolonial repute, capable of supplying the needs of the country with the finer as well as the more homely grades of glassware. But his utter lack of providence had already made this eleventh-hour struggle futile before it was begun. No conceivable profits from any likely lottery could, in the summer of 1773, have put him on his financial feet. And when this venture, for the success of which he had evidently drawn largely upon the good will of his most influential friends, not only proved a failure, but still further weakened his credit and injured his already waning reputation by the scandal connected with the handling of the receipts, his affairs seem to have gone quickly from a state of secret to one of public hopelessness.

His Charming Forge interest was already slipping away from him when the lottery was being organized. For the "Pennsylvania Gazette" of June 2nd, 1773, contains an advertisement stating that on June 8th, in pursuance of a writ dated April 10th, Stiegel's half interest in Charming Forge and the adjacent lands, as well as several tracts in Bethel Township, would be exposed for sale by Sheriff John Nagel of Berks County. And

Paul Zantzinger, who was then occupying the Forge under a lease from Stiegel, bought it in.

Numerous tracts of Stiegel's land in Elizabeth and Lebanon Townships were also advertised for public sale by the owner during 1773, as witnessed by a broadside preserved at the Historical Society of Pennsylvania; although the sale, if it took place, does not seem to have been successful. And already the foreclosure of the Cox mortgages on Manheim, and of the Bennezet mortgage on Elizabeth Furnace, were threatening, and were casting before them their shadows over Stiegel's affairs.

By the end of the year Stiegel was arrived so close to the limit of his resources that he was forced to curtail, if not to abandon, his making of the finer grades of glass at the Manheim factory, and to devote such activities as he was still able to maintain there to the making of the cheaper grades and more immediately marketable ware. About this time, from October 8th, 1773, to May 5th, 1774, he kept, on some of the blank leaves of the Elizabeth Furnace Day Book for 1771–72, a sort of running diary and account; and in this, on January 23rd, 1774, he states: "This evening set three small bottle pots on the Bottle side and one large Bottle pot on the Flint side." And on February 22nd he writes, "Were set 4 large Flint Pots, the hoods being taken off them to melt bottle metle in them." And he adds a list of some 22 hogsheads and 12 casks of glass shipped to various dealers and customers in the surrounding country — Lebanon, York, Carlisle, Elizabethtown, &c. But money was tight, and these efforts evidently proved of slight assistance to him; for he repeatedly complains in his correspondence that he is unable to collect bills owing him and that his glass is unsalable for cash.

The end, although he resolutely refused to recognize it, was now in sight. On February 3rd, 1774, John Feree, Sheriff of

Lancaster County, sold Stiegel's Manheim estates to Michael Dieffenderfer, and on February 9th Paul Zantzinger, who had evidently purchased Stiegel's ½ interest in Charming Forge at the Sheriff's sale advertised for June 8th, 1773, deeded this half of that property to George Ege, the nephew of Mrs. Stiegel. Ege subsequently became the owner of the entire property, built himself a fine stone residence there (the house is still standing although in bad repair), and here, in the middle of the next decade, gave Stiegel his last asylum in the days of his abject want.

These sales and foreclosures left Stiegel, who was, in addition, tormented by creditors and bombarded with judgments and suits, with Elizabeth Furnace as his sole remaining possession, and that only held on sufferance pending action by Bennezet. But he seems to have been quite incapable of believing that Fate would allow him to be finally overwhelmed. All through the spring and summer of 1774 he moved heaven and earth to get his influential friends to come to his assistance, constantly trying to arouse in them the faith in his own future which he still preserved unshaken. On August 4th, 1774, he wrote to Jasper Yeats from Manheim saying in part, "I am at present in a distressful situation, being persecuted by almost everybody. George Ross my attorney is often from home and employed in Publick affairs. Speak to Messers Ross and Biddle who generally appear for me, that no judgments may be obtained as I am assured that I can get over them by this fall." He also mentions having hopes of paying Mr. Singer £100, and having given his wife's watch to Nicholas Steel, and adds, "Fred Stone was sued as they say for my sake and have made a great noise about laying the blame to me for his being in Gaol, for which I should be very sorry if it were so." Again in the same letter he says, "Let them give me time and I will pay every dollar. Can it be that my former friends in Lancaster County will drive me to ruin when I have increased the wealth of the county by at least £150,000?" And finally he ends with, "I beg therefore you will take pity on an honest man that wants nothing but to satisfy everybody and maintain my cause. I could not send you a fee at present, money being too scarce, but shall satisfy you with honor and gratitude."

Seven days after this letter was written, on August 13th, 1774, Sheriff John Feree of Lancaster County advertised a third of Elizabeth Furnace and all the Brickerville property, "being the estate of the said Henry William Stiegel Seized and taken in execution and to be sold by virtue of a writ of Levari Facias." One of the original broadsides is owned by the Historical Society of Pennsylvania. And on August 23rd Stiegel wrote at considerable length to John Dickinson, and sent the appeal, together with a detailed statement of his liabilities and his assets as he optimistically figured them, by the hand of his wife who was to explain the situation and, evidently, to try to get Dickinson to step between her husband and his more pressing and relentless creditors. The letter is so indicative of Stiegel's attitude, and the statement throws such light upon his actual financial condition, and upon the persistent and fateful optimism with which he constantly masked his true position from himself, that I print both documents in full. The letter is as follows, —

MANHEIM August 23d, 1774

SIR

This comes to you by Mrs. Stiegel and have also by her sent you a copy of Jacob Hubers last will. The Heirs would not sign the Deed and according to the Will I can't see it Necessary. John Huber has signed it, but as the Will alters the case I think another writing must be Framed for him & the Executors to sign the Titles to the Swamp Place can find nothing of them. I shall be Glad to hear what you have Done about the Works whether there is to be a survey as you proposed, also if you Got Them Titles from Mr. Giles I sent you Mr. Olds and John Hubers hereby. I am at present hard pushed by sundry of my Creditors as Mrs. Stiegel will inform you. I have a Good Estate as Mrs. Stiegel will show you the situation of. I could pay them all If they would but give me Time. Mr. Cox having Entered up his Judgment Keeps me Tied hand and feet that I can make no sale or use of my estate to Advantage. They all wait for a Sheriff's sale. All this might be altered if I hath but a friend to Assist me and take my part. Mrs. Stiegel will show you the Situation of my Estate and inform you of our Distressed Situation which is in your power to Relieve — or else I must be ruined. Mr. Cox is too hard as I am sure I can make the money out of the sales in the Estimate mentioned in 12 or 18 months if the people only were out of the Notion or Expectation of a Sheriff's sale which can be done no otherwise than taking up the Mortgage and Judgment from Mr. Isaac Cox and Entering satisfaction in the office for which purpose I am ready to grant a Deed or fee Simple or as you will advise to you for that part of the Estate mentioned in the Estimate at £5015 to satisfy Mr. Cox's Demand of £2815 which I think is the whole Principal and Interest due to him to August the 2d or thereabout. This being Done I would set about selling of it as fast as I could and send the people Down with the money and Security (after the Terms of Sale should be settled between us) for you to Give them Deeds till the whole sum and Interest was Reimbursed to you, and then leave it to your Generosity to Divide with me or Do as you please; this would be befriending me Indeed. At this rate I should Get the rest of my Estate free. Collect my Debts and Enabled to pay my friends, honorably raise and Establish my Credit and carry my Factory on with Spirit which would make Considerable Profits Especially if a non importation Agreement should take place, but in my present situation I am quite discouraged; most every one imposing on me and taking advantage of my Distress.

I am flattering my Self of your best Inclination of obliging me and whilst you are but Safe, more I expect not and that will Appear very Clear by the Estimates. The Satisfaction that will arise within your own breast must be very great when you reflect that by Assisting a man struggling with Difficulties and one who Does all in his power to pay everybody with the Strictest honor, you may prevent the Ruin of a Family.

Upon the whole, Suffer me once more to Entreat and Beg your Assistance. Depend on it you will not Suffer. I Remain after my Humble Compliments, with Great Esteem
  Sir
   Your most Afflicted and much Distressed
    Humble Servant
     HENRY WM. STIEGEL

And the statement of his affairs which accompanied this communication—it is in Stiegel's own hand and is preserved among the Dickinson letters in the Historical Society of Pennsylvania —runs thus,—

Daniel Bennezet Mortgage	£3000		
Interest to March next	270		£3270.
Isaac Cox Mortgage on the Forge	1000		
Manheim Estate	3000		
Interest due	500. 5. 2		
A bond of	100		
A debt	87. 5.11		4687.12. 1
Judgments to Discharge			
Wischard and Edwards	250		
Michael Blessing	124		
Adam Wilman	67		414
Actions in Suit			
Heidelberg Lottery	390		
Henry Kupell	360		
Balser Helzor	100		
Eberhard Michale	350		
Adam Diefenderfer	80		1280
Bonds			
Frederick Juirer	100		
Matthias Burk	350		
Isaac Wikoff	150		
Joseph Shansbery	67		
George Glass	50		
Jo. Armstrong	34		751
	TOTAL		£10,402.12. 1

Value H.W.S.

⅓ Elizabeth Furnace................................	£4000	
½ Charming Forge.................................	2500	
Mill built near furnace, rents £50 per annum...........	800	
Heidelberg Estate, 2 houses & 8 acres land............	250	
Tavern House & Stables & lots at Newmanstown.......	100	
A Plantation near the above 100 A. Rents £6..........	100	
Mill at Manheim & 20 acres of land..................	600	
Lots sold to Toubeberger for	200	
Two lots with Tavern and Stable....................	300	
4 ten acre lots....................................	400	
Sundry squares and lots............................	400	£9650

Glass Unsold

Phil. Store, William Smith exclusive of orders..........	260	
N. Y. James and Arthur Jarvis......................	215	
Baltimore, Jo. Littele..............................	57	
Melchor Keener	23	
York, Mr. Sleeg...................................	23. 1	
Hanover, R. McCalister	91.14	
Frederickstown, Conrad Geork......................	140	
Hagerstown, At Mr. Harzo..........................	67. 8	
Frederick Bonner..................................	39.10. 4	
Carlisle, Jo. Wilkins...............................	64. 0.10	
At Glass House....................................	200	
Boston. Cushing Esq.	140	1320.14.2
	TOTAL	£10,970.14.2

The within sale being completed there will remain for me and family the Estate (Manheim) now mortgaged to Isaac Cox. All the ground Rents of Manheim amounting to £240 per annum actually received last October £4000. its capital. The Large Brick House & Buildings adjacent with 92 acres of the best land £2500. The Glass House, Houses, Stores, Lots and Buildings thereto belonging will run at £150 per annum. £2500. £9000.

Some action Dickinson seems to have taken in consequence of this and other similar appeals from Stiegel, but just what that action was, — whether he advanced money to him, or whether, as it seems likely, he joined with Bennezet in the bidding in of the Furnace at the Sheriff's sale, it is not possible to ascertain. Certainly Stiegel from this time on, as long as he continued to entertain any hopes whatever of recovering his property and his position, appears to have regarded himself as not only beholden to Dickinson, but as in some sense at his mercy and under his orders. We will come to the evidence of this later on.

On the other hand, Stiegel's appeals to Jasper Yeats seem to have brought him no practical aid, and the last of these letters of which I have found any trace is dated October 14th, 1774; it says in part —

> "Sir; I have been awaiting your answer to my last letter. Singer" — (to whom in a former letter to Yeats he had promised to pay £100, but who does not figure in his statement to Dickinson) — "has come home, but I have received no answer yet. Let me therefore beg the favor of you hereby to send it and if possible to prevail on Mr. Singer to send me his answer to my last. I doubt not that if he were to come here we might think of some plan that would help me and at the same time secure him and Mr. Stone" — the man for whose being in gaol Stiegel was said to be responsible.

Meanwhile Stiegel had, as evidenced by numerous entries on the books in his own handwriting, been in some sense, or in some capacity, continuing his connection with the Manheim Glass House. On May 5th, 1774, there is an entry in his own writing which states, "Glass House shut down. Manufactory left off making glass and all hands discharged out of Mr. Stiegel's employ and on and after May 5th as above mentioned are to account for the same with Messrs. Smith and Simund. They having leased the works and Manufactory." There were, at this time, 13 men working, but whether this indicates a bona fide lease of the Glass House, and Stiegel's subsequent entries on the books were made in the capacity of an employee, or whether the alleged lease was a move in the defensive campaign against his besieging creditors, does not at all appear from the documents at hand. In August and September there are entries referring to the profits and expenses of the lottery.

On August 17th there is an entry showing payments to Isaac
Cox of interest as follows, —

On Forge Bond for Oct. 1772 in full thereof July 19th 1773 .... £ 45
On Manheim Bond, 2 years as above £2500..................... 67. 4
On Glass House Bond from August 2nd 1774 on £560. 2 years..... 300
On 2 final Bonds amounting £196. 6. 2 years.................... 11.15.1
                                                              _____
                                                              £423.19.1

In October there are entries showing that certain workmen
began work. In the early part of November there are recorded
statements of loss and breakage at a vendue of glass held by
Templeton and Steward, in New York. And on November
14th, in Stiegel's own handwriting, there is the following statement of profits and losses:

"Elizabeth Furnace sale.. £2250
Manheim Estates sold by Isaac Cox lost............................ 5562. 7. 8
Manheim improved lots.. 42. 9.10
Glass House tools.. 50
House Furniture.. 342.19
Store and Goods.. 65. 3. 6
Elizabeth Furnace Mill, Bennezet................................. 550.

Elizabeth Furnace

To stock ⅓ part of land and premises............................ £2500
To Elizabeth Furnace Plantation................................. 1200

By Daniel Bennezet sold on his judgment and mortgage for sum of....... 1450

Profit and loss... 2250

MANHEIM ESTATES
To stock.. £8262. 7. 8
By Isaac Cox, sold Feb. 3rd...................................... 2700

Profit and loss... 5562. 7. 8

Philadelphia Store.. 356. 3.11
By stock.. 232. 8

Profit and loss 123.15.11
Lottery Creditors' account paid £168.11 from sale of glass by William Miller.
Henry Smith, Printer Lottery ads. paid £39. 15."

In short, during these months the books are carried on in
very much their usual haphazard fashion, with about the usual
number of entries in Stiegel's writing; and, except the note

about the lease itself, there is nothing to indicate that the management of affairs had passed out of his hands. As neither Smith nor Simund appear in any of the subsequent affairs of the Glass House, I am inclined to believe that they were mere dummies, raised for a moment above the breastwork of his last ditch, to distract the fire of the enemy. But be this as it may, even this last ditch was now become untenable. Both the Cox and the Bennezet mortgages had been foreclosed. Whatever aid Dickinson was able, or saw fit, to afford him, did not run to the paying of his debts and the giving to him of a free chance to recoup his fortunes. And, late in the fall of 1774, he was not only driven to abandon his Manheim hopes, but was, either at the instance of some of his many creditors, or through some development of the scandal attending the abortive undertaking of the third drawing of his lottery, cast for a time into prison. The last entry in the Manheim books in his own handwriting bears the date of November 24th, 1774.

CHAPTER IX

THE STIEGEL IMPRISONMENT

T HAT Stiegel was imprisoned for debt after his failure, and that he was liberated on Christmas Day, 1774, are two of the facts that have, from the first, maintained their place in the Stiegel tradition. And while there have been times when the elusive and contradictory character of the contemporary documents bearing on the case have made me almost doubt whether he ever actually saw the inside of a gaol, yet on the whole it seems pretty certain that for a short time, — say from late November until Christmas, 1774, — he was in sober reality behind such bars as were then provided — either in Lancaster or in Philadelphia — for the detention of the insolvent and the unfortunate. But the utmost limits of his possible incarceration lie between November 24th, 1774, when the last entry in his own handwriting appears on the Manheim books, and January 24th, 1775, when he again writes to John Dickinson from Manheim, saying,

> " According to my promise sent you hereby, the situation of the Furnace, Estates, Plantations, anything in my power I can do for the best of the Estate to save you and the other gentlemen command me, I shall do it with pleasure, but should be glad to know your sentiments in Time, that I might Engage me self otherwise. Mrs. Stiegel joins me in our best compliments to you and spouse and I am, Sir,
>
> Your most Obedient Humble Servant
>
> HENRY W. STIEGEL."

His term of imprisonment has been given as lasting as long as two years; and much has been said about the effect of confinement upon his health, and of the pallid and broken man who emerged at the end of the ordeal. But this is merely our old friend Tradition at her tricks of cutting an ample garment of detail out of the cloth of a limited knowledge.

The facts are as follows: On November 24th, 1774, Stiegel was still in Manheim.

On December 15th, 1774, he sent out (presumably to all his creditors) the subjoined printed communication, the name of the addressee and the changed day of the week being written in. Mr. George H. Danner owns the copy here reprinted: —

Philadelphia, December 15th, 1774

Sir;

Please to take notice. That I have appealed to the Honorable House of Assembly for a Law to relieve my Person from Impris-

Thursday

onment. If you have any Objection please to attend ~~Monday~~ next at three o'clock in the afternoon, at the Goal in this city, before the Committee of Grievances.

Your humble servant
Henry W. Stiegel.

To John Brubaker

In the news columns of the " Pennsylvania Gazette " of December 28th, 1774, it is stated that,

> "On Saturday last the General Assembly adjourned to the 20th of February next. During their sitting the following laws were passed" (here follow the titles of four laws and then) "5th. An Act for the relief of Henry William Stiegel languishing prisoner in the gaol of Lancaster County with respect to the imprisonment of his person."

The act above noted is referred to in the printed Acts of the General Assembly of Pennsylvania, John Penn Lieutenant Governor, 1774, Chapter DCCXI, as a "Private Act Passed December 24th, 1774. Referred for consideration to the King in Council July 21st, 1775, and allowed to become a law by lapse of time in accordance with the Proprietary Charter." The act states that Stiegel was "willing to assign over all his effects for the use of his creditors, for the payment of his debts, and to discharge such as shall thereafter remain unpaid, as soon as by his industry he can find means of satisfying such creditors; yet by his imprisonment he is disabled from putting into execution his just intentions and reduced to great distress." It provides that the "Justices of the County Courts of Common Pleas for the County of Philadelphia, or any three of them, on application to them for that purpose in writing made by Henry Wm. Stiegel, shall appoint a certain day and place for holding a special Court of Common Pleas." And it allows an exemption in his favor of "wearing apparel and bedding for himself and family not exceeding 10 pounds in value in the whole."

It also there appears that, at a Council held in Philadelphia, on Saturday, December 24th, 1774, at which were present the Honorable John Penn, Esq., Governor, Richard Peters, Benjamin Chew, James Tilghman, Andrew Allen and Edward Shippen, Jr., Esquires, the governor laid upon the board for consideration two bills, the 2nd of which was the bill for Stiegel's relief; and that this was read, considered and immediately returned to the House with the inserted amendment, "nor any debt due to any distant or absent creditor, to whom notice shall not have been given pursuant to the Direction of this Act." And that the Assembly agreed to this amendment at 2 P.M. and that the Speaker presented to the Governor five bills, of which this formed one, and that his Honor enacted them into laws and signed a warrant for affixing the seal to them.

As a matter of fact, however, the warrant for the affixing the Great Seal of the Province to this act was not signed until April 28th, 1775. It is now in the possession of the Historical Society of Pennsylvania and runs as follows: —

THE HONORABLE JOHN PENN ESQUIRE, Governor and Commander in Chief of the Province of Pennsylvania and Counties of New Castle, Kent and Sussex on Delaware

To EDMUND PHYSICK of the Great Seal of the said Province Esq.,

GREETING

These are to authorize and require you to affix the said Seal to the Exemplification of Laws passed by me the 24th of December last." (Here follow three Acts and then) "An Act for the relief of Henry William Stiegel a languishing Prisoner in the Gaol of Philadelphia County with respect to the imprisonment of his person." (Then follow ten other acts.)

WARRANT:

Given under my Hand on the lesser Seal of the said Province at Philadelphia the 28th day of April 1775."

And, among the original documents owned by the New York Public Library, is the following letter:—

To the Right Honorable the Lords of His Majesty's most High Privy Council for Plantations.

MY LORDS:

Pursuant to your Lordships' order of the 21st of July last we have taken into our Consideration Twelve Acts passed in the Province of Pennsylvania in December 1774 & March 1775 Titles of which are contained in the List hereunto annexed whereupon we beg leave to Report to your Lordships

That these Acts being passed for the purposes of internal Police & Economy or for the relief of insolvent debtors languishing in confinement and Richard Jackson, Esq., one of His Majesty's Counsel whom we have consulted thereupon, having reported to us that they appear to him to be proper in point of Law, we see no reason why all the said acts may not be allowed to take effect.

We are &c. &c.

WHITEHALL,
Nov. 24, 1775

JAMES JENYNS
BAMBER GASCOYNE
WHITEHED KEENE
G. F. GREVILLE

But these latter documents are merely the final knots in the legislative red tape which the authorities evidently continued to tie around the Stiegel case long after it was disposed of by the more common-sense methods of actual practice. By the proprietary Charter of the Province of Pennsylvania, all laws passed by the Assembly and signed by the Governor had, in order to become valid, to be referred to London and either approved by the King in council, or allowed to become laws by failure of that body to disapprove of them. But it is quite evident that in practice the colonial authorities sometimes took the action of the Home Government for granted, and put acts that dealt with minor local affairs into instant execution. And this is evidently what was done in Stiegel's case. The act, as we have seen, was passed on December 24th, 1774. It was sent to the Governor the same day; it was amended and returned to the Assembly; the amendment was accepted and the bill again sent to the governor and signed by him; all on this same afternoon. And though nearly a year had to elapse in the ordinary course, before the final imprint of validity could be given to the act, we know that Stiegel was a free man within the month. He was doubtless liberated as soon as the bill was signed and probably reached home for Christmas.

But there is something about this imprisonment of Stiegel's that, while equally mysterious, would appear to be more darkly significant than the mere matter of its duration. To be imprisoned for debt was doubtless a terrible blow to the pride of a man of Stiegel's temperament, and almost any conceivable breaking down of his energies, and of his self-confidence, might reasonably be ascribed to the effect of so definitive and public a disclosure of the weak foundations that underlay the structure of his fortunes, his generosity and his ostentation. But although a debacle of this sort would be sure to alter the

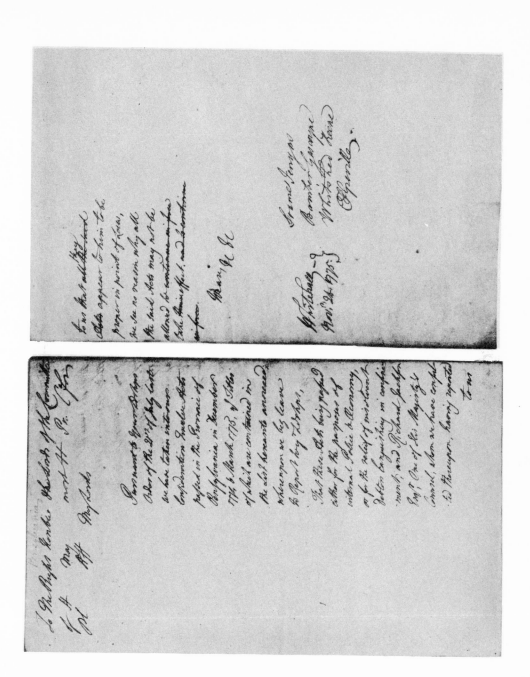

WHITEHALL LETTER, NOV. 21, 1775

attitude of his self-seeking adulators, and of the horde of followers who doubtless flocked to his feasts and fattened upon his foolishness, the complete change visible in the treatment accorded him by his more influential and disinterested friends after his release, — the coldness shown him by Dickinson and the loyal but evidently aloof charity manifested toward him by George Ege, — inevitably raise in the mind of the investigator a question as to whether there was not, in what led up to this detention, something (perhaps connected with the lottery) which the public opinion of the day regarded as differentiable from mere insolvency. That Stiegel himself felt this, and that he believed himself innocent of any wrongdoing, would seem to be shown by the wording of a prayer which he wrote down during his imprisonment on the fly leaves of a book of prayer, afterwards preserved among the Ege family effects. The prayer runs as follows —

"Honored and truthful God. Thou hast by Thy laws earnestly forbidden lying and false witness and hast commanded on the contrary that the truth shall be spoken.

"I pray Thee with all my heart that Thou wouldst prevent my enemies who like snakes are sharpening their tongues and who, although I am innocent, seek assassin like, to harm and ridicule me, and defend my cause and abide faithfully with me. Save me from false mouths and lying tongues, who make my heart ache and who are a horror. Save me from stumbling stones and traps of the wicked which they have prepared for me. Let me not fall among the wicked and perish among them.

"Turn from me disgrace and contempt; and hide me from the poison of their tongues.

"Deliver me from the bad people and the misfortune they utter about me may recoil on them. Smite the slanderers and let all lying mouths be stopped of those who delight in our misfortunes and when we are caught in snares so they may repent and return to Thee.

"Take notice of my condition, Oh, Almighty Lord, and let my

innocence come to light. Oh, woe unto me that I am a stranger and live under the huts of others. I am afraid to live among those who hate friends. I keep the peace.

"My Lord, come to my assistance in my distress and fright amongst my enemies, who hate me without a cause and who are unjustly hostile, even the one who dips with me in the same dish is a traitor to me.

"Merciful God, who canst forgive transgressions and sin, lay not this sin to their charge. Forgive them for they know not what they do. Forbear with me so that I may not scold again as I have been scolded and not reward the wicked with wickedness but that I may have patience in tribulation and place my only hope on Thee, O Jesus and Thy Holy Will.

"Almighty God if thereby I shall be arraigned and tried for godliness then will I gladly submit for Thou wilt make all well. Grant unto me strength and patience that I may through disgrace or honor, evil or good, remain in the good, that I may follow in the footsteps of Thy dearly-beloved Son, my Lord and Saviour who had to suffer so much for my sake.

"Let me willingly suffer all wrongs that I may not attempt to attain my crown with impatience, but rather to trust in Thee, My Lord and God, who seest into the hearts of all men and who canst save from all disgrace. Yet Lord hear me and grant my petition so that all may turn to the best for mine and my soul's salvation for Thine eternal wills sake. Amen."

CHAPTER X

FINAL YEARS

FOR some time after his liberation from gaol, Stiegel (who by the terms of the act that freed him had had to turn over his entire remaining possessions, except ten pounds worth of clothes and bedding, for the benefit of his creditors) seems to have continued to hope. He entertained, — on what possible grounds it is now impossible to imagine, unless in the basic grounds of his own temperament, — the belief that he might yet pay off his debts, recover his property, and resume the position that he had lost. We have already seen his letter to Dickinson, offering to look after the interests of the Furnace and the Manheim Estate. On the same day, January 24th, 1775, he wrote to Jasper Yeats,

E. I. Jan. 24 1775

DEAR SIR, — I told you last week that Conrad Mark had agreed to take up the action which he did, but since sent a few lines he would not stand to it. Now sir! you know my poor situation, all I have is through the indulgence of the assignee and judgment creditors and the charity of my friends and as I am not in any business have enough to do to maintain me and family with what little I have to do and besides he has no more right than any other creditor after I assigned all my estate. Let me therefore beg of you for the sake of me and my poor family to get him to drop the action which I believe he will do on your advice — I have to get in business as soon as Times will Turn. In the mean time I hope you will act my friend and as soon as I get able shall make satisfaction. Remain, Your most obed't Hble Servant,

HENRY WM. STIEGEL

On March 30th, 1775, John Feree, Sheriff of Lancaster County, gave Michael Dieffenderfer a deed to all Stiegel's

Manheim holdings including the glass house, — the same having been purchased by him at the Sheriff's sale of February 3rd, 1774. And it appears that Stiegel then moved to Elizabeth Furnace and, on somewhat questionable authority and informal terms, acted as its caretaker. This appears from the following letter, addressed to John Dickinson in the fall of 1775.

ELIZABETH FURNACE Oct. 25, 1775

MOST HONOURED FRIEND

Since mine of April, hath not the pleasure of hearing from you. As I know you are constant overwhelmed with the business of our present unhappy Country affairs, I was afraid to be troublesome to you, but could no longer Hesitate to write hereby, and inform you, that since I saw you last, — Mr. Isaac Cox completed my ruin by the sale of my whole Manheim Estate for a Title more Mean one fourth of its value as it does not pay near for My buildings. Though he hath given me the fairest Promises, still he gave Me fatal Blow — I could therefore not stay any longer there, seeing all my hopes frustrated and everything taken out of my hands to make that Valuable Manufactory now fully completed either serviceable to me or my Country, — therefore at the desire and order of Mr. Charles Stedman, with a promise to inform you and Mr. Bennezet to Get both Your Concurrence of which I would not have the least doubt by your Genteel behaviour to me and Family: I moved to the Furnace and took Possession of the Premises and have lived there since and taken care of the Estate, having no further orders from you or the other Gentlemen, I could not undertake any Thing further. Mr. Bennezet was since here and Told me that neither he or you approved of my living or remaining here, — which Surprised me very much, — his reason was that he was afraid it would Detain others from buying, — I should be very sorry, that should be the case, but am Assured of the Contrary. I told him I Intended, and am still in hopes, to make us friends, to satisfy Mr. Bennezet and have my shares again; and Towards which he made me a most generous Proposal and should have Succeeded before now if it was not for the present alarming situation of our Country.

I must say hath Mr. Cox acted with such Generosity I might be yet in the possession of my Glass factory and hath it completely at Work, for mine and my Country's Benefit. But Alas! Now I am ruined and a poor man, that Supplicates your Commiseration for me and my poor Family and hope you will be favourable to us. You may rely on my Industry

and faithfulness that I shall use all my Endeavor to Promote your Interest and to Deserve the Confidence and Trust you will confer on me. I am Assured you can't at the present Time make any thing to save your money and as soon as anything is to be done, or can be done, I think I can bring it to a bearing sooner than any Body. I shall be glad to hear from you and also of your Esteemed Family by the Bearer my Nephew Elias Wood my poor Wife and Mother joins me, to be remembered to you, and Mrs. Dickinson. In love and friendship and I remain with Esteem
Honored Sir, Your most Obligd. Hble Servant

HENRY WM. STIEGEL

Sometime before this the Höltz family had adopted the English form of their name, as so many Pennsylvania German families did, which explains Stiegel's reference to his "Nephew Elias Wood."

But whatever may have been Dickinson's actual interest in the properties formerly owned by Stiegel, it is quite evident that either his generosity, his patience, or his faith in the unfortunate man's ability, had become exhausted. There is no evidence that he did anything toward rehabilitating his fortunes. Meanwhile, sometime during the months between the transfer of the Manheim properties to Dieffenderfer and Stiegel's writing of the above letter, a company had undertaken the operation of the Glass House.

I. Daniel Rupp, in his History of Lancaster County, says that the factory was run, after Stiegel's failure, by a Mr. Jenkins. Ellis and Evans attack this statement and say that no positive proof of its accuracy exists, averring that the works were carried on by David Rittenhouse of Philadelphia. The Mr. Jenkins here referred to was, doubtless, the James Jenkins who for a time occupied the Stiegel mansion after Robert Morris, who bought it in September, 1777, and lived there with his wife and mother-in-law until the evacuation of Philadelphia, in the summer of 1778. It is possible that David Rittenhouse (who had, as we have seen, had special work done there for him in the past) subsequently leased the factory for a short term, or made some arrangement with the blowers to make tubing and special vessels for his experimental work. But I have been unable to find any evidence of his having used the factory for commercial purposes.

The real proprietors of the factory after Stiegel's failure are identified by the following advertisement, which appeared in the "Pennsylvania Gazette" of October 21st, 1775, — four days before the date of Stiegel's letter to Dickinson, quoted above:

LANCASTER, October 21st 1775

Notice is hereby given to all persons who have lots in the town of Manheim in Lancaster County and are in arrears of groundrent for the same, that they pay off and discharge the same on the 10th and 11th days of November next, otherwise they may expect that their lots will be seized by the proprietors of said Town. Attendance will be given on the same days at the house of Jerome Heintzelman in said town by the sub-scribers. They have likewise for sale several houses and lots in said town; any person or persons inclining to purchase any of the said houses or lots may be informed of the terms by applying as aforesaid. And Whereas the subscribers do now carry on the Glass Manufactory in said town and now have a large quantity of green glass upon hands, they flatter them-selves that the gentlemen, merchants and shopkeepers will favor them with their custom. William Bosman, Michael Deffenderfer, Paul Zant-zinger, Casper Singer, Frederick Kuhn.

N.B. They will likewise give Two-pence per pound for broken flint, and a Half-penny per pound for broken green glass, delivered at the Manufactory.

In Volume X. of the Pennsylvania Magazine of History and Biography, in an article entitled "Notes of Travel of William Henry, John Heckenwelder, John Rothrock and Christian Clewell to Gnodettern on the Muskingum in the Early Summer of 1797, Edited by John W. Jordan," the statement is made that "Manheim contains about 150 mostly small houses.

Glass works were formerly carried on here," and in a foot note "Erected by the eccentric and unfortunate Baron H. W. Stiegel, but since 1780 have not been operated."

Trouble continued to develop for many years over the collection of ground rents upon the Manheim lots. In 1856–57 a series of suits were brought to enforce payment, and considerable sums were collected. Finally, in 1880, a committee was appointed to make a settlement, and on March 29th, 1881, claims to the amount of some $13,000 were settled for $6,500 and the various ground rent holdings transferred in fee. Mr. George H. Danner has the following receipt in the rent book of Manheim:

November 12th, 1811

Received from Jacob Meyers for the half of the purchase money of 8 lots and the Glass House in Manheim 450 dollars whereof William Bousman received $70 and $80 is acoming to him from John Bousman on account which was signed the 31st of March 1812 and Mr. Heister receipt is $150 which will show by his signing

JOHN BOUSMAN
GABRIEL HEISTER

Mr. Danner tells me that, when his father was a boy, it was considered quite a feat to throw a ball over the old domed building of the glass house, which was then standing. This building was pulled down in 1812 and the bricks were taken to Neffsville, Lancaster County, where they were used in the construction of the Neffsville Hotel. They are a deep red and measure $2\frac{1}{8}'' \times 4\frac{1}{8}'' \times 8\frac{1}{8}''$. This building, which is still used for its original purpose, bears a marble tablet under the gable of its front wall which reads, —

BUILT BY
LEONARD FIDLER
AND
BARBARA FIDLER
A.D. 1812

The sign the Fidlers hung out in front of this house of entertaining bore the effigy of a green tree. But there was nothing to show that it was rooted upon all that remained of the "First Flint Glass Manufactory in Pennsylvania."

In 1776 Robert Coleman leased Elizabeth Furnace for a term of 7 years, at an annual rental of £450, and is said to have made Stiegel foreman of the works. Coleman subsequently purchased the property and it is still owned by the Coleman family. Stiegel undoubtedly held a position under Coleman at the Furnace, and appears, through his acquaintance with Jasper Yeats, to whom he wrote concerning his condition in January, 1777, to have secured orders for the Continental Army from Congress. At one time Elizabeth Furnace is said to have been the only source upon which the American Army could rely for cannon balls; and that many were made there is amply evidenced by the number that have been exhumed on the ground.

Washington is said, soon after the Battle of Trenton (December 25th, 1776), to have sent a force of the captured Hessians to Stiegel in order to dig a canal to supply the furnace with a greater water supply. A number of the prisoners taken at Trenton were camped in Reading, Pennsylvania, on a spot still known as Hessian Camp. And it was doubtless from these prisoners, so held in the neighborhood of the furnace, that this work gang was drawn. The canal they dug is said to have doubled the capacity of the works.

Tradition long claimed that Washington had, at this time, visited Stiegel at Elizabeth Furnace; but the report seems to have been derived from two events, neither of which had any connection with Stiegel. One of these is the fact that Washington did visit Elizabeth Furnace, but it was long after Stiegel's death. The visit was paid to Robert Coleman, in 1792, when Washington was President of the United States. The party consisted of the President, Robert Morris, David Rittenhouse, Dr. William Smith, provost of the University of Pennsylvania, and Trench Francis, the legal advisor of the Penns, who, as State Commissioner, accompanied the President. It is said that Washington presented Mr. Coleman with a portrait of himself, painted by Gilbert Stewart, as a memento of the visit.

The second fact which is doubtless responsible for the story of Washington's visit to Stiegel, is that on September 18th, 1777, the Continental Army under Washington were (as is shown by a letter from Washington to General Wayne) at Warwick Furnace, a depot for the manufacture and repair of guns, situated on French Creek, about 8 miles north of Yellow Springs, and about 9 miles from the Schuylkill River. On the old maps the region to the northwest of Manheim was also called Warwick, and the Rev. Thompson P. Ege, evidently misled by this similarity of names, gives this date as the occasion of the supposed Washington visit to Elizabeth Furnace.

Much disagreement has existed, first and last, among the recorders of the Stiegel tradition, as to whether Stiegel was a Tory or a Patriot. The Stedmans were Tories, and two of them, Alexander and Charles Jr., were later attainted of treason and their property confiscated. And doubtless Stiegel's known connection with them may have led to the assumption that he, too, was opposed to the cause of the colonists. Israel Smith Clare, for instance, in "A Brief History of Lancaster County," published in 1892, says, "he was a tory and was visited at various times by the British Generals." But there is no possible question about his loyalty. In the Pennsylvania Archives there is a return of Captain George Volich, of the 9th Battalion of the Lancaster County Militia, commanded by Colonel John

Huber, running from May 25th to October 26th, 1778, which is signed by order of Captain George Volich and Henry Wm. Stiegel as a true return from the rolls dated October 2nd, 1778. Anthony Stiegel was also loyal to the colonies. An enrollment of the Pennsylvania Militia for 1782 shows him rated in the second class. George Ege, Stiegel's nephew, was also an ardent patriot, and was a member of the General Assembly of Pennsylvania in 1783.

As to Stiegel's son Jacob, however, there is reason to be doubtful. It is possible that he was influenced by the Stedmans. At any rate, there appears to be some foundation for the tradition that he raised a company of Tories in Lancaster County for the King's cause. It is said that once, being short of both provisions and money, he pledged his watch with a Lancaster County farmer for a bullock, and that the watch remains to this day in evidence for the truth of the story.

In India it is said that Hanniman, one of the old Hindu gods, being hard put to it to reach an enemy that had taken refuge in Ceylon, went up to the Himalayas, grabbed an armful of mountains, carried them down to Cape Comorin, and filled in enough of the straits of Palk to make stepping stones to cross by. And the scattered rocky hills that stretch down the middle of the Indian peninsula are pointed to as the pieces he dropped on the way and as proof of the story.

Moreover we have it from Stiegel himself that one of the Stiegel watches at least, — his wife's, — he gave himself to Nicholas Steele. But, the seat of war having changed to the South, the orders from the army ceased toward the end of 1778; and as there was probably no other business to be had, Stiegel's employment at the Furnace seems to have come to an end. Certainly, in the spring of 1779, he left and took up his residence at the parsonage in Brickerville. This move was made, as recorded in the second Church Book of the Brickerville congregation, on the 1st of April and by the consent of the church council. On May 23rd the same record shows that he was instructed by the congregation to draw up a call for Pastor Schroeder, and it is supposed that he now maintained himself by teaching, giving music lessons and such like services to the residents of the region.

His destitution is further testified to by the fact that, at this time, he sold to George Ege his faithful slave Cyrus, as well as a negress named Anne who for years had been his cook. He still seems to have had in his possession the Elizabeth Furnace Day Book for 1771–72 which he had so long used as a diary and account book. Under date of September, 1779, in this book, the following memorandum appears in his handwriting—

"Dr. Daniel Bennezet's account Sept. 1779........£3000
Bonds and mortgage........................ 720
To 4 years interest on the same................ 540
Ditto to Sept. 1779 interest.................. 900 "

This, to my mind, is the most pathetic thing in the entire discoverable record of Stiegel's life. One can see him, stranded and penniless, a refugee on sufferance in the parsonage of the church he had represented in conferences and befriended in its time of need; doubtless sitting by the light of a single candle, after trudging back along the Horse Shoe Pike from giving a lesson to some farmer's brat, and figuring on a blank page of the Day Book of his first successful venture how many pounds it would take to retrieve his ruin.

The ruin, however, was irretrievable. The Third Church Book of the Brickerville Congregation shows that on April 17th, 1780, he vacated the parsonage and moved into the Thurn Berg, or Castle, at Schaefferstown, which, in the spendthrift days of 1769, he had built on the hill near that village, out of the very £3000 on which we have but now seen him figuring the interest. This property, according to Mr. A. S. Brendle, was now owned by his brother Anthony, who, while never possessed of any means during the years of his brother's prosperity, had married into comfortable circumstances on his second venture. But a year later Stiegel was again obliged to move, and for a time he taught school in Shaefferstown, in a building on North Market Street, which was also owned by Anthony.

Stiegel at this time was but fifty-one years old, and this fact, together with his evident inability to take a fresh hold on affairs, or even to retain such slender holds as he secured, shows us, in a manner at once pitiful and conclusive, how utterly the framework of his abilities and the fabric of his self-confidence had crumpled and collapsed, when his supporting faith in his own star was removed. The history of the last years of his life is almost as obscure as that of his first years in America, and we can only follow his footsteps by the faint and fast-fading traditions of his presence at various points in Lebanon and Berks Counties. In 1781, he is said to have held a clerkship at the Reading Furnaces, near Robesonia, in Berks County. On January 11th, 1781, his mother, Dorothea Elizabeth, died, presumably at her son's house in Schaefferstown. In 1782 and 1783 Stiegel again taught school in Schaefferstown, according to Mr. Brendle; and, on August 13th of the latter year, we get one of the few authenticated glimpses of him that these years afford, through a letter of that date, written from Schaefferstown to Jasper Yeats, about some old debts that he was desirous of collecting. This letter is vouched for by Rev. Joseph Dubbs.

In 1782 his second wife died while on a visit to Philadelphia, and is said to have been buried in that city because of lack of funds to bring her body back. Finally, presumably late in 1783 or early in 1784, Stiegel's nephew by marriage, George

Ege, who then owned and operated Charming Forge, and lived there in the large stone mansion he had built in 1777, took him in. And for a time local tradition has it that he daily tramped into Wolmansdorf, and taught school there, in a small schoolhouse that has only been torn down in recent years, and that stood on the site of the present club house. Local tradition also points out the room on the third floor of the old Ege house where Stiegel slept. And here, on the 10th of January, 1785, he died, his brother Anthony having died in Schaefferstown the day before.

The location of Stiegel's grave is unknown. It has been said that he lies in Schaefferstown; in Wolmansdorf; and in the Brickerville Church burying ground; besides other less likely places. But either the conditions of the time, or some family carelessness in such matters, has prevented the grave of the Stiegels from being so marked as to retain their identity. Anthony Stiegel's grave is also unknown, as are those of Stiegel's second wife and of his mother.

In the Brickerville Church burying ground, alongside of Elizabeth Huber Stiegel's grave, and of the grave of Stiegel's grandson, James Old, who died in 1777, there is an unmarked grave. It is possible that Stiegel rests there. But while the records of the Weather Bureau have no data between the years 1777 and 1798, the Philadelphia office of this service was able to inform me, from tables collated from old diaries and other documents by Charles Pierce in the early years of the last century, that the winter of 1784–85 in Pennsylvania was tolerably mild although much snow fell; and it seems extremely doubtful whether the body of a pensioner, for whom the past and its associations had barely secured an asylum, would have been carried over the miles of wintry and mountainous roads intervening between the Forge and Brickerville for interment.

On the other hand, there are three unmarked graves near the orchard behind the Forge Mansion, and, while local tradition has it that these are the graves of slaves, it was no uncommon thing at the time for farmers and even landed proprietors to be buried on their own land. It is at least possible that Stiegel's body lies under the apple trees at Charming Forge. But however this may be, his spirit — or at least the spirit with which Legend, and the modern Festival of the Roses at Manheim, and the orators of the Lutheran Church in Pennsylvania, have invested him — goes marching on at the head of one of America's most picturesque traditions.

CHAPTER XI

SUCH, then, was the life of the man whose memory has survived for a century and more as one of the most conspicuous pioneers of American manufacturing enterprise, and as the hero of a legend in which a tradition of spendthrift extravagance and ostentation is strangely joined to a tradition of exemplary piety.

We have no portrait of Henry William Stiegel, and no description of his appearance or of his person has come down to us. But it is evident from what we know of his career that he had, as the saying is, a way with him. He had been dowered by nature with really fine abilities. He was a passionate lover of music. He was a discriminating connoisseur of beauty. He had an aptitude for science. He had a keen eye for business possibilities; was possessed of both energy and initiative; was a persuasive promoter and had a talent for organization. But some disgruntled fairy had endowed him at birth with the ironic gift of a too great facility. So that, while he was brilliantly destined to do many things well without effort, he was doomed never, until too late, to learn his own limitations. And since, in the beginning, he knew no need to focus his ambitions and concentrate his endeavors, so to the end he found it more congenial to dazzle his inferiors than to retain the confidence of his equals.

In fine he was an illustrious example of a temperament and a type whose less conspicuous possessors and exemplars are legion. He wore the stars of a general in that army of martyrs of whom it is commonly said that they are their own worst enemies.

It would be but a superficial statement of the truth to say that Stiegel was the victim of his own vanity. His vainness was only the smoke that showed what fires of self-confidence burned in his heart. He was so supremely certain of his own potentialities and of the favor in which Fate held him in consequence, that he was not only led into dissipating his talents as freely as he squandered his substance, but actually, later on, came to regard as his own enemies, and as the enemies of God, those of his creditors who dared to question the validity of his good intentions.

He ran his many-sided life in very much the same happy-go-lucky, borrow-from-Peter-to-pay-Paul way that he ran his many-sided business. And he kept his conscience quite as naïvely as he kept his books. The proof of this lies in that astounding trial balance which he submitted to heaven in the prayer written during his imprisonment.

And this brings us to one of the curious developments of modern Stiegelism. Of the essential kindliness of Stiegel's nature there is no possible question. Of his lord-bountiful generosity there is superabundant evidence. To the defining of the splendid concrete achievement of his esthetic taste, his personal initiative and his executive talent, the balance of this book is devoted. But no unbiased decipherer of his career and student of his character would think of picking him out as a candidate for canonization. Yet, if ever it was possible to see a saintship in the making, that interesting process is to-day visible in the celebrations of his memory that are annually held in Manheim and its vicinity.

It is true that Stiegel, in the sense in which that term is rather loosely used, was a notably religious man. He was a staunchly orthodox and a helpfully active member of the Lutheran Church. He was to the full as prominent in its councils as he was in the community, and to the full as generous toward its needs as he was toward his neighbors. But so far from there being any reason to think that religion modified his character, he seems, like the majority of mankind, to have expressed his character in terms of religion exactly as he expressed it in terms of life.

In life he was always either the patron or the postulant; either the dispenser of lavishness or the pleader for dispensation. And in religion he was no otherwise. He was the patron of the church exactly as he was the patron of Manheim. He was the preacher of the church's hospitality exactly as he was the dispenser of his own. And his prayer to God, written in the day of his distress, is exactly as humble, as self-exculpatory and as vindictive, as his letters written to John Dickinson under like circumstances.

But no doubt the superstructures of saintship often rest on even stranger foundations. And, meanwhile, Manheim, thanks to a once common clause in an old deed, to the enthusiastic and contagious sentiment of Dr. J. H. Sieling, and to a happy conjunction between public psychology and the fullness of time, has become the seat of an annual celebration which promises to make it the Lourdes of Lancaster County, and which we Americans, poor enough in such colorful customs, should rejoice to see flourishing in the bleak garden of our folk lore.

Stiegel's most permanent and personal religious interests were centered in the Brickerville Church. But in 1770, when he was in the full swing of his development of Manheim and of his reckless building extravagancies based on the Bennezet loan, he set aside one of the Manheim lots, built a small church on it which he named the Zion Lutheran Church, appointed a board of Trustees and made the congregation responsible for half of the cost. In 1771, Dr. Frederick A. C. Muhlenberg was elected its first pastor, and in 1772, the burden of financial responsibility proving too heavy for the small congregation, Stiegel, at their urgent solicitation, deeded the property to them.

Now, at this time, it was the very general custom to sell property for a cash consideration plus an annual ground rent in perpetuity. And when, as in this case, the deed really represented a free gift, it was the custom to specify, in addition to a purely nominal cash consideration, a purely nominal substitute for the annual rental. Five shillings was then, as one dollar is to-day, the usual cash sum specified as the consideration of transfer; and some natural product, so easily come by as to be the equivalent of a snapped finger or a doffed hat, was usually chosen for the annual acknowledgment. One grain of wheat was a favorite choice. One peppercorn was another. And a June rose, a more poetic but equally plentiful provision of nature, was a third. We need not go beyond the annals of American glassmaking to illustrate this. In 1757, when Matthew Earnest was allowed by the Common Council of New York City to construct a dock on city land for the use of the Glass House Company, he was required to pay one peppercorn per annum for the privilege. And it was the habit of Stiegel's one rival as a glassmaker, Casper Wistar, of Philadelphia and Wistarberg, to require, in lieu of ground rent, the annual payment of a rose in his deeds.

But there is nothing more quickly forgotten than the casual conventions of abandoned legal formalities. So that when Dr. Sieling (who had developed a passionate interest in the Stiegel traditions through an early friendship with some of the older inhabitants of Brickerville and Manheim) discovered among the records of the Manheim church the original deed of December

4th, 1772, conveying, for a consideration of five shillings, the described lot Number 220 on the general plan of the town to "Peter Ereman, Henry Wherley and Wendell Murzell Trustees and Wardens for the only use, purpose and benefit of the German Lutheran Congregation settled and established in the Town of Manheim," he instantly seized upon the covenant, "Yielding and paying therefor unto the said Henry William Stiegel his Heirs and Assigns at the said Town of Manheim in the month of June yearly forever hereafter the Rent of One Red Rose if the same shall be lawfully demanded" as a unique and exquisite example of his hero's ability to mingle poetry with princeliness.

And, as matters turned out, no guile in propaganda could have proved so potent as this ingenuous error. At that time, in 1891, a new church was in course of construction; and Dr. Sieling was influential in having a red rose made the central ornament of the "rose window" that was placed above the chancel. It was a pretty conceit and the press bruited it abroad. The Stiegel story was refurbished and retold. A descendant of Stiegel, of whose existence Manheim was then in ignorance, wrote to know the meaning of the rumors. He was instantly urged to come in person and receive the tribute that was his by inheritance. On the second Sunday in June he was received in the traditional Stiegel fashion, with the blare of bands and the booming of guns, and was handed the rose by the pastor of the church. And thus was inaugurated that Feast of Roses which is already become the cherished expression of Manheim's civic pride, and bids fair, if the sermons preached on recent occasions are any criterion, to become the festival of its patron saint.

PART II
STIEGEL GLASS

PART II: STIEGEL GLASS

CHAPTER I

GLASS IN GENERAL

THE making of glass antedates the making of history. But neither glass nor glassmaking assumed much importance until the invention of the blowpipe by some forgotten benefactor of mankind during the second or third century before Christ. Egypt imported this new process from Asia Minor, and, when the Romans conquered Egypt, the blowpipe was one of the trophies they took home with them; and they were the first to develop its possibilities and to place glassmaking among the minor arts. Moreover, the whole western world of Roman times learned the craft from them. And a sort of glass furore developed, so that, by the middle of the second century of our era, Europe was making more glass than at any time since, until our own day.

But this activity ended with the fall of Rome, and little glassmaking was carried on in Europe during the next thousand years, except the so-called Green or Forest glass of the Middle Ages.

In the twelfth century, however, glassmaking was revived and brought to great perfection in the region between the Persian Gulf and the Mediterranean; and, in the fifteenth century, the art of enameling on glass was learned by the Venetians from the Saracens, and soon the genius of Venice had solved the problem of making colorless glass and her factories were producing the famous *crystallo*, and her master blowers achieving the technical triumphs in its manipulation, which gave her undying fame. This crystalline, white, transparent glass of the Venetian factories was obtained through great care in selection of materials, but more especially through the discovery and skilful employment of manganese as a chemical neutralizer of the greenish tinge inherent in the normal product. It is because of this cleansing effect that manganese is often called "glassmakers' soap."

After the decline of the Venetian industry, Germany took the lead in European glassmaking; introducing, toward the end of the seventeenth century, a product which was a compromise between its own early "green glass" and the new methods. Then, for a hundred years, Bohemia led the western world. And finally, toward the middle of the eighteenth century, the English flint glass was introduced, and became, for a short time, the most sought-for product of the European glass pots.

Glass is a fused mixture of silica (usually in the form of sand) and of at least two alkaline bases, one of which is some form either of potash or soda, and the other some form either of lime or of a metallic oxide. A glass-like, vitreous substance is obtainable from silica and soda, or potash alone, but it is very inductile and is soluble in water. The addition of the second metallic base renders the resultant material highly resistant, not only to water, but to acids; of which latter hydrofluoric acid alone is capable of attacking it with any ease.

The hardness, denseness, specific gravity and optical properties of various forms of glass are dependent upon the nature and proportion of the ingredients used in their manufacture; and the number of formulæ which have been devised for special purposes is very great, and has very greatly increased in recent years. But we are only concerned, broadly speaking, with two kinds, one in which lime is the second base, and one in which an oxide of lead is used for this purpose. The former is variously spoken of, according to its quality, as "bottle glass," "green glass" and (when it has been rendered colorless by careful manufacture and the use of manganese), as "crown glass." The lead glass is commonly called "flint glass."

As the attributes of glass depend upon the ingredients used, so does the quality depend upon their freedom from impurities. Coarse sand and crudely made alkalies produce the dark, scarcely translucent, glass known to the early makers as "black metal." The various dirty brown, dull olive and olive green glasses, with which we are familiar in most old bottles and in many new ones, are conditioned as to color by the sands used, with their attendant mineral impurities. Even the "green glass" from which most early windowpanes, and many household vessels such as bowls, pitchers, mugs and so forth, were made, requires the greatest care in the selection and preparation of material. And this "green glass" — of a light sea-green tint and of an excellent quality — was the highest technical attainment of the American glassmakers before Wistar and Stiegel.

A typical formula for the making of such a glass is:

Sand, purified................. 100 parts
Chalk or limestone............. 35 to 40 parts
Sulphate of Soda............... 40 to 45 parts

The sea-green tint of the resulting glass would be due to such traces of iron or alumina as were present in the sand, and for the making of "crown" — that is to say of colorless glass of this same kind — minute amounts of peroxide of manganese and white arsenic would be added. The term "crown," for years used to denote a white glass with a lime base, originally referred to a specific method of blowing window glass. It then came to be applied to the glass of which the best of these windowpanes were blown. "Flint" glass is said to have derived its name from an early use of crushed flint as a source of silica; but, whether this explanation is legitimate or apochryphal, the term is now universally used to denote glass in the making of which lead has been used as the second base.

Lead glass possesses, to a degree only excelled by the diamond, the attribute of dispersing white light. It is also much softer than lime-glass, and hence lends itself readily to cutting and engraving, and is thus susceptible of very brilliant and decorative effects. On the other hand it is very expensive, and was never used except for such purposes as would warrant its greater cost. A typical formula for flint glass is:

Carbonate of potash..............	1 cwt.
Red lead or Litharge.............	2 cwt.
Sand, washed and burnt..........	3 cwt.
Saltpeter.......................	14 to 28 lbs.
Oxide of Manganese..............	4 to 12 oz.

This is taken from Apsley Pellot's "Curiosities of Glass Making," published in 1849. And now, as we shall have frequent occasion, beside speaking of "bottle glass" and "green glass" and "flint glass," to refer to glass (both of lime and of lead derivations) to which various coloring ingredients have been intentionally added, it may be well to glance at the following typical formulæ supplied by the same author for the obtaining of colored glasses.

The materials intended to be fused into glass are, when mixed together, technically called "batch." After fusing they are called "metal." The "6 cwt. of batch" in the following table refers to the flint glass formula given above.

For Blue Transparent Glass add, to the above 6 cwt. of batch, 2 lbs. of oxide of cobalt.

For Ruby Red add, to above 6 cwt. of batch 4 oz. of oxide of gold.

For Amethyst or Purple add, to above 6 cwt. of batch, 20 lbs. of oxide of manganese.

For Common Orange add, to above 6 cwt. of batch 12 lbs. of iron and 4 lbs. of manganese.

85. Blue Flint Vase. 8½ inches high

PLATE I

61. Amber Flint Mug. 6 inches high

PLATE II

91. Amethyst Flint Toilet Bottle. 5³/₄ inches high

PLATE III

106. Emerald Green Flint Creamer
3³⁄₄ inches high

98. Blue-Green Flint Salt Cellar
3 inches high

PLATE IV

99. Deep Amethyst Flint High Bowl. 3¾ inches high

PLATE V

140. Mug, Rooster Design   139. Mug, Parrot Design   141. Mug, Steeple Design
5 inches high   5⅝ inches high   5⅜ inches high

PLATE VI

140. Mug, Rooster Design   139. Mug, Parrot Design   141. Mug, Steeple Design
5 inches high   5⅝ inches high   5⅜ inches high

PLATE VII

143. Blue Flint Drug Bottle,
Conventionalized Floral Design
6 inches high

142. Cordial Bottle,
Dove Design
4¾ inches high

PLATE VIII

Excavated Specimens from Elizabeth Furnace Site

Excavated Specimens from Manheim Glass House Site

For Emerald Green add, to above 6 cwt. of batch 12 lbs. of copper scales and 12 lbs. of iron ore.

For a Gold Topaz color add, to the above 6 cwt. of batch, 3 lbs. of oxide of uranium.

For Soft White Opaque Enamel add, to above 6 cwt. of batch, 24 lbs. of arsenic and 6 lbs. of antimony.

For Hard White Opaque Enamel add, to above 6 cwt. of batch, 200 lbs. of putty, prepared from tin and lead.

In making either flint or green glass, it is found that better results are obtained when, to the new materials of the "batch," there are added anywhere up to a quarter in bulk of broken glass of the same kind. This broken glass is called "cullet," and its use explains the constant advertisements we find in the early American papers, offering to pay a penny a pound for broken green glass and two pence a pound for broken flint.

The chemistry of glass is a very complex subject; glass being an amorphous compound and the authorities more or less agreeing that no chemical statement of "normal glass" can be given. Moreover, the processes of manufacture are such that it appears nothing in the way of identification is to be arrived at by means of chemical analysis. I was therefore forced to abandon any idea of a chemical or analytical identification of the Stiegel output. Even the nomenclature of the subject is very variable. And it is therefore clearly stated here, for the purposes of clarity, that in the following pages the term "bottle glass" is used to mean lime-glass of various brownish, olive and olive green tints; "green glass" to indicate the finer, sea-green or artificially colored grades of lime-glass; and " flint " to indicate either white or intentionally colored glass in which lead (either as litharge or as red lead) has been used as the secondary base.[1]

In practice, red lead is preferable to litharge, because of its finer state of subdivision, and of the better chemical reactions from its decomposition. The Stiegel account books show that he used litharge first, and later took up red lead.

We will now glance rapidly at the methods of making and

manipulating glass used during the eighteenth century, in order sufficiently to familiarize ourselves with the processes and the tools to be able to understand some of the problems that will present themselves in considering the individual pieces.

The pots in which glass is made are of the finest fire-clay, and the greatest care is needed in their construction. No grit, sand or other extraneous particles must be present; and a single air-cell in the clay wall of a completed pot is liable to cause it to burst or crack when subjected to the tremendous heat (at times approximating to 10,000 degrees F.) of the furnace. The pots are therefore built up, layer by layer, from a putty-like paste, prepared from the most carefully washed clay, and from a powder made by grinding up old pots; and over a year is given to the gradual drying of them under ever-increasing temperatures, before they are put into use.

In making glass, a pot is filled with batch, and, as this melts and sinks down, more is added until a full pot of molten metal is obtained; and this is subjected to greater and greater heat until all the impurities have risen and been skimmed off and all the air bubbles expelled. From 16 to 36 hours is required for this cooking process. The small bubbles, or "tears," so often seen in old bottles, are due to imperfect "cooking." Once the metal is properly prepared, the pot and its contents are allowed to cool down to the point at which the glass lends itself most readily to manipulation — a red heat — and the blowers and their assistants begin their part of the manufacturing process.

The tools of the glassblower are of the simplest, and the results of his operations depend almost entirely upon his expert skill. Of course the blowpipe is his chief implement. This is an iron tube from 4 to 7 feet in length, tapered at the blowing

end and slightly enlarged at the end upon which the glass is
to be gathered. Next in importance to the blowpipe is the
pucellas, — the tool that, to the glassblower, is as variously
serviceable as is the axe to the woodsman. This (*A* in
the accompanying cut) closely resembles a pair of spring
garden-shears, but is used for anything and everything
except cutting, the edges of the blades being dull. A
glance at the accompanying illustration of a workman

seated at the glassmaker's
chair and holding the pucellas in such a way as to fashion the neck of a vase, will
instantly suggest its possibilities.
Held inside of a rotated vessel in the
course of production, it is equally
serviceable in enlarging the opening
or giving a flare to the edge of a wineglass, or bowl, or vase.
The next most important implement of the trade is the short
bladed shears used to trim the edges of glasses and other
vessels. Much skill is required to shear a wine glass. It is
held upon the iron by the left hand and rotated toward the
shears, which are grasped in the right.
A skillful workman can shear a glass
entirely round the bowl at one operation. These shears are shown in C on
the accompanying cut. Here too, at B
and D respectively, are shown the
tongs with which the blower picks up
half-formed handles and other bits of

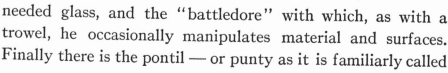

needed glass, and the "battledore" with which, as with a
trowel, he occasionally manipulates material and surfaces.
Finally there is the pontil — or punty as it is familiarly called

—a solid iron rod which is fastened by means of a little molten glass to the end of the piece opposite to where the blowpipe is attached, thus affording either a supplemental or a substitute handle by which to hold it.

In addition to these tools the glassblower uses a flat iron plate raised on four legs, like a low table, on which to roll into shape the glass he has gathered for blowing on the end of the  blowpipe. This is called a marver (from the French "marbre," the early habit being to make them of marble) and its use is shown in the accompanying cut. He also uses a work bench called the glassmaker's chair, with two inclined wooden arms supplied with iron surfaces, upon which the blowpipe is rapidly rolled back and forth in shaping the objects being formed. The typical form and useful purpose of this chair are quickly grasped from the cut on page 127.

In practice a workman called the gatherer generally begins each operation by inserting a blowpipe (the end of which has already been heated) into the pot, through a hole provided in the wall of the furnace, and gathering a small quantity of glass around its end. This he allows to cool for a moment in order to give a supporting surface, and then he again inserts the pipe into the pot and gathers as much metal thereon as he judges is needed for the intended article. He then blows gently through the pipe, thus inflating the gathering (sometimes called a "paraison") somewhat; and then he rolls it into a symmetrical shape on the marver, reheats it to the proper working temperature, and hands it to the blower.

The latter then, by blowing and by aid of rotation and the

pucellas, obtains a bubble of the required thickness and of a partially satisfactory shape; and an assistant having brought the prepared punty and attached it to the closed end of the bubble, the blowpipe is detached by running a wetted iron round the desired line of fracture, and the piece — now open at what was the blowpipe end and attached to the punty at what is going to be its base — is finished with the punty for a handle, by which it is rotated on the chair or stuck into the furnace for reheating.

In some cases a piece will be drawn out to a greater length while the blowpipe and punty are both attached to its opposite ends. In others (as in fashioning the long necks of some bottles, or the tubes of funnels) the blowpipe is swung sharply in a circle over a pit provided for the purpose. And again a graceful twist is imparted to a decorative design by turning the blowpipe in one direction and the punty in the other while both are fast to the glass.

After glass objects are finished, great care is necessary in cooling them to avoid a liability to fracture in sudden changes of temperature or from slight impacts. This is due to the fact that glass is a very poor conductor of heat; so that if the outside of a piece cools too quickly, the inner portions of the glass will cool at varying tensions, and structural strains will be set up, which, at the slightest excuse, will release themselves by fracture. The finished pieces are therefore immediately placed in what is known as the annealing oven — an arrangement of heated chambers in which the temperature of the included objects is only allowed to fall by the degrees needed to keep pace with the internal as well as the external cooling of the glass.

Other manipulations, more especially related to the Stiegel product, will be discussed and described when we come to consider the pieces in whose production they were employed. But before leaving this subject of glass in its general aspects, it will be well to say a few words about the effect which moisture and other destructive agents have upon its texture, and about the modifications which its color (or colorlessness) undergoes under the influence of long exposure to light.

We have already seen that the introduction of the second metallic alkaline base in the composition of glass renders it proof against the attacks, not only of water, but of most acids. But this invulnerability is relative, not absolute. Once the original smooth outer surface is impaired, either by scratches or by the growth of fungus, the carbonic acid or the ammonia salts contained in the atmosphere find a secure lodgment, and, given the presence of moisture, the work of decay begins. It is not necessary to enter into the chemical processes involved, further than to state that they depend upon the power of carbonic acid, in the presence of moisture, to decompose the alkaline silicates; and upon the subsequent washing away of the soluble carbonates of soda or potash thus formed. When this process is finally complete (as in cases of long burial in moist earth), there remains an acid silicate of lime, alumina, or lead, as the case may be, retaining perhaps the shape of the original vessel, but consisting either of layer upon layer of iridescent scales, or of an opaque pearly crust.

Blown glass, because of the complicated series of inflations, involutions and doublings to which it is subjected, is very easily attacked. And on the other hand, a large percentage of lead tends to protect glass from these changes. The iridescent effect noted even on glass that has been buried but a few years, and which reaches its maximum of beauty in such long-buried specimens as the excavated pieces dating from Roman times, is due to the breaking up of the light by its passage through these fine superficial films, and its partial reflection from the back of scales at varying depths. All the excavated fragments that I found at Elizabeth Furnace, and later at Manheim, show an iridescent scaly formation resembling that of the shell of an oyster. And to a less extent this is even true of glass manufactured as late as 1840, 1850 and 1860, uncovered by me in Salem, Gloucester, Cumberland, Burlington and Ocean Counties, New Jersey.

I have already referred to a piece of a light green, open pot, sweetmeat dish (similar to the one illustrated in Figure 7) that I uncovered at the Elizabeth Furnace site on August 15th, 1913. It was broken into three pieces by the grubbing hoe. And I wrapped each of these in paper and put one in my pocket, one in my wallet, and the third in the side pocket of the automobile. But in each case, when I reached home and opened the papers, I found nothing but a talc-like, procelainous powder.

The action of sunlight upon glass is less destructive, but scarcely less disconcerting. I remember happening to be in Boston as a boy, at the time of the Blue Glass craze; when the population of the United States was obsessed with the belief that to let light fall upon them through panes of blue glass was equivalent to drinking from the fountain of youth. And while walking on Beacon Street on this occasion, I noticed, as doubtless hundreds of thousands of Americans have noticed, panes of purple glass in a majority of the windows facing south across the Common. But while I do not doubt that this phenomenon has puzzled many observers, to me it merely suggested that purple glass had superseded blue in the *materia medica* of vitreous therapy; and as I wished to keep up to date in such developments, I made inquiries and learned that these purple panes were not panaceas, but very old panes of originally colorless glass which had turned purple in the sun. There are fewer of them there than when I was a boy, but it speaks volumes for the stability of Boston that they are still a familiar sight on that fine old street.

The effect is due to the fact that the colorless protoxide of manganese (used in the crown glass of which these panes were made) has been reduced to a purple bin-oxide by the action of the sunlight. The same effect can be seen in many of the flint flasks, wine glasses and flips, contained in the collection of Stiegel glass which I presented to the Metropolitan Museum in New York. Frequent references to this collection will have to be made from now on and for convenience it will be spoken of as the Hunter Collection.

Numerous other changes of color, or developments of discoloration, take place in glass; a fact which was noted as early as 1823 by Faraday, Bontemps and Fresnel. One of the commonest of these discolorations is the yellowish tints that develop in glass where sulphate of soda has been used as the source of the alkali. The sulphate of soda being reduced by any protoxide of iron that is present, the resulting sulphide of sodium and sesqui-oxide of iron both tend to produce yellow tones.

The following is quoted from a communication made by Thomas Garfield to the Chemical section of the American Association for the Advancement of Science, at its meeting in Boston, on August 27th, 1880, and printed by the Salem Press in 1881; this communication being a report upon a series of experiments and observations carried on through a considerable period of years by Mr. Garfield as to the effect of sunlight upon glass.

"Every specimen of colorless glass exposed for 10 years has changed in color, except some white flint glass.

" Diffused light will also color glass, but with greatly diminished effect.

" There comes a time when coloring action of sunlight ceases.

"Purple tint develops less rapidly than yellow tint in glass containing sulphur, but goes on increasing in depth of color beyond 10 years.

"Amber, Olive, Blue and Purple change to darker tints of the same color.

"Brown-yellow to tints of purple and greenish.

"Greenish white to bluish.

"A piece of glass affected by sunlight exposure may be restored to its original color by a single firing in the kiln; and after being exposed to sunlight will reproduce same color as before."

NOTES

1. It is important to remember that throughout the text dealing with glass Mr. Hunter's application of the terms "bottle glass," "green glass," and "flint" or "lead" is arbitrary and that the chemical composition of the pieces so designated had not been determined. Composition of glass cannot be determined by its look, color, or ring, as was one time assumed, but by analysis only. The collectors' use of spectographic analysis and of the chemical spot test to ascertain the presence or absence of lead in glass is comparatively recent in the United States and apparently was unknown to Mr. Hunter in 1913. At that time and for long afterwards all clear (white) glass and all brilliant blue, amethyst, emerald-green or other artificially colored glass which was fashioned into table or decorative wares was assumed to be flint or lead glass. Actually many such pieces were made from non-lead metal. Insofar as I have a record, all of the engraved and the enameled pieces such as Figs. 113-138 and 145-157 to which the spot test has been applied have proved to be non-lead glass. The same test has proved that amethyst diamond-daisy bottles like Fig. 108 were blown from non-lead metal. However, bottles in a similar pattern were made from lead glass; so it is likely that, as Mr. Hunter assumed, some of the diamond-daisy bottles were also.

HMcK

CHAPTER II

MOST of us, first or last, have made our own mental pictures of the beginnings of America. We have landed with the Pilgrim Fathers. We have sallied forth through the frozen drifts from their hunger-haunted cabins, hoping to add a lucky turkey or a starved rabbit to our dwindling larder. We have ploughed their stony fields with a blunderbuss slung over our shoulders and one eye focused on our furrow, while the other vigilantly watched the edge of the forest. We have, too, in our imagination, settled in Virginia; campaigned with Captain Smith; fallen in love with Pocahontas; escaped scalping by treacherous Indians; and grown tobacco. We have swapped schnapps for furs at what was not yet Albany. We have been familiar with a Philadelphia that was but a Quaker village straggling on the shore line of the Delaware; and with a New Amsterdam that still clustered phlegmatically about a flimsy fort on the tip of a wooded wilderness. In short we have, we think, re-lived the lives and re-captured the outlook of our seventeenth-century ancestors.

But the chances are that the nature of at least one of their privations and the object of at least one of their longings has never dawned on us. The chances are that it has never entered our heads to think how precious a possession a single glass bottle, miraculously preserved amid the perils of migration, may have been in the domestic economy of our great grandmother's great grandmother. Nor is it likely to have occurred to us how much of light, life, comfort and luxury may have centered, in our great grandfather's great grandfather's dreams, in the fancied possession of a single pane of wavy window glass. The truth is that we take glass so completely for granted as one of the axiomatic necessities and omnipresent factors of our daily lives, that it is only by a deliberate exercise of the awakened imagination that we can realize the meaning of its scarcity to a people, transplanted from less arduous surroundings, where they had been moderately accustomed to its employment.

The consciousness of this need on the part of the colonists is writ large in the fact that the first attempt at establishing a manufacturing industry ever made in America was the building and equipping of a glass house; and the difficulties that stood in the way of this need's satisfaction are summed up by the further fact that one hundred and thirty years elapsed after the inception of that initial and short-lived undertaking before the first successful American glass house was at last founded. And it was twenty-five years later still before the second successful glass factory, with the history and output of which we are to be immediately concerned in this volume, came to a beginning.

Thus Franz Daniel Pastorius, before he laid out the site of Germantown, Pennsylvania, in October, 1685, built a small house in Philadelphia, the windows of which, for want of glass, were glazed with oil paper; and having finished it he placed the following inscription over the door: *Parva domus sed amica bonis, procul esto profanis*. And the governor, seeing it, laughed and encouraged him to build more. No wonder that an early poet (the verse is quoted by Holme in 1689, in discussing the industries of the Province of Pennsylvania) was moved to write: —

"The window glass is often here
Exceeding scarce and very dear;
So that some in this way do take
Isinglass windows for to make."

The obtainable facts about the earlier attempts to put glass-making on a commercial footing in the colonies are extremely meagre. History seldom refers to them. The very tradition of them is often all but forgotten. And the following data — the poor harvest of a search whose labors have been out of all proportion to its results — are all that I have been able to gather.

JAMESTOWN, VIRGINIA. FIRST FACTORY, 1608

On the 13th of May, 1607, one hundred and five colonists, under the leadership of Captain Christopher Newport, landed on the site of the future village of Jamestown, Virginia, and established the first quasi-permanent English settlement in North America. In the Weeks report on the manufacture of glass, in the United States Census Report of 1880, it is stated that Captain Newport, on his second voyage in the later part of 1608, brought over eight Poles and Germans who were qualified to make pitch, tar, glass and "soap ashes"; and that a glass house was erected, about a mile from Jamestown, where glass was made. Smith's "History of Virginia" states that some of the products of this factory constituted part of the first cargo of goods ever exported from this country, the shipment being made in 1609. Little more is discoverable about this early undertaking. In Howe's "Historical Recollections of Virginia" we find a quotation from Smith under date of 1615 that, "for a long time the labor of the colony had been misdirected in the manufacture of ashes, soap, glass and tar, in which they

could by no means compete with the Swedes and Russians."
And Governor Argall, on his arrival in 1617, is said (Weeks
report) to have found the glass house in decay — a statement
we may well credit, seeing that Smith says that Argall found
"but five or six houses, the church down, the palisades broken,
the bridge (to the mainland) in pieces, the well of fresh water
spoiled and the storehouse used for a church."

JAMESTOWN, VIRGINIA. SECOND FACTORY
1620–22

The need of glass, however, was even more urgently felt
after the reorganization of the colony by Governor George
Yeardly, in 1619, and the establishment of family life in Virginia. Moreover, the possibility of manufacturing beads with
which to trade with the Indians seems to have appealed to the
promoting instincts of these early Americans. In 1620, a sub-
scription list was started in Jamestown, looking to the establishment of a second glass house; the subscribers to share in the
profits, and the making of beads being one of the emphasized
features of the undertaking. In 1621, one Captain William Norton arrived by the ship George with four Italian workmen
whom the London Company sent over; and in Neal's "Virginia
Company of London," on page 231, it is stated that the Company, in a letter written in July, 1621, and forwarded by this
same ship George, commended Captain Norton to the Governor
and directed that he be lodged in the Guest House, together with
his "gange," until he found a convenient place for his furnace.
This letter also directed that care be exercised in the choice of
a site, so that Norton and his men might be as secure as possible
from surprise, and so that "the commoditie of glass should not
be vilified by too common sale to the Indians."

The factory thus established actually flourished for a time, as is amply testified to by the various output inferable from the fragments still found near its site (Dr. Edwin A. Barber, Bulletin of the Pennsylvania Museum, January, 1906). But its life was short. It is referred to in a letter from the colony dated June, 1622, saying that the Italians had not been killed in the Indian Massacre of March 22nd of that year, and that the bead factory had escaped destruction. But again, in February, 1623, in another letter, the suggestive question is asked as to what should be done with the Italian workmen. And the rest, as Hamlet says, is silence.

A number of the beads made at this early factory are shown in the Pennsylvania Museum in Memorial Hall, Fairmont Park, Philadelphia. Most of them are round — about the size of a pea. Others are elliptical and a few rectangular. And they are of various colors and decorations — light transparent green with longitudinal white markings; opaque white; translucent turquoise. Dr. Edwin A. Barber, in the Bulletin of the Pennsylvania Museum for January, 1906, calls attention to bits of window glass picked up on the site of this factory, and to a broken fragment of the top of a bowl or other vessel then recently secured for the Museum, and suggests that the fine grade of work evidently done by these Italian glassblowers may, by its unsuitability to the rough needs of the colonists, have militated against the success of the experiment. In view, however, of the uniformly similar fate which for many years overtook glassmaking experiments that by no stretch of the imagination could be accused of over-refined workmanship, it would seem unnecessary to lay this early failure at the door of "counsels of perfection."

SALEM, MASSACHUSETTS, 1638–42

The honor of the next try belongs to the North.

In 1638 Lawrence Southwick, a Quaker, John Concline, a glassblower, Ananias Concline and Obadiah Holmes, erected a glass house in Salem, Massachusetts. It is recorded in Felt's Annals of Salem that in December, 1641, the General Court of Massachusetts authorized the town of Salem to lend the proprietors of this undertaking the sum of thirty pounds sterling; which sum was to be deducted from the next town rate, and was to be repaid by the glass men when they were able and if the works succeeded. But the factory ceased operations about 1642; for in 1645, in a petition to the General Court, John and Ananias Concline state that the undertakers of the work had neglected it for the past three years. Lawrence Southwick and his wife were subsequently banished from the colony during the persecution of the Quakers and died on Shelter Island in Long Island Sound from privation.

Mr. Edward Southwick, of Salem, a lineal descendant of the original Lawrence, informs me of the family tradition that hollow ware and bottles were made at this factory in light green, dark green, blue and brown glass. Also "bulls eyes" for windows and doors. Also that earthenware as well as glass was made there. He says that the glass house was located about five hundred and fifty feet south of the south point of the old Quaker burying ground, now enclosed in a high fence in the rear of number 30 Aborn Street; and that, south of this point again, Abbott Street now runs through the original Southwick lot at about where the dump heap, or refuse pile, of the glass house was situated. I have made three visits to Salem, and while Mr. Southwick, on account of his age and ill health, has upon no occasion been able to accompany me to the site, I have pretty thoroughly canvassed the ground. But it was for a long while used as a town dump before more recent building operations began on it; and while fragments of glass may easily be found there, some of them exhibiting the surface signs of long burial, none of them suggests an authentic connection with the original works. Nor has either the Essex Institute or the Peabody Institute in Salem any pieces of glass made at this factory. Aborn Street was originally the road from Salem to Boston. Mr. Sidney Perley, in an article on "A Part of Salem in 1700," published in the "Essex Antiquarian" in 1902, says that this road was, in 1707, called "the highway that leads past the field called glass house field" and that it is again referred to in 1735 as "the way to the glass house fields." It became Aborn Street in 1804.

NEW YORK, NEW YORK. JAN SMEEDES, 1654

New Amsterdam was the next to take a hand in the glass game.

But although the fact is undoubted, the details are no longer discoverable. Jan Smeedes was among the earliest settlers of Manhattan Island, and was one of the first to receive an allotment of land. This was situated in the present neighborhood of William Street, between Wall and Pearl Streets. Here, on the East side of the street, just north of the present Hanover Square, stood his residence. And here, at the present corner of William and Stone Streets, on the present site of the New York Cotton Exchange, he is discernible in 1654 engaged in the business of making glass.

NEW YORK, NEW YORK. EVERT DUYCKINGK
1655

Near by, on the land now known as numbers 20 and 22 South William Street, his fellow townsman Evert Duyckingk was, in the year of grace 1655, carrying on a rival glass works. So much emerges from the records, but little more that is pertinent to our inquiry. William Street was originally known as Glass Makers Street. Afterward it was known as Smee Street; from which fact we might perhaps infer that Jan Smeedes, or Smee as he was also called, got the upper hand in the rivalry. Under British auspices Smee Street became Smith Street and then William. Duyckingk was a native of Barcken, in Westphalia; a small town beyond the boundary of the Netherlands. He was a glassblower and received a grant of something more than half an acre on the north side of Slyck Steegh in 1643. The records show that he sold the property in 1674 to Jacob Melyer; and advertisements in early New York papers show that his descendants continued to engage in the glass trade.

Jan Smeedes, or Smee, left New Amsterdam in 1664 and took up his residence on Long Island; having first for an instant become visible among the mists of antiquity as the defendant in a suit instituted in 1658 by one Routoff Jansen for the recovery of five beaver skins. He was one of the patentees under the Nicoll patent of the Town of Newtown in 1666–67. He was appointed commissioner to lay out and regulate roads in that town in 1670, and died on his farm at Dutch Kill in 1671. But what he made at his glass house, or what was the output of his rival, is unrecorded and is now undiscoverable. I tried to get some information as to glass fragments or other indicative remains from the contractors who made the excavations for the New York Cotton Exchange, and for the buildings at 20 and

22 South William Street; but, as was to have been expected, without results. The one clear fact that emerges is that glass-making, which had proved too much for Virginia, and had downed Massachusetts, also beat the Dutch.

PHILADELPHIA, PENNSYLVANIA, 1683

Pennsylvania, if we may so construe a hint or two contained in the records, next entered the lists for a moment, though in no very determined spirit. In a letter from William Penn to the Free Society of Traders, dated August 16th, 1683, he refers to a "tannery, saw mill and glass house, the last two conveniently posted for water carriage." And one "John Tittery, glass maker and servant to Ye Society Board," is found arriving at Philadelphia on June 20th, 1682, by the ship America from Newcastle-on-Tyne, indentured to serve for four years at 88 pounds stirling per year. But Dr. Moore's letters, which were printed in 1687 and refer to a number of industries in Pennsylvania, do not mention glassmaking. And although all the trades which flourished in the colony are listed in "Letters and Abstracts of Letters from Pennsylvania" (Bishop's "History of American Manufacture"), glassmaking is not among them. Probably no quantity of glass was ever made for commercial use at this unidentified glass house.

CHAPTER III

MORE than fifty years now elapsed during which one finds no hint of further attempts on the part of any of the colonies to manufacture their own glass. Doubtless the increasing facilities of transportation from Europe made their need less pressing. And possibly, too, it was being gradually borne in upon the minds of the ambitious, that the establishment of a glassmaking industry requires, by the very nature of the undertaking, a large outlay of capital and ample backing. At any rate the colonial press during the early years of the eighteenth century abound in advertisements of imported glass, while even tradition is silent on the subject of local efforts looking to competition.

In 1739, however, Casper Wistar, Brass Button Maker of Philadelphia, a merchant of standing and a man of parts and of property, began the construction of a plant in Salem County, New Jersey — the Wistarberg (or, as it has occasionally been called by an anachronistic transposition of local nomenclature, the "Allowaystown") glass works, destined to prove the first successful venture of the kind made on American soil. But the history of this factory has a certain direct bearing upon the subject of this volume, inasmuch as the Wistarberg plant was a flourishing concern with (colonially speaking) a long and honorable history of successful activity behind it when Stiegel landed in America, was the immediate and recognized rival of the Manheim works during the whole period of the life of that concern, and survived it some years before itself succumbing to the Revolutionary depression and disorganization of business; we will pass it by for the moment and dispose of the other pre-Stiegel glass undertakings before taking up its history.

CONNECTICUT. THOMAS DARLING, 1747

The first of these is but a flash in the pan. In 1747 the legislature of Connecticut granted to Thomas Darling a patent giving him the sole privilege of making glass in that colony for the period of twenty years. The patent lapsed, however, owing to Darling's inability to fulfill the conditions of the act.

BOSTON, MASSACHUSETTS. BOWDOIN VENTURE
1749

About the same period Massachusetts seems to have made several attempts to establish a glass industry. Justin Winsor, Librarian of Harvard University, in his excellent "Memorial History of Boston, 1630 to 1880," mentions the name of Bowdoin as appearing in a petition in 1749 asking the legislative grant of wood land in aid of such an enterprise. But nothing tangible can be seen to have resulted.

BOSTON, MASS. GERMANTOWN FACTORY
1750–1760

In 1750, however, Joseph Crellins organized a company which actually managed for a decade to maintain a precarious and ineffectual existence. Crellins was a native of Franconia, and had originally migrated to Philadelphia. Here, he was a close friend of Benjamin Franklin, whose "Plain Truth" he translated into German in 1747. In 1750, he moved to Boston. And here, together with John Franklin, tallow chandler (Benjamin's brother), Morton Quincy, merchant, and Peter Etter, stocking weaver, all of Boston, he organized a company which leased a hundred acres of land from John Quincy, at Shed's Neck in Braintree, for ten shillings an acre, and prepared (although it did not actually proceed) to begin building.

Isaac C. Winslow now joined the company, which, on August 27th, 1752, re-leased its holdings to General Joseph Palmer and Richard Crouch, who, by the terms of the lease, were to begin immediate operations. And they would seem to have wasted no time in doing so, since, under date of November 6th, 1752, the Rev. Edward Holyoke, President of Harvard, enters in his diary: "Yesterday saw ye Glass Works established in Braintree in 1752 by a company of German Protestants."

On November 27th of the same year Isaac Winslow petitioned the legislature to grant him the exclusive right of manufacture for the colony for a term of years, alleging that it would be necessary to incur expenses of two thousand pounds sterling before any advantage would accrue from the enterprise. The patent was granted in December, 1752. On April 2nd, 1756 (prior to which time the company's glass house appears to have been destroyed by fire), Joseph Palmer petitioned for the privilege of establishing a lottery to raise twelve hundred and fifty pounds sterling. This permission was also granted on the twelfth of the same month.

The whole project seems to have grown out of an unsuccessful attempt to establish a German settlement in Massachusetts. But the site chosen for this project — Braintree, in that part of Quincy still known as Germantown; a neck of land on the west side of the Fore River just where it enters Boston Harbor and the present site of the Sailors' Snug Harbor — was about as

inconvenient, inaccessible and unsuitable a site for a manufacturing village as could have been picked out. Nothing but the
coarsest of green bottles and the primitive glass known as
"Black Metal" were ever made at the works. And as there
was little demand for such wares in the well-supplied market
of Boston, the company finally, in 1760, acknowledged failure
and ceased operation.

NEW WINDSOR, ORANGE COUNTY, NEW YORK
1753–1785

Meanwhile, after a hundred years of inaction, New York
once more began to attempt the establishment of the glass industry. About 1753 a glass factory was started at what is now
the village of New Windsor, in Orange County, on the banks
of the Hudson not far from Newburg; the founders of the enterprise being Christian Hertell, Samuel Bayard, Loderwick
Bamper and Mathias Earnest. Hertell was the resident manager, and the location of the factory seems to have been chosen
owing to a belief that the peculiar stone underlying "Butter-
hill," as Storm King was called, was a superior material for
glassmaking purposes.

An agreement, made on the 3rd day of January, 1752, is
reproduced in Mr. Edward M. Ruttenber's "History of the
Town of New Windsor," printed in 1911 by the Historical Society of Newburg and the Highlands, by the terms of which
some nine residents of the village agreed to sell 12 lots to
Samuel Bayard and company for the purpose of founding this
glass house; it being stipulated that should the factory not be
built and operated, the land should revert to the original
holders. And a deed, dated August 18th, 1752, is on record in
the Register's Office in New York, conveying, for £320, some

10,360 acres of land in Orange and Ulster Counties to Mathias Earnest, Samuel Bayard, Loderwick Bamper (all described as shop keepers of New York City) and to Christian Hertell (described as a mariner).

That the factory was running in 1755 is attested by the following advertisement, which was printed by the "New York Gazette or Weekly Post Boy" in its issues of August 18th, September 8th, 15th and 22nd, 1755:

"All persons that have any demands of the Company of the Glass House at New Winsor are desired to bring in their Accounts to Loderwick Bamper in New York as speedilly as possible in order to have them adjusted by the said Company. Said Bamper has also to sell a parcel of choice good molasses and New York Rum by the Hogshead."

And it is said that the company continued to operate the works until after the Revolution, and were quite famous in their day and that mail, brought by sloops and post-riders, was distributed from there to the settlers in the regions for miles around.

I visited New Windsor and made every possible endeavor to get some clue to the nature of the factory's output. But I finally discovered, by the aid of a map of the village, made from the original survey of the site in 1749 by Charles Clinton, and from information furnished me by residents, that the clay surface of the land on which the factory had stood was long ago excavated and used by brick works, and that the excavations thus made had been filled in. No pieces of the glass made there are now to be found, therefore, on the site of the works, which stood on lot 22 of the old map. This lot now lies west of the Shore Road and a hundred feet or so north of Broad Street — a winding road which ends opposite the machine works of Joseph H. Turl. In the factory's day this lot faced the river.

NEW YORK, NEW YORK. GLASS HOUSE COMPANY, 1754–1767

If you happen to be at all familiar with the intricacies of New York City real estate titles, you are pretty certain at some time to have encountered that bugbear of local searchers, the Glass House Farm. Yet if you are never so interested in the early glass industry of the United States, you are unlikely ever to have heard of any 18th-century factory on the banks of the Hudson, in what was then known as Newfoundland. I have, as it happens, experienced both interests. Yet my earlier, legal acquaintance with the Glass House Farm suggested nothing to me as a new student of glassmaking history, until I happened recently to come across the designation again on an old map, and looked at it with a fresh eye. But when I thereupon set out to discover the origin of the name, I found myself for a long time lost in no-man's land. The standard reference works all claim to offer complete information as to the farm titles underlying present New York City holdings, but all hasten to add, "except the Glass House Farm." But I finally struck a clue in "The Rapelje Narrative," by George Rapelje, published in 1834 by West and Trow. Here I came across a casual reference to the fact that the glass house stood originally "north of a country seat called 'Content,' a delightful place, the summer residence of Mrs. McAdam." And by the aid of Mr. Thomas H. Kelby, Librarian of the New York Historical Society, I finally identified this lady as Anne McAdam, wife of William McAdam, a merchant in the city of New York. And with this hint as to location as a starter, but by a course too dryly technical to be interesting, I finally reached an approximate identification of the glass house site as lying some 400 feet east of the shore of the Hudson River in the neighborhood of the present line of 37th Street. And about 20 feet south of 37th Street, in what are now the freight yards of the Pennsylvania Railroad, I found enough pieces of glass mixed with the soil, and showing many marks of long burial, to make it seem probable that this was the authentic location of the vanished works.

Later, an unexpectedly brilliant light was thrown on the nature and scope of the company's output by the following advertisement, which I discovered in the "New York Gazette or Weekly Post Boy" of October 7th, 14th and 21st, and of November 4th, 18th and 25th, 1754:

> "Notice is hereby given. That there is to be sold by Thomas Lepper Storekeeper to the Glass House Company, living at their Store on the late Sir Peter Warren's dock at the North River near Mr. Peter Mesier's, all sorts of Bottles from 1 Qt. to 3 Gallons and upwards as also a variety of other Glass Ware too tedious to mention, all at reasonable rates; and all gentlemen that wants Bottles of any size with their names on them, or any Chymical Glasses or any other sort of Glass Ware, may by applying to said Lepper, have them made with all Expedition. N.B. Said Lepper gives ready money for Ashes and old window glass."

Esther Singleton, in her "Social New York Under the Georges, 1714–76" (Appleton, 1902), publishes an illustration of several bottles preserved in the Van Cortland Mansion, in Bronx Park, New York, and describes them as "bottles of the kind Mr. Lepper was able to furnish." One of these bears the name of "Sidney Breese" and the date "1765." Another has "F.V.C. 1765" incised in the glass inside of a raised, heart-shaped border. I went up to Van Cortland Mansion and examined these bottles, and, in my judgment, they bear every evidence of having been made at Wistarberg. There were also some half-pint bottles of Wistarberg make, but without inscriptions, in the Van Cortland Mansion collection.[1]

The "said Lepper" (as appears in an advertisement which he signed as "Thomas Lepper from London," and which appeared in "The New York Gazette Revived in the Weekly Post Boy" on May 28th, 1750) kept a Gentlemen's Ordinary at the Sign of the Duke of Cumberland, opposite the Merchants' Coffee House, for a time. On November 19th of the same year, another advertisement in the same paper shows that he had removed to the Ferry House, Staten Island, where he "will continue to keep good Entertainment." And the minutes of the Common Council of the City of New York for Tuesday, February 8th, 1757, show that on that date Matthew Earnest was granted liberty to construct a dock, "fronting his land in the Out Ward of the City, commonly called and known by the name of New found Land, having on the south side thereof the land of the late Sir Peter Warren and on the north the land of one Mr. Mandawell and contains in breadth toward the River between four and five hundred feet." This is the central portion of what was afterward known as the Glass House Farm and the part on which the Glass House stood. And this dock was quite possibly intended for the use of the Glass House Company, in place of the dock spoken of in the advertisement of 1754 as "the late Sir Peter Warren's," on which at that time the Company's store was located.

Again, in the "New York Mercury" of October, 1758, there appeared an advertisement reading:

> "This is to inform the Publick that the new erected Glass House, at Newfoundland within four miles of this City, is now at work, and that any Gentlemen may be supplied with Bottles, Flasks of any sort of Glass agreeable to directions.
>
> " N.B. Any person that has Oak Wood to dispose of, by bringing it to the above mentioned Place, will receive the New York Price upon Delivery by
>
> MATTHEW EARNEST."

I have failed to find any record of Earnest's associates in the Glass House Company; but in four deeds and leases, recorded in the Register's office of the City and County of New York, David Provost and Elias De Breese were associated with him, and it may be that they were also connected with him in the Glass House venture.

I have also been unable to discover the exact life of the undertaking. But Governor Moore of New York, in a letter dated January 12th, 1767, from Fort George, New York and addressed to The Lords of Trade and Plantations, is found saying: "The Master of a Glass House which was set up here a few years ago, now a bankrupt, assured me that his ruin was owing to no other cause than being deserted by the Servants he had Imported at great expense and many others had suffered and been reduced as he was by the same kind of misfortune."

And "The New York Gazette and Weekly Mercury" of February 29th, 1768, contains an advertisement of "the noted farm on which the Glass House stands adjoining the North River, and is now in the occupancy of Matthew Earnest," to be sold on the 2nd of the following March "at publick vendue, at the Merchants' Coffee House to the highest bidder."

Finally, in "The New York Gazette and General Advertiser," from January 27th to February 5th, 1813, the following advertisement appears:

> "To LET OR LEASE —That part of the old Glass House Farm adjoining the Greenwich Road situate about three miles from town and containing about 35 acres an excellent situation for a milkman. Inquire of A. L. Stewart, 235 Broadway."

Sic transit gloria mundi.

Roughly speaking, the Glass House Farm tract extended from Thirtieth Street on the South, to Fortieth Street on the North, and from Eighth Avenue to the Hudson River. This property had consisted of three farms, the southernmost of which belonged to Sir Peter Warren; the middle one, on which the Glass House stood, belonged to William McAdam; and the northernmost to Mr. Jellis Manderville (erroneously called "Mandawell" in the minutes of the Common Council). And these were first brought together under a single ownership by Rem Rapelje after the Revolution, he having purchased the McAdam farm from the legatees and devisees of Sarah Arnold on June 4th, 1773, she having procured title in 1768 from Matthew Earnest, then a bankrupt. Mr. Francis Halpin, in "The History of the Chemical Bank," published in 1913, and containing the history of the Chemical property in this region, states that the Glass House was built of wood.

BROOKLYN, NEW YORK. LODERWICK BAMPER
1754

Loderwick Bamper, one of the founders of the New Windsor Glass House, is said to have started a glass house in Brooklyn in 1754, at a location corresponding to that portion of the south side of State Street now lying between Hicks and Columbia Streets. Bamper, according to Henry R. Stiles in his "History of the City of Brooklyn," published by J. Mensell, Albany, 1869, was a son-in-law of the Dutch governor of Surinam; came to New York between 1720 and 1730 in a vessel owned by himself, with a cargo of dry goods and horses; purchased ground at the northwest corner of Gold and Beekman Streets, where he erected a residence; was a large buyer of land in the northern and western parts of New York province, and also in Brooklyn, where, on Brooklyn Heights, he had his summer home, and, as above located, his glass factory. Bamper had a store in New York City in 1753, where various advertisements published in the local papers show that he sold Linens, Glass, Molasses, Raisins, Writing Paper, Tea Kettles, Twine, &c. &c.

To all intents and purposes, nothing whatever is known of this Brooklyn glass enterprise of his. But at least, if the New York Glass House has lent its name to a muddle of legal complications, its Brooklyn brother has sent a phantom bottle careering down the halls of history.

Deming Jarvis is his "Reminiscences of Glass Making," published in 1865, says (and please note the mixture of personal statement and doubly unascribed quotation):

"The Historical Society of Brooklyn, N.Y., has in their collection 'a glass bottle, the first one manufactured at a glass works started, in 1754, near the site of the present glass works on State Street. This enterprise, we are informed, was brought to an untimely end for want of sand, — that is the right kind of sand.' From this we infer it must be a flint glass bottle, as the sand suitable for green or black glass abounds on their coast."

And this bottle, projected into history by Mr. Jarvis's unnamed informer as the first of its race, "inferred" by Mr. Jarvis to be a flint glass bottle by reason of the nature of the Long Island sands, soon comes to figure in the pages of Mr. Jarvis's successors and quoters as "stamped with the name of Mr. Bamper and the date 1754," and, in Bishop's "History of American Manufacture," in the Weeks Report in the United States Census of 1880, and in Stiles' "History of the City of Brooklyn," it is paraded as Exhibit A in the case for American glassmaking.

It might, indeed, so figure here, had I not happened to be born with a drop of Missouri blood in my veins. But, chancing to have a curiosity to see this bottle, I sought an introduction to it in the rooms of the Long Island Historical Society of Brooklyn (the only institution of the kind to which Mr. Jarvis's reference can possibly apply). And lo, it was not to be found, nor did interested search reveal its hiding place. And finally, after some inquiry and correspondence, I received the subjoined letter from the institution:

Long Island Historical Society
Brooklyn, N.Y., Nov. 18th 1913.

Mr. F. W. Hunter,

127 East 37th St.,

New York,

My dear Mr. Hunter: —

Miss Ingalls, the former curator of the Museum, has been interviewed, and she says that she has no recollection whatever of the "Bamper bottle" ever having been in the Museum.

I have also looked through the catalogue of objects in the Museum and find no mention of the bottle in question.

If we ever owned it, it must have been while the Society rooms were on Jeroleman and Court Streets, and have perished in transition.

Regretting very much that we no longer have it to produce,

Very truly yours
(signed) Isabel Beers
Assistant.

Like the sword, Excalibur, the Bamper Bottle has vanished into the depths from which it rose. Was it flint, or black metal? Did it bear on its rotund side the historic name of "Bamper," or was it plain? Was it a real bottle, or was it a "hant"? We shall never know. For ever and for ever, from this time forth for ever more, it is the Man in the Iron Mask of American glassware.

PHILADELPHIA, PENNSYLVANIA, 1763?

And now, since we are dealing in riddles, here is another. The " Pennsylvania Chronicle and Universal Advertiser " of July 24th, of August 2nd and of September 4th, 1769, and the " Pennsylvania Gazette" of August 17th and of December 14th, 1769, all contain the following notice:

"Broken Flint Glass single or double is wanted and if brought by any person to Jacob Barge or Jacob Morgan in Market Street, James White in Front Street near the Drawbridge or to Jacob Reno in Second Street next door but one to Edward Duffield, shall receive for the same 2 d. per pound.

" As it is intended again to be worked here a New Glass House it is to be Hoped that all Lovers of American Manufacture will encourage what lies in their Power and particularly in this instance, save collect and send such Broken Glass as above directed.

" N.B. No duties Here."

At this late day this comes to us like a thin cry from the void; a faint "C.Q.D." whose vibrations just reach our aerials and then fall silent. Was the former Glass House, whose existence is implied in this admirable Dutch-English, the one we glimpsed, "conveniently posted for water carriage," in 1683? We cannot tell. Was the New Glass House, encouraged by what lay in the power of patriots, ever "worked here"? Again, as the lawyers — those incomparable finalists — have it, "the deponent saith not."

Yet one other whisper reaches us from the rustling pages of those curiously uncommunicative eighteenth-century newspapers. In the " Pennsylvania Journal and Weekly Advertiser " and in the " Pennsylvania Gazette," in the issues of December 7th, 1774, the following advertisement appears:

"AMERICAN GLASS

" The Proprietors of the Glass House, near this city, having now procured a set of good workmen, and the works being in blast, the public are therefore informed, that they may be supplied with most kinds of White and Green Glass Ware, such as are usually imported from Great Britain, and at moderate prices, which it is hoped will induce the friends of their country and their own interest to promote the undertaking.

" JOHN ELLIOTT, AND CO.

"Orders from Store Keepers and others, both of town and country, will be executed with care and despatch, and a reasonable price given for white and green broken glass.

"A person who understands the making of window glass, in the English method, may find encouragement, by applying as above."

John Elliott and Company were located, in the Philadelphia of that day, on Front Street between Chestnut and Walnut Streets. And while the Glass House for which they bespeak custom in the above quoted advertisement does not (since it came after Stiegel instead of preceding him or competing with him) properly belong in the present review, the notice is reprinted here as a matter of possible interest. It is evident that there had long been a desire, intermittent, but persistently reviving, to establish a glass industry in Philadelphia. That desire finally, and at about this time, came to fulfilment in the beginning of that century of success that fell to the lot of the establishment later so well known as the Kensington Glass Works. It is possible that the New Glass House which was "intended again to be worked here," in 1769, and the enterprise the Elliotts call attention to in 1774, may have some connection with the history of that factory. At any rate the clippings are here tossed, like bits of bread, on the waters of investigation.

NOTES

1. Mr. Hunter did not weigh all the possibilities in the case of the wine bottles. "Black glass" bottles, the orthodox common wine containers in the 18th century, would have been the product of any glasshouse making bottles. Unless marked, those produced in one house would have been practically indistinguishable from those of other glassworks. During the period of the Wistars' operation the wine bottle passed four milestones in changing form. It was growing taller and developing a higher kick-up. While the Glass-House Company of New York operated, it would have produced bottles of the same forms, colors and sizes as those made at Wistarberg during the first decade or so of Richard's regime. The bottles at the Van Cortlandt Mansion could equally well have been blown at Wistarberg, New York City or almost any contemporary European glasshouse.

HMcK

CHAPTER IV

CASPER WISTAR, the founder of the first successful glass industry in the American colonies, was born in Wald-Hilspach, in the then Electorate of Heidelberg and the present Grand Duchy of Baden, in Germany. Family tradition has it that the family was of Austrian extraction and titled. And, judging from the position made for himself in the community of his day by the founder of the American branch, by the character of his career in colonial Philadelphia, the simplicity and solidity, initiative and originality, of his undertakings, as well as by the prepotency of the stock, as witnessed by the patriarchally noble presence, exquisite courtesy and fine courtliness of one of his direct descendants, Mr. Josiah Wistar, of Salem, New Jersey, to whom I am indebted for some of this information, the tradition is more convincing than the majority of such cherished American beliefs.

Casper Wistar was twenty-one when, on September 16th, 1717, he landed in Philadelphia. He brought little money with him, but as it soon became evident that the things he touched had a quiet way of turning into that commodity, the lack was negligible. He soon came to be recognized as a merchant of position, and early acquired a more than local repute as the manufacturer of a brand of brass buttons, "warranted for seven years," the reputation of which was among the assets bequeathed to his heirs, and the manufacture of which was continued even after his death in 1752. In 1726 he married Catharine Johnson (or Jansen), of Germantown; a Quakeress who was doubtless responsible for the fact that he himself, in 1725, joined the Society of Friends. His eldest son and successor in the conduct of the Wistar works, Richard, was born on June 7th, 1727.

By the middle thirties of the eighteenth century, Casper Wistar was a man of mark in Philadelphia, and, for the day, of wealth. And he then, by what inducements led it is now impossible to discern, turned his attention to what was evidently an undertaking close-knit with his desires and his ambitions — the starting on American soil of a well found and effectively conducted glass industry. For reasons doubtless connected with the plentifulness of fuel and sand, and with the accessibility of convenient water transportation, he chose Salem County, in the then province of New Jersey, as the site of his enterprise. And here, on January 7th, 1738, he purchased 39 acres of land from one Clement Hall, and, adding to this bit by bit, he had, by the spring of 1739, acquired some two thousand acres in all. Some hundreds of acres of this land, Mr. Josiah Wistar informs me, are still in the possession of the family. The tract upon which the glass house was actually erected was bought from Amos Hilton on April 27th, 1739. This land lay on both sides of the highway from Salem to Pilesgrove, about a mile beyond Thompson's Bridge (now Alloway), and on a branch of Alloways Creek. The factory stood about fifty or sixty yards south of the road, in what is now, and has been for many years, a well-tilled field; and some of the buildings connected with the plant were located on either side of the highway — the present road from Alloway to Daretown.

At the present time nothing is left of any of these buildings. But R. M. Ashton, in a paper read before the Salem Historical Society in 1885, describes as still standing, "an old dwelling built of logs neatly squared and dovetailed at the corners, carrying the scars where the joists have been sawed off which at one time extended several feet beyond the first story to support the projecting roof, so common to the homes of the first German settlers." He adds that "this was the principal dwelling in the small village of Wistarberg, the kitchen of one story attached to the west end of the house has been removed within the last forty years. The store for the sale of merchandise (the removal of which has been of comparatively recent date) stood on the edge of the highway, on the same side as the dwelling and about fifty yards west of it, shaded by the stately sycamore still standing on the opposite side of the road."

Wistar started his factory with the aid of expert help imported from Holland; and almost all the subsequent output of the works bears evidence of the persistence of this early Dutch influence. A document still extant and bearing date of December 7th, 1738, sets forth an agreement between "Casper Wistar, brass button maker," and "John William Wentzell, Casper Halter, John Martin Halton and Simon Kreismeier, experts in glass making." By the terms of this agreement Wistar undertakes to pay to Captain James Marshall fifty pounds and eight shillings sterling, the price of these men's passages from Rotterdam; they, to teach the art of glassmaking to him and his son Richard, and to no one else; and he, to provide land, fuel, servants, food, and materials for a glass factory in the province of New Jersey, to advance money for all expenses including their support, and to give them one third of the net profits of the enterprise. This, by the way, is one of the first instances of coöperative industry in this country.

The factory was built during the summer and fall of 1739, and began operation late in that year. Under date of July 31st, 1740, Charles Carkesse, Secretary to the Commissioners of the Customs in London, writing to Thomas Hill, Secretary to the

Lords Commissioners for Trade and Plantations, says: "Mr. William Frasor Collector of the Customs at Salem in West Jersey having informed the Commissioner that there has lately been erected a Glass Work within eight miles of that Port by one Casper Wester a Palatine and is brought to perfection so as to make glass; I am directed to give you an account thereof for the Information of the Lords of Trade."

In 1748 a church — the original building, plus an addition which doubles its size, is still standing, and known as Emanuel's German Lutheran Church — was built at Freasburg, a few miles from Wistarberg on Upper Alloways Creek. And it is recorded that many of its members, among others German emigrants named Freas, Troelinger, Ridman, Dielshower, Sowder, Knieal and Tabal, had come to work for Wistar at his glass house.

It happens that we have, through an advertisement printed by Richard Wistar in the "Pennsylvania Journal" of October 11th, 1780, offering the then inoperative works for sale, a most interesting inventory of the buildings at that time. The description runs as follows: —

"Two furnaces with the necessary ovens for casting glass, drying wood &c. Near by are two flattening ovens in separate houses, a store house, a pot house, a house with tables for cutting glass, stamping mill, rolling mill for preparing glass for working pots. Dwellings for workmen. Mansion House, 6 rooms to a floor. Bake house and wash house. Store house. Retail shop kept for 30 years being a good stand $1\frac{1}{2}$ miles from the Creek where shallops land from Philadelphia, 8 miles from Salem, $\frac{1}{2}$ mile from good mill. 250 acres of cleared land in fence, 100 acres of mowable meadow for large stock of horses and cattle. Stalling for 60 head of cattle a barn, granary, wood house and wood lot."

Casper Wistar died in 1752, and by his will, dated February 13th, and probated March 28th, of that year, he left the glass works, all tools, &c., to his son Richard, who, however, was

directed to give annually to his brother Casper 400 boxes of
the best 8x10 glass, 400 boxes of the best 7x9 glass, 100 boxes
of the best 9x11 glass, three dozen half gallon case bottles,
six dozen pocket bottles, one dozen pint bottles, &c. His
executors (named in the "Lancaster Gazette" in its first issue,
July, 1752) were his wife Catharine Wistar, his son Richard,
David Deshler and Richard Johnson — the latter being his
wife's brother. Richard Wistar never lived at Wistarberg, but
he continued the operation of the factory, and employed Benjamin Thompson as manager of it. And on August 11th, 1752
(three months before Stiegel gained his first foothold in Lancaster County by marrying Elizabeth Huber of Brickerville), the
following advertisement appeared in the "Lancaster Gazette":

> "Richard Wistar hereby gives notice that he is removed from
> his Father's House in Market Street Philadelphia to a house
> higher up in the same Street next door to the Spinning Wheel
> almost opposite the Prison. Where may be had Glass 9x11,
> 8x10, 7x9 and all other sizes of Window Glass and Bottles,
> wholesale and retail. He likewise carries on the trade of Making
> Brass Buttons where merchants shop keepers and others may be
> supplied as usual."

The same notice appears in the "Pennsylvania Gazette" of
November 23rd, December 7th and 14th, 1752. In the "Pennsylvania Chronicle" of July 31st, 1769, and in the "Pennsylvania Gazette" of September 28th, 1769, the following advertisement appears: —

> "Made at subscriber's Glass Works between 300 and 400 boxes
> of Window glass consisting of common sizes 10x12, 9x11, 8x10,
> 7x9, 6x8. Lamp glasses or any uncommon sizes under 16x18
> are cut on short notice. Most sort of bottles, gallon, $\frac{1}{2}$ gallon, and
> quart, full measure $\frac{1}{2}$ gallon cafe bottles, snuff and mustard
> bottles also electrofying globes and tubes &c. All glass Amer-
> ican Manufacture and America ought also encourage her own

manufacture. N.B. He also continues to make the Philadelphia brass buttons noted for their strength and such as were made by his deceased father and warranted for 7 years.

RICHARD WISTAR."

It is at least conceivable that this advertising, the only commercial advertisement of the Wistarberg products that I have found, except the one already quoted, was resorted to because of the successful rivalry of the Stiegel works, then in the heyday of their Manheim activity.

The next glimpse of Richard Wistar afforded by the press of the day, is a notice inserted in the "Pennsylvania Chronicle and Universal Advertiser" (printed by William Goddard and R. Towne in Market Street next above the P.O.) on April 18th, 1770, and offering a reward of $20 for "two German Servant Lads run away" — these being described as, "Jacob Stenger aged 18 years 5 feet 8 inches well set, good countenanced, light complexioned, dark hair," and " John Kindiel 17 years 5 feet 3 inches, old look, freckled face, black hair, thin long visage of a slender make." The incident is of interest in connection with the early history of American glassmaking in that Jacob Stenger was one of the Stenger brothers who, in 1775,[1] started the first glass plant that has survived to the present day — the factory which is now running as the Whitney Glass Works at Glassboro, New Jersey; and where, amid an orderly but clangorous turmoil, thousands of bottles are turned out per day by batteries of automatic machines. One wishes that Richard and his run-away-servant-lad could stand for a moment before one of these clanking monsters; could watch its sixty bottles a minute lifted from its opening molds by its ghostly steel fingers; and thus see with their own astounded eyes what America has done by way of "encouraging her own manufacture."

It has been supposed that the Wistarberg works were kept

in operation until the death of Richard Wistar — he died in Rahway, on August 4th, 1781. But his advertisement of October 11th, 1780, quoted from above, makes it certain that the works were already idle at that time. It is certain that the general business stagnation due to the Revolution gradually sapped the vitality of the enterprise during the '70's, and Mr. Josiah Wistar says that he has reason to believe that actual operations ceased early in 1780. Richard Wistar, by his will, gave his executors authority to lease or sell his glass house.

It is, I think, quite evident from the above data that the Wistarberg glass works relied for their commercial success — at least during the earlier years of their activity — almost entirely upon the making of window glass and bottles. This was the natural course of development for such an undertaking to adopt; a direct addressing of itself to the paramount needs of the day; and was, as we shall see, also true of the Stiegel works. But even in these earlier years, the Wistarberg glass house turned out many articles of household utility — bowls, dishes, and pitchers of various quaint shapes in crude brown, green or bluish green glass; as well as snuff canisters, preserving jars and attractive bottle-like vessels for, one supposes, the storing of pickles and sweetmeats. Later on — perhaps after the advent of the German workmen — the factory's range of output was much broadened and the management's leanings toward the employment of colored glass developed along lines of greater and greater refinement. Technical skill also increased with the demands made upon it. And at last — during an as yet unidentified period of the factory's prosperity — it produced, apparently in considerable quantities, esthetic-utilitarian wares of striking individuality and real beauty. For the most part these Wistarberg pieces are characterized by a fine primitive feeling for form, and by a richly refined sense of color, the two expressing themselves (whether separately or in conjunction) with, in general, a certain crudity, but almost invariably with distinction.

During the summer and fall of 1913 I paid several visits to the site of the Wistarberg works; very thoroughly canvassed the ground; made exploratory excavations; and gathered enough fragments of the glass made and used there, and enough pieces of the factory's finished output, to form an excellent and illuminating basis for a determination of the kind of work done, and for a critical sorting out and identification of at least the more markedly characteristic Wistar pieces from the surviving specimens of early American glass.[2] Judging from the specimens of flint glass (both clear and colored) that can be ascribed with certainty to this factory, and from the fact that Stiegel himself limited his own claim to being "the first flint glass manufacturer in Pennsylvania," the priority in this important branch of the industry must, I think, be accorded to Wistar. And it follows that, in the present state of our knowledge, he must, provisionally at least, be regarded as the first American maker of flint glass.[3] He is even more definitely entitled to rank (we make our bow in passing to the beads of the second Jamestown glass house) as the first American maker who fused different colored glasses for the obtaining of bi- and tri-colored pieces in whorled and concentric waved designs — using clear flint with opaque white; clear flint with brown; emerald green with opaque white; emerald green with brown; blue, green and opaque white; blue, amber and flint; and variations of these combinations. The factory also made a very lovely grade of opaque turquoise blue glass. And the exquisite transparent turquoise glass from which many of its earlier and cruder bowls and dishes are made, as well as the bluish golden opalescent glass found in some of its most delicate and dainty pieces, are recognizable at sight by anyone who has once made their acquaintance.

The factory seems to have made comparatively few pieces in dark blue, although a very rich shade of this glass was made there; and in this it differs widely from the Stiegel works, where blue was preponderantly the favorite color. On the other hand, it turned out many fine pieces in a very rich dark brown flint — dark, yet with a glowing amber sort of fire in it. It also made pieces in pale amber, and in a faint smoky brown. But in the plain colors, green was its favorite; and in the variety and glossy richness of the effects thus obtained, it stands quite alone.

The Wistar technique is also characterized by various schemes of decoration, based upon manipulations of a coating of glass superimposed upon a part of an already partly finished piece. A pitcher, for instance, when partly blown and still attached to the blowpipe, and before the base had been welded to it, would be dipped for about a third of its height into the molten glass, and the extra coating thus obtained tooled into a spiral or grooved pattern, or drawn out over the thinner glass above it in a friezelike design suggestive of breaking waves.[4] Covers of vases were treated in the same way, to match the bodies of the vases they belonged to. Another favorite decorative device, sometimes used alone, and often in conjunction with the dipped decorations described above, was the twining of a slender thread of glass spirally about the neck of a pitcher or the upper portion of a mug. Expanded designs also (that is to say designs impressed on the original "gathering" or "paraison" of glass by blowing it into a small pattern mold, and afterwards expanded as the piece is blown in the usual way) were used to some extent. For the most part these were simply perpendicular ribbings, which gave a corrugated effect to the sides of the flasks or jugs on which they were used. But there is reason to suspect that more intricate patterns were at one time used — doubtless in emulation of the Stiegel methods — at Wistarberg.

I regret that space forbids the insertion of illustrations showing some of this factory's work, but for the present at least I must content myself with giving a partial list of the identified products of the factory.

Among the earliest pieces, rough bowls and queer squat pitchers very Dutch in appearance, and made of a crude, open pot, brown glass are found.

The early bottles produced were extremely heavy, characterized by a deeply indented bottom, showing a semi-globular hollow; had sharply rounded shoulders, tapering necks, and had the lips for the most part finished with a deeply divided double head. They came in many shapes, no two being exactly alike; and now and then one finds one with an elliptical bottom — a sort of amphora shape. The glass used was mostly a coarse green, but occasionally, probably in the period of the first color experiments, one finds a golden green with blue streaks. Many carboys were also manufactured, the lips being reamed over to form a trim.

Later, bowls of good quality, sea-green glass were turned out, some of them large enough for washbasins. The edges of most of them are reamed, and, as the decorative instinct developed, some of these were made with the edge gracefully flared and the wave design frieze worked out upon their lower parts in superimposed glass. The latter range in size from a couple of inches high to a gallon or more. Bowls also come in white flint with a "watered silk" design in opaque white.

Like the New York Glass House Company factory, Wistarberg also seems to have made a practice of blowing bottles with the orderer's name impressed upon them in a sort of glass seal attached to the side. One of these bears the inscription "John

Smith. 1750." This is not a ghost bottle, like the celebrated Bamper "hant." It is owned by Mr. J. B. Kerfoot of New York.

Flasks of considerable variety were also made, both early and late. One curious specimen has the neck inserted[5] after the Dutch method, and has its flattened body covered with small knobby protuberances. Others are perfectly plain, with sheared mouths, in clear flint and in light amber. Others, in rich amber and deep brown, have the expanded ribbed decoration running from their mouths some two thirds of the way to their bases. And, in the finest period of the factory's workmanship, flasks in two and three colors were made with an expanded pattern as above.

Pitchers seem to have been a great standby of the Wistarberg factory. The great majority of them are in greens; and it is in these that some of the finest effects were produced. They are almost always very bulbous in the body and with flaring necks. They come plain and in both styles of the superimposed decoration — the heavy corrugated double coating and the frieze wave-pattern. And they range in size from the tiniest individual creamers to pitchers that will hold a gallon. Bicolored pitchers are also found — green with whorls of brown, clear flint with brown whorls, clear flint with opaque white "watered silk" wave patterns, and so forth.

One of the factory's characteristic shapes was a sort of bulbous bodied bottle with a jug handle. These come in all sizes from an ounce to a gallon. They come plain, with the superimposed wave frieze, and in the expanded ribbed design. They are almost always, if not always, green.

Bowls in great variety were among the factory's output; some thoroughly utilitarian, and others extremely decorative in the characteristic Wistar style. They made bowls of green and

turquoise green glass as large as a foot high and fifteen inches
opening. And they made others with the superimposed decoration as small as a couple of inches either way. Many blue
bowls of very rich hue were made there too; as well as others
in the rich brown that the factory produced in such perfection.
And a curious and extremely handy device that they were very
fond of using, was the blowing of glass balls to use as covers for
their pitchers and their bowls. Some of these balls measure
more than a foot in diameter and are slightly flattened at the
bottoms so as to fit the larger bowls. Others, in light green,
dark emerald, amber, and various shades of blue, come in all
sizes from blue balls to cover large bowls to little green marbles
to keep the flies out of the individual creamers already mentioned. I found the pieces of several of these balls in excavating
on the factory site; and have since seen beautiful bicolored
pitchers, with the original balls, made to match them, still
closing their graceful mouths.

Scent bottles were another specialty of the Wistar works, and
belong for the most part to its best period. Exquisite little
bottles in a delicate ribbed and twisted decoration are found;
some about two inches long, and of a size and shape fit to slip
into a lady's glove. Others have their tails drawn out and curled
back against their bodies till they look at a little distance like a
sea horse. Others, again, are miniature flasks, with the expanded
ribbing running down from their mouths. Finally, many are
made in gourd shape, with three, or more often four, ribbons of
glass crinkled perpendicularly up their four sides. The latter
are mostly in green. The small flasks come in amber. The
"sea horses" and their tail-less brothers come in dark-blue,
light blue, smoky brown, golden opalescent, and in various bi-
and tri-colored combinations.

Mugs in blue, green and brown, also exist. And some of the

large flip-shaped glasses, with handles added, and the spiral thread wound round their upper edges are extremely effective.

Finally — doubtless made by the workmen from the glass left in the pots at the end of the day's work — some wonderful pieces are found in the shape of canes, pipes and toys. The pipes are sometimes finely worked from the richest of the factory's emerald green flint. Others are in the deep amber brown glass already described. Others in white flint. And some of the canes, splendidly executed in triple or double color schemes and showing the rich Wistar hues, are as beautiful as they are fragile.

Altogether, the history and output of this glass house offer most interesting and rewarding subjects for study and investigation; and I hope that some day they will be thoroughly looked into and the results made public. It is a strange thing, and yet typical of the complete indifference shown toward our early glass and its history, that no one seems to have even suspected that this factory not only rivalled, but in some ways entirely outrivalled, the Stiegel works. Yet in the use of color there is no comparison between their achievements. And in virility and individuality of design the scales fall quite sharply, to my mind, on the Wistar side. The Stiegel staff included skilled workmen from the chief glass centers of Europe, and his output shows the influence of them all. In delicacy, in variety of decoration, in sophistication of technique, the Manheim products belong to another world from those of Wistarberg. Yet I freely confess that as a result of continued and familiar association with both, the Wistar glass is steadily gaining ground in my estimation. I began my investigation of it simply because I wished to have as full a knowledge as possible of what had gone before Stiegel in American glassmaking; and at first I looked rather coldly upon the fine crudity of design and the effective and colorful simplicity of the Wistar products. Later, I found myself frequently feeling that "I could be happy with either were t' other dear charmer away." And, more and more, I am coming to see that the early American factories worthy of the collector's best endeavors and of the esthete's hearty interest, are two, not one, and of practically equal appeal.

NOTES

1. Present evidence indicates this house began operating in 1781.

2. If Mr. Hunter had described in detail and elaborated on both the fragments and specific pieces attributed to Wistarberg the real value of his attributions would perhaps not be so questionable. Many described types doubtless were Wistarberg but most pieces in this category have been traced to other houses in South Jersey, New York or New England or to those areas. Hence the generic term "South Jersey type" should be substituted for "Wistarberg" throughout the discussion.

3. I know of no proof or even evidence that the Wistars ever made any lead glass. Seemingly Mr. Hunter was led astray by the current misconceptions about identifying flint or lead glass. (See note page 133.) In his statement that his was the first flint glass manufactory in Pennsylvania, Stiegel was limiting his claim to his own state not because an out-of-state competitor made flint glass before he did. Advertisements, apparently not discovered in 1913, prove Stiegel was asserting his priority in this field over his rival, the Philadelphia Glass Works.

4. The usual method of forming this and similar superimposed decoration was first to attach a "pearl" (blob of glass) to the bottom of the parison and then pull it up over the parison, tooling it into the desired device.

5. Neck inserted or "inserted neck" is another misleading collector-coined term. The neck was not inserted. That appearance or effect resulted from the so-called German half-post method of bottle blowing: a second gather of metal was made upon the first and called a half-post because it usually terminated on or just below the shoulder of the piece.

HMcK

CHAPTER V

BEFORE proceeding to a detailed description of the individual articles so far discovered and identified as specimens of Stiegel's glassmaking enterprise, it will be well to pass in rapid review, first, the sources of our knowledge; second, the history of the factory with regard to the ascertained scope and the specific nature of its activities; and, finally, the derivation of its esthetic inspirations, and the qualities and distinguishing features of its output.

And in order to make the first of these summaries as simple and sequent as possible, it is advisable to recall that, when I was moved to undertake my inquiry into the history of the man and the nature of his glass, the emphasis of tradition was almost wholly laid upon the spectacular events and habits of his personal career, and upon the bare fact of his having established and conducted a factory for the manufacture of glass. Many articles of English, German, eighteenth-century American, and nineteenth-century American make, were then confidently and in good faith offered as specimens of Manheim manufacture; and while there was a certain core of unanimity in regard to the ascribing of certain articles to the Stiegel glass house, and while there was a considerable amount of scattered family tradition in regard to the acquirement of various individual pieces, which, once subjected to comparison and analysis, offered valuable evidence by no means to be disregarded, no logically synthetised theory as to either the specific character or the general characteristics of Stiegel glass existed.

In these circumstances, three sources of possible information presented themselves. First and most obvious, the collecting and collating of the surviving family traditions with regard to pieces of glass which had come down from previous generations with the story of their having been bought at the Stiegel works. Second, an exhaustive examination of the files of contemporary newspapers, and a search for any documents which might have been preserved and which might relate to the matter. And third, if such an undertaking should prove feasible, a series of excavations on the site of the old factory.

The first of these inquiries I pursued in conjunction with my assembling of the Hunter Collection. And while the histories of certain pieces will be, from time to time, referred to, and the inferences drawn from information thus obtained will, from time to time, be set forth, it is obvious that, in the vast majority of cases, evidence of this kind is contributory to one's conclusion rather than determinative of them, and that often, while its influence has been a factor in a final judgment, that influence is too remote to be worth recording.

One example, however, of the value and serviceableness of this source of information may be cited. In the case of those salt cellars made in white, blue, and purple flint glass, and decorated with the Venetian Diamond pattern (the ones which, as we shall see, Stiegel himself called "Chain Salts"), there proved to be so widespread and absolutely unanimous a tradition as to their origin, that the point appeared to be established beyond a reasonable doubt. And, naturally, this at least tentatively satisfactory identification immediately extended one's inferential knowledge to all other pieces of similar glass, decorated with the same pattern; and, by analogy, placed under a most significant suspicion similar pieces, made from the same material, and decorated with designs derived by obviously cognate methods.

Once this start had been made, other family traditions, relating to pieces or types not so widely recognized or claimed as of Stiegel origin, but bearing a close kinship in material and method of production to these, acquired significance. And thus many a farmhouse tradition, unnoted and possibly unsuspected, has made its minute contribution to the structure of conviction.

A similar body of tradition, similarly collected, collated and analysed, formed the foundation of my judgment in regard to the mugs, screw-topped bottles and other articles decorated in color with vitrifiable enamels after the German style. And in both of these classes — in the mold-impressed and subsequently hand-blown pieces, and in the enamel-painted ones — a careful comparison of the best authenticated Stiegel specimens with the known work of the European factories, with whom Stiegel was competing, not only afforded a wholesome check upon the always fallible testimony of family tradition, but gradually disclosed marks of decisive difference, and bases of less obvious differentiation, which, taken together, afford a consistent and in most cases a conclusive guide to authoritative judgment.

As regards the second source of information — contemporary documents — much information as to the character of the Stiegel output has been derived, as we have already seen, but as will be presently more specifically shown, from the advertisements which he inserted in the colonial press. But the most valuable information in this matter — a mass of various and often detailed data that the most sanguine investigator would not have dared to hope for — we owe to the diary-like account books of the Stiegel enterprises, an incomplete series of which proved to have been preserved among the uncatalogued possessions of the Historical Society of Pennsylvania, at Philadelphia, among the John Dickinson papers.

From this source not only much information as to the history and development of Stiegel's various glass houses has been drawn, but also a highly instructive catalogue of articles manufactured and on hand in the spring of 1770, as well as many scattered and hereafter assembled facts as to the nationality of his workmen, the nature of his raw materials, the prices paid for the making of various articles, and the sums for which he sold them.

There remains the third chief source of information as to the nature and quality of Stiegel's glass, — the excavations prosecuted on the site of the Manheim factory. And as these resulted in evidence which is, in a sense, basic to almost all the determinations hereafter noted, I will set down a somewhat detailed account of the proceedings.

I have already described the investigations of this nature carried on at the site of the Elizabeth Furnace plant; and it may be pertinent to state that, during the summer of 1913, Mr. J. B. Kerfoot and I had made at least a dozen examinations of old glass factory sites, and excavations thereon, in southern New Jersey, hoping to find evidence bearing upon the date and location of the manufacture of the elaborately decorated table ware blown in full size, three-piece, contact molds, and specifically characteristic of the extensive wave of American glassmaking which succeeded the Revolution, and whose dates, roughly speaking, are probably statable as lying between 1800 and 1840.[1] So that I was pretty fully posted as to the relation which fragments thus found would bear to the output of the factory from which they emanated.

On Saturday, July 26th, 1913, being in Manheim, I determined to make a house-to-house canvass in the neighborhood of the glass house site, and see what information I might come upon, or what relics I might possibly find. But meeting with no success, I proceeded to interview the children of the neighborhood, offering premiums for fragments of glass from the old factory. Here again, I met with no success, and, in the course of these inquiries, I was repeatedly told that such a search was vain as the factory had been built originally on very low ground, and that the site had subsequently been filled in to a depth of 8 feet; also that Pitt Street had been cut through in the 1840's. But I was also informed that many families in Manheim were possessed of fragments of old glass, picked up at the time of the tearing down of the factory; and indeed I had already seen certain of these in Mr. George Danner's museum. Subsequent inquiry confirmed the rumor of the scattered possession of these relics, but unfortunately I could find no one able to lay his hands on the pieces, although Mr. Nathaniel W. Long remembered that his father had had some specimens put away, and promised to try to find them for me. Before leaving Manheim, however, I repeated my house-to-house canvass (several householders having been away from home on the occasion of my first visit), and this time, at 152 South Charlotte Street, the residence of Mr. H. H. Schenck, I was told that a piece of glass had been found when excavating their cellar, and, after a search, Mrs. Schenck found it and brought it to me. It proved to be the stem of a wine glass of the variety known as "cotton stem," and the inescapable inferences forced upon me, as to the technical skill of the Stiegel workmen, and as to the character of his finer products, naturally not only astonished me, but induced me to make the most searching inquiry as to the identity of the piece, and the depth and location of its unearthing. Having been satisfied on these points, and having finally obtained the specimen (it is illustrated in Figure 159), I was ready to make the most determined efforts to secure the chance of excavating on the surrounding properties.

Mr. George H. Danner has in his possession an old map,

inscribed, "A Draught of the Town of Manheim and Sundry Out Lots thereto adjoining Situate on a branch of Ebiecus Creek in Rapho Township in the County of Lancaster belonging to Messrs. Isaac Cox and Henry William Stiegel 1769." This map was evidently drawn by Thomas Lincoln, and many of the lots shown thereon bear the names of their purchasers written across them in Stiegel's handwriting. This map shows that Pitt Street was already laid out, and, from the various Stiegel deeds,

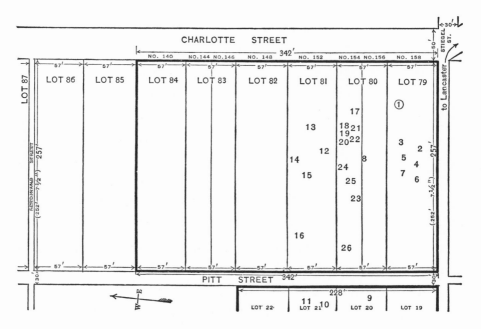

as well as from his mortgage of the Glass House to Isaac Cox, dated February 2nd, 1770, it appears that the glass house premises occupied the lots numbered on this map as follows:

Facing on Charlotte Street, with a total frontage of 342 feet, and a depth of 257 feet, lots numbered 79, 80, 81, 82, 83 and 84, and fronting on Pitt Street, with a total frontage of 228 feet, and a depth of 257 feet, lots numbered 19, 20, 21 and 22.

The following residences, at the time of my investigations, occupied the old site:

Old lot 79	F. P. Ruhl	No. 158 South Charlotte St.		
Old lot 80	{ Morris Stoner	No. 156	"	"	"
	{ John Walter	No. 154	"	"	"
Old lot 81	H. H. Schenck	No. 152	"	"	"
Old lot 82	C. Bomberger	No. 148	"	"	"
Old lot 83	{ Levi Hess	No. 146	"	"	"
	{ J. S. Beckin	No. 144	"	"	"

With these data in mind, therefore, I set out, on the afternoon of Sunday, October 19th, 1913, to visit the owners of these properties and obtain permission to dig in their gardens; and having that afternoon obtained the desired privilege from Mr. H. H. Schenck, I was on hand early Monday morning, meaning to tackle the job. But Mr. Schenck was away for the time being, and, while I was examining the adjacent back yards, Mrs. John Walter called me and said that she had found pieces of glass in her rose bed, and that if I cared to I might dig there. So I borrowed a spade and went to work. But, by the time I had sunk a shaft some four feet deep, I made up my mind that while I was not ashamed to beg, I was very far from being much at digging, and concluded to get help. And a short search was rewarded by finding two men from Columbia, Pennsylvania, a Samuel Warfel of 614 Plain Street, in that town, and a friend of his, who had come to Manheim in search of work; and, these agreeing to give me the morning, we returned and went at what proved to be a sizeable and arduous undertaking. We three worked till half after one in the afternoon, and at half after two, Mr. Schenck, who had returned meanwhile, kindly offered me the services of his man, and he and I worked till about five.

The excavations made were from 2 to 7 and 8 feet deep, and some of them as large as 8 feet in diameter. Below the filled-in soil (a layer that varied considerably in thickness), a hard clay was encountered, which not only made digging difficult, but led to the breaking of many of the fragments embedded in it.

No pieces from the surface soil were retained or considered, their presence being merely taken as indications for digging.

In all, 25 excavations were made, and in order to show the relative positions of these, their locations are indicated on the accompanying diagram by numbers, and the nature of the fragments unearthed from each is given in the following summary:

Location No. 1.	The old well of the glass house is here, in the cellar of the residence of F. P. Ruhl.
Excavations Nos. 2 and 3.	Bricks 2⅝x4⅛x8⅜. Fragments of light green, blue-green, amethyst and flint glass, and pieces of broken hollow ware.
Excavations Nos. 4, 5, 6, 7.	Fragments of flint glass of blue, amethyst, light and emerald green, amber and dark red-brown glass. Window glass and bits of hollow ware.
Excavation No. 8.	Window glass. Flint, light green glass. Pieces of broken bottles.
Excavations Nos. 9, 10, 11.	Flint, light green and window glass in small quantities. Probably the site of a shed or store house for finished product, as no glass drippings or pieces of glass-pots were found here.
Excavations Nos. 12, 13, 16 and 26.	Pieces of flint, blue, light green-glass, window glass and bits of hollow ware.
Excavations Nos. 14 and 15.	So few specimens of any kind found that no diggings were made further north.
Excavations Nos. 17, 21 and 23.	Quantities of window glass, light green, nile green, olive and olive-green glass as well as of white and blue flint; also bits of hollow ware.
Excavation No. 20.	Flint flashed with opaque white, as well as the commoner run of glass.
Excavations Nos. 18 and 19.	Uncovered two glass-pots and a brick and tile walk; also quantities of glass.
Excavations Nos. 23, 24, and 25.	Window glass. Flint, light green, nile green, olive-brown and blue glass. Many drippings and also fragments of hollow ware.

A typical selection of these fragments, illustrative of the range of color represented by them, is reproduced in color in Plate VIII.

Up to this time (which antedated the finding of the Stiegel account books and the searching out of the contemporary Stiegel advertisements), I had taken as authoritative the tradition and the generally expressed conviction that Stiegel had made neither bottles nor window glass, and that his output had consisted entirely of white flint,[2] blue, emerald green and amethyst pieces. When, therefore, I here unearthed any quantity of window-glass fragments, measuring $\frac{11}{128}$ and $\frac{5}{64}$ of an inch in thickness, as well as open pot glass of light green, nile green, olive green, olive, olive brown and dark red-brown colors, besides portions of different sized bottles and closed pot flint glass of blue, blue and green mixed, amethyst, emerald green, pale amber, amber and white transparent flashed with opaque white, I was not only dumbfounded, but forced immediately to alter my entire attitude toward the question of the Stiegel output, and to broaden and reconstruct both the scope of my inquiry and the character of my collection.

At the time of these excavations my study of the presumable types and alleged specimens of Stiegel glass, carried on along the lines already indicated, had proceeded far enough and had developed enough tangential inferences and enough collateral suggestions awaiting confirmation, for the results of the day's work to afford immediate clarification on many points; especially those connected with the Stiegel work in color. For example, I had already acquired the beautiful blue flower vase illustrated in color in the frontispiece of this volume, and believed it to be Stiegel, although, at this time, I had no irrefutable evidence of Stiegel's having used the sunken-panel form of molded and expanded decoration with which its sides are adorned. The finding, therefore, of a fragment of just such a vase, with a portion of the panelling upon it, and showing the identical color and quality of glass,[3] not only instantly established the identity of my specimen, but opened up the entire field of flips and other pieces similarly treated.

But while my ideas were thus immensely clarified, and my investigations vastly facilitated in the lines of colored glass and manipulative methods, the finding of vast quantities of plain flint fragments, and the evidences of an extensive manufacture of household hollow ware neither molded nor colored, gave me a disconcerting glimpse of a territory for the exploring of which I possessed at the moment neither guide nor compass. And it was primarily for the mapping of this territory — for the gradual identification of the Stiegel plain flint pieces — that the lists of the factory's output, soon thereafter uncovered in the factory's advertisements and in the Stiegel account books, afforded me the much-needed bench marks of departure and bases of comparison. I will summarize the information thus obtained in the most easily graspable form.

The Manheim Glass Works account books, in the possession of the Historical Society of Pennsylvania, have a list for the year 1769, and another from January 1, 1770, to April 1, 1770, some of the figures in Stiegel's own handwriting, showing lists of glass ware, either on hand at the Manheim glass store, out on consignment, or sold since the beginning of 1769, summarized in the following list:

Quart Decanters molded	923
Quart Decanters plain	1968
Pint Decanters plain	6374
Half Pint Decanters plain	3319
Sundry large Tumblers	29
Pint Tumblers	3153
Half Pint Tumblers	8900
Gill Tumblers	4740
Half Gill Tumblers	2
Half Gallon Tumblers	3
Quart Mugs and Bowls	527
Pint Mugs	1387
Half Pint Mugs	940
Half Pint cans	475
Large Glasses	29
Salts	301
Plain salts	508
Common salts	5748
Chain Salts	207
Salts with Feet	585

Tall Salts	757
Beer Glasses	32
Sugar Boxes and Covers	312
Pocket Bottles	6214
Cream Jugs	2057
Vinegar Cruets	791
Smelling Bottles	584
Fine Wine Glasses	223
Plain Wine Glasses	5648
Bulbed Glasses	77
Phials	6318
Glasses	3
Free Masons	2
Junk Bottles	345
Toys	251
Mustard Bottles	1354
Wine Water Glasses	24
Fine Beer Glasses	48
Mustard Pots	1152
Pocket Bottles	292
Junk Stands and Glasses	130
Candle Sticks	4
Blue Flower Jars	3

The books also show that window glass had been made in sizes of 10 × 12, 8 × 10, 7 × 9, 6 × 8, 5 × 7 and 4 × 6.

In addition to this list the discovered Stiegel advertisements are summarizable as follows, in so far as they bear upon the articles manufactured and offered for sale:

March 1769
All sorts of Bottles, Window Glass and Sheet Glass, also retorts and other glasses for doctors and chymists.

March 1770
Flint and Blue Flint Glass.

July 1771
Patterns sent with orders will be exactly executed.

January 1773 (New York)
Decanters, Quart, Pint, Half Pint.
Pint Crafts.
Double flint fine.
Tumblers, Pint and Gill.
Syllabub and Jelly Glasses.
3 feeted Salts and Creams.
Wine and Water Glasses.

Vinegar and Mustard Crewets.
Phials and other bottles for Chymists and Apothecaries.

February 1773
Flint and Common Tumblers, Pint, Half Pint, Gill and Half Gill.
Carrofts enameled.
Wine Glasses Mason and Common.
Syllabubs and Jelly glasses with and without handles.
Mustard and Cream Pots. Flint and Common.
Salts.
Salt linings.
Crewets.
Wide-mouthed bottles for sweetmeats.
Rounds and phials for doctors.
Wine and water Glasses.
Ink and pocket bottles.
Orders taken for all kinds of glasses for chymical and other uses agreable to patterns.

It will, I take it, be obvious to the least practiced student of such matters that the identification of articles of ordinary household utility, made of uncolored and undecorated flint glass, presents difficulties much more baffling than those presented by articles in which distinctions of color, schemes of decorative design, characteristic marks of manipulation, and idiosyncrasies of painting or of engraving traceable to individual workmen, are present.

But here, too, local tradition offered at least a basis of inquiry. And, again, the greater and greater frequency with which certain types, and types combining certain features of structural character with certain points of material quality, were noted as one approached the region immediately supplied by the factory under examination, tended to concentrate and direct the investigation. And of course the authentic testimony of the list and the advertisements above quoted, immensely aided in correlating these indications. Moreover, all such studies are helped by the cumulative character of the knowledge acquired in prosecuting them, and by the many and illuminative cross-references that increasingly develop between specimens of different character that have been made by the same men. The

shapes of handles, the configuration of pitcher lips, the contours
of wine-glass stems, the weltings of wine-glass feet, — all these,
and many more, come to be eloquent, though silent, witnesses
of origin. And all these have borne their part in the discrimina-
tions and discardings, the siftings and selections, the gradual
isolations and identifications, represented by the articles, plain
as well as colored, molded as well as enameled and engraved,
which are hereinafter described.

But, when all these sources of information and springs of
judgment have been enumerated, there still remains the most
subtle, yet at times the most convincing, of them all. I refer to
those delicate nuances of characteristic color, and those intimate
attributes of textural value and surface quality, with which local
habits of chemical process and manipulative procedure, often
emphasized by the effect of time, inalienably imbue all articles
of man's making, whether they be of pottery or of porcelain,
of enamel or of glass. By the very necessities of its derivations,
Stiegel Glass is *sui generis,*[4] and it is only, as Pater says, the
"roughness of the eye" that prevents our recognizing the mere
material of it at sight. But although such a recognition is often
beyond the border of our limitations, it is also frequently well
within the circle of our capacities. And it is in the training
and refining of such capacities that so-called "expert" equipment mostly consists, — in the possession of a certain aptitude
for fine perceptions; a trainable color sense and a developable
responsiveness to textural and qualitative stimuli; and in the
schooling of these by the constant handling of many examples.
Such qualifications as I possess in this line are based, in general,
upon nearly twenty years of constant study and collecting of
Chinese porcelains, lapidary work and glass, and, in the present
instance, upon nearly three years of investigation, in the course
of which I have doubtless examined more pieces of actual and

alleged Stiegel Glass than it has fallen to the lot of any one man to handle since the close of the American Revolution.

Nevertheless, both the assembling of the Hunter Collection, and the contentions and conclusions of the present volume, are essentially pioneer work. No one can be more conscious than myself of the problems that remain to be worked out and of the ambiguities that remain to be resolved. And while I have tried to err on the side of conservatism, and while I confidently hope to be convicted of more sins of exclusion than of inclusion, I entertain, neither on the one side nor on the other, any false notions of infallibility.

NOTES

1. Failure of readers to grasp and remember the significance of such statements as this was responsible, in part at least, for the attribution of this 19th century glassware to Stiegel. Mr. Hunter tentatively and in cautious wording considered the possibility that some of it was Stiegel but nowhere did he make a definite, unqualified attribution even of the pieces in Figs. 109-113.

2. See note on page 133.

3. The consensus among students today is that neither the fragment (now at the Metropolitan Museum of Art, New York City) nor the portion of some sort of panel on it were large enough to have justified this conclusion. It is believed also that the vases are 19th century and, judged by the geographical distribution of those traced, were probably made in a New England glasshouse, possibly at Cambridge or Sandwich.

4. This chapter is an important object lesson in methods of research and study— methods to emulate. But, while Mr. Hunter's methods were right beyond a doubt, subsequent studies of glass, American and foreign, seem to indicate that the specimens available to him were insufficient for a comprehensive comparative study and a determination of exactly what the "sui generis" of Stiegel's glass is.

HMcK

CHAPTER VI

BOTH at Elizabeth Furnace and at Manheim, Stiegel made bottle glass, green glass and flint glass. At Elizabeth Furnace, the making of bottles and window glass was the chief industry, and the making of flint was doubtless more experimental than commercial. But the character of the bottle glass was the same at both places — nile green, olive green and olive; and in both places excellent "green glass" was made, as well as a good quality of dark red-brown glass of the same type. With a single exception, I have made no attempt to distinguish any specimens as deriving specifically from the Elizabeth Furnace plant. This exception is a pair of sauce dishes in light green glass very much under "cooked," and hence full of minute air bubbles, which have been included in the Hunter collection on the strength of their perfect resemblance to the fragment of such a vessel uncovered by me at Elizabeth Furnace, which disintegrated because of its long exposure to the chemical action of the earth.

Sand, limestone and clay all abound in the neighborhood of Manheim — Stiegel owned a limestone quarry two miles from the Furnace. Yet once at least, on October 7th, 1765, he purchased a load of clay from William Crawford, in Philadelphia, for which he paid £3. 2. 6. This may very well have been imported clay from which to make glass-pots. For the latter purpose a clay found near Stourbridge, in England, is said to be the best obtainable, and is often exported for use by foreign glassmakers. Nor is the purchase of such a material as great an extravagance as appears, since the ground-up bodies of the worn-out pots is a most valuable ingredient for the making of new ones that are better than those constructed wholly of new clay. But while the Stiegel account books are full of references to the men being "busy with the clay" or "cleaning the clay" — so much so indeed that one unacquainted with the necessities of the situation might think the works were potteries with glassmaking on the side — no other mention of any purchase of this material appears.

Potash, on the other hand, is frequently charged up as bought and paid for. It is possible, since Stiegel exported much glass to Boston, and since the Boston papers of the day teem with advertisements of potash and pearl ash, that he procured his supply from there in exchange for his finished product. In the earlier days of his Manheim works, he purchased much litharge (a yellow lead monoxide used in the making of flint glass), but later on bought chiefly the more costly, but more desirable, red lead (minium). I found no formulæ anywhere mentioned, either for the composition of "batch," or for the obtaining of his color effects.

We will not here concern ourselves with the methods of making either the window glass, the sheet glass, or the bottles turned out at the Stiegel factory. It is likely, from the wording of his advertisements, that both the "crown" method (by which an opened bubble of glass was spun into a flat circular disc from which windowpanes were cut) and the "sheet" method (in which an oblong cylinder of glass was first fashioned and then cut longitudinally by a diamond and allowed to open and flatten out under the influence of heat), were practiced at the works. On the other hand, the common run of bottles were usually, at this time, blown in crude clay molds that were open at the top and about as deep as the body of the bottle. The body of the bottle being thus formed, the punty rod was attached to the bottom (driving it in a bit in the operation), and the neck of the bottle drawn out by means of the blowpipe. This dent of the punty, made in attaching it to the bottom of the hand-blown bottle, is the parent of all those larger and more sophisticated hollows by means of which quart bottles have so long been made to hold a pint and a half.

But leaving these staple articles of manufacture out of the question, the manipulations of glassmaking as practiced at the Stiegel works, divide themselves, for the purpose of our study and classification, into four groups. The first of these is the blowing and fashioning of plain-surfaced articles of all descriptions and grades, with no other accessories than those already described — the blowpipe, the marver, the pucellas, the shears, the punty and the glassmaker's chair. The second group includes all the articles with ribbed, fluted, whorled, diamonded, paneled and otherwise modeled surfaces, which, at the Stiegel factory, were mostly obtained by the use, at one stage of the blowing, of small, open-topped, perpendicularly incised molds, and by the subsequent manipulation, with the ordinary tools and by the ordinary processes of hand blowing, of the impressions thus given to the gathering or paraison.

The third division includes the cutting and engraving of designs upon the otherwise finished pieces, by means of a diamond point and of a small copper wheel and emery or pumice. The fourth includes the decorating of otherwise finished pieces in vitrifiable enamels.

As glasses of various types formed a large proportion of the articles made by the simpler process, and as we have the authority of H. J. Powell, in his "Principles of Glass Making" (1883), for the statement that every principle of glassblowing is illustrated in the making of a wine glass by the early methods, we will briefly follow the making of one of these bits of table ware. The stems of wine glasses are either drawn out from the substance of the bowl itself, in which case they are called "straw shanks," or are made from a separate piece of glass and attached to the bowl while hot, when they are known as "stuck shanks." Both methods were used at the Stiegel factory; although there, as elsewhere, the latter method was by far the more common one. In the case of a wine glass with a straw[1] shank, the blower, after receiving the blowpipe with its small gathering of glass upon the end, proceeded to blow a bubble of the required size and thinness; whereupon, from the end of the punty rod, a small quantity of molten glass was dropped upon the end of this bubble and a small knob formed from part of it with the pucellas, and the balance drawn quickly out into a stem. Another, smaller, bubble was now blown upon another blowpipe, and its end attached to the bottom of the stem previously formed. The end of this small bubble was then "wetted off" (that is to say a line was drawn round it with the wet point of a punty rod and the glass fractured along this suddenly cooled line), and the open-ended bulb thus formed was further opened by the insertion of the pucellas point and then spun out into the foot of the wine glass by rapid rolling on the arms of the glassmaker's chair. At this stage of the proceeding, the upper part of the bowl of the glass was still attached to the original blowpipe, which still formed the handle by which the glass was held for working. And a punty rod was now attached, by means of a little molten glass, to the center of the foot, and the blowpipe "wetted off" from the end of the bowl. Then, with the punty for a handle, the bowl was reheated, given its final shape either with the pucellas or by spinning, sheared, and the sheared edge rounded off by being, for a moment, inserted in the furnace. Last of all, the punty was "wetted off" and the finished glass taken to the annealing oven. This left upon the foot of the wine glass, or other piece, the rough protuberance with fractured edges with which we are familiar on early specimens of hand-blown glass, and which is called the pontil mark — "punty" being the glassmaker's alocution for the Italian name of the tool. Toward the end of the 18th century it became the custom to grind out these blemishes, at first very crudely and in a manner that left an irregularly circular depression in place of the protuberance. Later on, a star, or other ornamental cutting, was used to disguise the meaning of the work done. A few Stiegel pieces are found, as we shall see, where a die seems to have been pressed upon the reheated bottom with the object of obliterating the pontil mark. The accompanying cut shows the foot of a Venetian diamond pattern toilet bottle in the Hunter Collection.

Not only the foot-rims of wine glasses, but the bases of bowls, the lips of pitchers, and the sheared edges of various vessels, were occasionally finished by what is known as "welting" — that is, by having the edge turned back and pressed flat upon the adjacent glass. In the case of wine-glass feet of English and of Stiegel make, the welting is always done from above downward and inward. But the rims of pitchers and other vessels may show the welting turned either in or out.

We have already seen that the great majority of wine-glass stems were made separate and attached to their bowls when finished. These are either plain rod (or cylinder) shape, or baluster shape, or decorated, either externally or internally, with spiral adornments. Those externally decorated in this fashion are usually what are called "rib-twisted" — that is to say, the small gathering of glass from which they are fashioned has had a series of longitudinal lines incised on its surface with the pucellas point, and has then been drawn out and twisted as it was drawn.[2] The internally decorated specimens with which we shall have anything to do, and in which Stiegel copied the Bristol technique, are known respectively as "cotton stems" and "bubble stems."

The cotton stems are formed by threads or bands of opaque white glass, laid longitudinally upon the surface of a small gathering of flint glass, and afterward covered by a second gathering, and the whole then drawn out and twisted in the drawing. The device is of Venetian origin, and for the finest work of this kind done in Bristol, and for the color effects similarly produced in the Netherlands, prepared rods of white and colored glass were, according to Dillon, probably imported from Venice.

The various forms of bubble stems are merely variations upon a hollow blown stem. Some show a large, pear-shaped bubble. (See Fig. 51.) Others have the sharper end of this pear-shaped bubble drawn out into a sort of tail that almost reaches the foot of the glass. (See Fig. 34.) Others show several small bubbles, or even symmetrically arranged groups of "tears," in a single stem (see Fig. 52), the effect having apparently been attained by puncturing the original gathering of glass with the tool point, and subsequently covering it with a second gathering.

We now come to the second division of our grouping of the manipulative methods employed at the Stiegel factories; namely, the pieces impressed in the early stages of their making with a design obtained from a small "pattern mold," and subsequently treated by the usual methods of hand manipulation and blowing. The basis of the process is explained by Apsley Pellatt, in his "Curiosities of Glass Making," under the caption of the Venetian Diamond, and the accompanying cut is taken from that volume. The metal molds, a cross section of one of which is shown in the illustration, were about a third of the size of the intended piece. And after the first gathering of glass had been allowed to cool somewhat, and a second gathering made upon this foundation, the whole was slightly expanded by blowing, and then blown into the hollow of the mold, and again withdrawn. The perpendicular moldings thus impressed upon the partly blown bubble of glass were then, in the forming of the so-called Venetian Diamond[3] pattern, pinched together with the pucellas at equidistant points, until the design was completed as shown in the dia-gram; and the blowing and other formative processes then continued as with the ordinary undecorated pieces. Of course all the effects produced by variations of this pattern-mold proc-

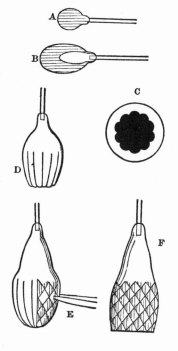

ess, together with many much more elaborate (and generally less beautiful) decorations, were later achieved, with more speed and less labor, by means of the molds made in hinged sections, and opened or closed at the will of the workman by means of a treadle or other lever. It was from molds of this variety, made in three sections and commonly known as "three-piece-molds," that the imitations of the English cut glass of the last years of the 18th century, so popular in America in the early decades of the 19th, were made. And there are rea-sons to believe that, at some time during his factory's lifetime, some devise of this later type may have been used by Stiegel. But of that we will speak later. The matter belongs to that penumbra of uncertainty that surrounds all such inquiries as the present one, but has no bearing whatever upon the matter now under discussion.

The Venetian Diamond pattern, and the above described method of producing it, was, as the name indicates, one of the technical devices of the Murano glass houses. But it was not from Italy, but from England, where the Bristol factories had developed great skill in its use, that Stiegel derived the idea. And it was, broadly speaking, in imitation of the Bristol products, then so extensively imported into the colonies, that he employed it. But of that, also, later on. For the present we are merely concerned with getting a clear idea of the molds used by Stiegel, and of the manipulations by which his resulting decorative effects were obtained.

Before proceeding to consider the other molds used, however, it is necessary to note that three sizes of the diamond pattern are clearly distinguishable on the Stiegel pieces. They of course vary in actual size according as the piece, upon which the original molding was impressed, has been more or less expanded in the subsequent blowing. But, for purposes of identification, they will be hereafter referred to as the large, the medium and the small diamond. Great differences are also observable, in each of these, in the nicety with which the pinching has been done. In some pieces it is very uneven, and shows places where the two moldings have not been quite pinched into contact. In others the technique is quite without flaw. This is doubtless due to the varying skill of the workmen.

A glance at the cross section of the mold used for making the diamond pattern will show that it was, as regards its inner or molding surface, a "female" die—that is to say that the design which it bore, and which it was intended to impress upon the glass, was cut intaglio upon a smooth surface. The impressions which it made upon the glass were therefore in relief. Another series of dies, very commonly used by the Stiegel factory, were also of this same character, only, instead of the perpendicular depressions in the inner surface of these molds being, as in the illustrated case, wide and close together, they were narrow and wide apart. The impressions which they made upon the glass gathering blown in them, therefore, were raised ribbings, symmetrically spaced as regarded any one mold, but of various spacings, and of various depths, as between different molds for the obtaining of different effects.

Here again, as pieces, made from glass blown in these molds with the spaced ribbings, were subsequently expanded, and as the amount of expansion differed widely in different pieces, it is impossible to deduce the exact size or the exact spacing of the various molds. But, broadly speaking, there seem to have been three types of the mold-form used; one which produced narrow ridges wide apart, one which produced similar ridges with a medium separation, and one which produced ridges close enough together to give them, when expanded, the appearance of a shallow fluting. And when to the effect of expansion is added the effect of the rapid rotation on the glassmaker's chair, and the intentional twist often given to the pieces, it will be found that these three types of ribbing develop into a variety of sharply twisted or slightly whorled ribbings and flutings, often appearing to have been derived from many and dissimilar molds.

This threefold division of these perpendicularly incised molds is intended to be explanatory rather than dogmatic. Yet, at the same time, it satisfactorily accounts for all the different forms derived from this type of initial patterning, and pieces will therefore be hereafter differentiated by being described as of the wide, medium or narrow ribbed types.

In addition to these three types, it appears from a single

specimen that I have seen and examined, and which is in the possession of Mr. Nathaniel W. Long, of Manheim, that a mold of this character was also used in which a series of single narrow incised lines were equidistantly engraved on the mold surface. And of course it is quite possible that other mold designs may turn up.

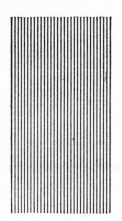

We have now to examine into the derivation of several other types of Stiegel pieces, in the making of which molds have been used. And the first of these are the vases, drinking vessels and other forms (see, for example, the frontispiece and Figures 82, 83, and 84), the sides of which are, for a part of their height, decorated by a variable number of slightly sunken panels, generally with rounded tops. These, like the forms already treated, were obtained from small, open-topped, pattern molds. But instead of the inner surfaces of these molds being so cut as to form "female" dies, they were so cut as to form "male" dies; the small, rounded topped pillars, which formed the slightly sunken panels on the inserted glass gathering, standing out slightly from their surfaces. This form of decoration was used on pieces varying in size from vases to cordial glasses, and many molds, differing not only in size, but in the number of their pillars, evidently existed and were in use.

Another type of Stiegel molding is represented by the drinking vessels illustrated in Figures 78, 79 and 145. These were also made with the aid of pattern molds. But in these cases the molds were so cut that the surface presented to the glass was a boldly fluted one — that is to say the deep perpendicular depressions cut into the face of the mold, and the sharp perpendicular ridges left between them, were about equal. The subsequent expansion of the glass in the blowing is probably responsible, more than any variations in depth of cutting in the molds, for the observed variations in sharpness or of depth in the fluted pieces when finished.

Among the most beautiful pieces produced at the Stiegel factory there are some, like the toilet bottle illustrated in Figure 108, which show a more intricate design than those we have hitherto dis-  cussed. One of these designs (see the accompanying cut) shows a series of daisy-like decorations enclosed in a series of squares. The other (see acompanying cut) shows four dots and four petals al- ternately enclosed in the four diamond- shaped divisions of a large diamond. The pieces upon which these patterns appear have been made by the pattern mold  and hand blown process we have just been considering. But, since their designs are not derivable from perpen- dicular lines cut in the face of the mold, and as any other sort of pattern cut into the perpendicular face of a mold would prevent the withdrawal of the glass blown into it, it follows that these pieces were either blown in a pattern mold very nearly dish-shaped, or in one that it was possible to open after the blowing was com- pleted.

We have now to consider the matter of those molded pieces already referred to as possibly of Stiegel origin, yet as standing for the present in the penumbra of doubtful authenticity. But before taking up the discussion of these pieces, which are all the product of full-sized contact molds, it will be well to describe

the simple, yet important, differences by which the expanded
pieces of pattern-mold origin, the pieces blown by hand in a
full-sized contact mold, and the later pieces "pressed" in a
mold by means of a plunger or piston, can be instantly distinguished.

To take the last first, the method of their production insures
that, while their molded exteriors shall show all the inequali-
ties of the mold in which they were made, their interiors shall
present a perfectly smooth surface.

On the other hand, in pieces blown with the blowpipe into a
full-sized contact mold, the air not only forces the soft glass
into the depressions of the mold surface, but *follows it in*. Any
piece thus made has, therefore, an internal depression corresponding with each external protuberance, and an internal protuberance corresponding with each external depression.

Finally, the pieces expanded in the open, after having been
impressed with a relief design in a small pattern-mold, show an
internal depression opposite each external depression, and an
internal protuberance opposite each external protuberance —
the exact opposite of the contact-mold-blown pieces. The reason for this is less obvious, but is equally cogent. Perhaps it
will be well to remember that if we make a few shallow incisions
on the surface of a fairly thick rubber band, and then stretch
the band, the smooth inner surface of the rubber bends in to
meet the cuts, while the uninjured portions of the material show
a corresponding tendency to assume slight bulges on both sides.
The action of the glass is similar. The comparatively thick
gathering of glass is partly forced and partly blown into the small
mold, and, when withdrawn, its surface has taken the impress of
the incised pattern, but its interior is unaffected. In the subsequent expansion by blowing, the thinner or weaker portions
of the material give on both surfaces, while the thicker and

stronger portions, because of their resistance, are left protuberant on both surfaces.

All the pieces which we have hitherto considered are expanded pieces, and show their respective pattern in identical, and not in reversed, fashion, on both their inner and their outer sides. The pieces which we have now to consider are blown in contact molds.

It will be remembered that Stiegel, in the list of glass made out by him in 1770, mentions "Quart Decanters Molded." In no other instance does he refer to any of the listed pieces by this term, although, if he was referring to the pattern mold so extensively used by his workmen, it is evident that he might, with equal justice, have added the same distinguishing designation to many of the other items in his list. It is also a fact that the small decanters made in white, blue and amethyst, and illustrated in Figures 111 and 112, share with the diamond patterned salt cellars the distinction of having been, for years, recognized by local tradition as of Stiegel make. It is also true that certain of these decanters (the same shapes, less finely executed and showing the three-mold lines where the molds were opened, and with a smooth bottom, were plentifully made later on and are frequently met with) bear evidences of a close relationship to the Stiegel material and careful workmanship. Moreover, a stopper of unquestionable Stiegel origin is shown in the Hunter Collection that would fit a quart decanter of this type. And on the score of all these facts, specimens of them have been included in the Hunter Collection and are here listed and described. The peculiar foot of the presumably Stiegel decanter of this type is illustrated in Figure 113. I have never seen a quart specimen that was not of much later make.

Finally, there are two pieces, a flint flip glass (Figure 109) and a flint sugar bowl (Figure 110), both of which bear such close resemblances to the glass made at the Stiegel factory, and both of which are decorated with designs that are so intermediate between the Stiegel designs and the subsequent American ones, that I have been able neither unqualifiedly to retain, nor unqualifiedly to reject them with any satisfaction. I have therefore chosen to regard them as possible missing links and to list them accordingly. They are both contact mold pieces; the mold marks on both have been carefully disguised by "flashing" — that is by a quick exposure to intense heat. And if it turns out that Stiegel, toward the end of his activity as a glassmaker, used the newly evolving contact molds for some of his work, these pieces, I believe, will be found to have been made by him.

There remain to be considered the engraved and the enameled decorations so extensively used by Stiegel, the first for some time, and the last after 1772.

There are four ways in which the surface of glass is cut, graven, or eaten away, for the purpose of esthetic decoration in the forming of figure work or other designs. One of these is by scratching or cutting, as it is called, with a diamond point. Another is by grinding with a large iron wheel and subsequently smoothing with a stone one and polishing with a wooden one, using abrading mediums in each case. A third is by a more superficial removal of the surface, with the aid of a small, rapidly revolved wheel of copper, with a very narrow cutting surface, and worked in connection with emery, pumice or other abrasive powder. And the fourth is by exposing the surface parts upon which it is desired to work to the erosive fumes of hydrofluoric acid.

The last-named method was not known until 1771, when the Swedish chemist Scheele discovered it; and it was probably not practiced in America until after the closing of the Manheim works. At any rate it was not used by Stiegel, and we can therefore dismiss it from consideration. The work done by its aid is of very inferior grade and is easily distinguished.

The chief uses of the large wheel are for the grinding down of rough surfaces, and for such deep cuttings as characterized the fascetted decorative designs of the English "cut glass." Here the surfaces left by the wheel are afterward polished. This wheel was never used at the Stiegel factory for the imposing of decorative designs on the pieces manufactured. I have, however, placed in the Hunter Collection two Stiegel pieces, which show a supplemental use of this wheel; one of them, a white flint, diamond-design salt cellar, with the lip ground and polished, and the other a tall, flint, diamond-design, salt shaker, the foot of which has been ground flat and polished. But of course in both cases the grinding may have been done later by the owners of the pieces, either to obliterate a nick in the lip of the one, or to remove an inequality from the foot of the other.

The two remaining methods, the engraving on the surface by means of the copper wheel and the ruling of straight lines upon it by means of the diamond point,[4] were the methods employed by the Stiegel workmen. As far as I know, the use of the diamond point was confined to the filling in of ellipses, circles and other outlines with trellis patterns of crossed lines and to other similar line work. The lines thus cut by the diamond point are, on the Stiegel pieces, appreciably deeper, and more noticeable to the finger nail when rubbed over them, than are the cuttings made by the wheel. Please note, however, that any representative collection of Stiegel glass is certain to contain pieces which show, on their bases or under parts, a letter or a series of two or three letters cut into the glass by means of a diamond. This is expecially true of specimens which have come from Lancaster, York or Berks Counties, where it seems to have been the custom for purchasers of such ware to cut their initials on the bottoms for purposes of identification. In a surprising number of cases, I have, in the counties mentioned, been shown such pieces and had the owners of them tell me proudly that his or her great grandfather had put the initials on — that, for instance "J. K. was put on by Jacob Kimmel whose son willed them to me."

The copper wheel used for glass engraving (and since semi-precious stones have been engraved in this way from ancient times the term is well used) is a thin copper disc from a quarter to an inch in diameter, capable of very rapid revolution upon a horizontal spindle, and propelled by a treadle. These wheels are of various sizes and types, and part of the skill of the artist lies in the selection of the wheel most suitable to his needs of the moment. Water and emery powder or pumice is used as the abrading agent, and the difficulties of the work are largely increased by the fact that the paste formed by these covers the surface being worked on, while the necessity of pressing the glass against the under surface of the wheel interposes this instrument between the workman and his work.

George Allers, John Casey and Edward Farrel (who later served as a teazer, or furnace stoker — a very responsible position — at the Manheim works) probably did the early engraving for Stiegel. It is likely that others also did this class of work and had apprentices who learned the trade from them. The contract signed June 4th, 1773, between Stiegel and Lazarus Isaacs, by which the later engaged to act as cutter and flowerer at the works, has already been referred to and its provisions noted. On August 10th, 1773, there is an entry in the Manheim books which reads, "Lazarus Isaacs is the Cutter and Flowerer." And in another of the account books, under date of

February 14th, 1774, and in Stiegel's own handwriting, Isaacs is charged 1 shilling for a quarter pound of pumice. And in the Manheim Ledger under the same date is found the following account:

Paid Lazarus for 6 months @ £5.10	£33
For ¼ pumice stone.	2.10
	£35.10

Lazarus Isaacs by 2 lottery tickets.	£ 3
For team hauling his goods.	1.10
	£ 4.10

From which it would appear that Isaacs left Stiegel's employ on that day.

I have distinguished, and will here enumerate, fourteen types of engraved design, stating in each case when the diamond-cut trellis work is found as a supplemental decoration.

I. Alternating figures, ellipse-like and diamond-shaped, formed by intersecting arcs of circles. With and without diamond-cut trellis work filling the ellipses and with dots and trefoil ornaments engraved in the angles formed by the intersecting arcs. Usually a single wavy line is engraved as a border above this design, which is the one most used on Stiegel pieces. See Figures 114, 115, 116, 117, 118 and 119.

II. Four segments of circles, filled with diamond-cut trellis work and finished at the top by a straight line engraved around the glass. A decoration of garlands and tassels is added below the circle segments. See Figure 120.

III. Floral design based upon a conventionalization of the tulip. Various treatments all showing diamond-cut trellis work filling the calix of the tulip. See Figures 121, 122, 123, 124 and 125.

IV. Alternating pyramids and inverted scrolls; the pyramids being formed by heavy graved lines and filled with diamond-cut trellis work; and the design being elaborately ornamented with dots, trefoils and other devices. See Figure 126.

V. An alternation of perpendicular wavy lines and a floral design. See Figure 127.

VI. A vine border. See Figure 128.

VII. An alternation of inverted foliated designs with double lined semi-circles enclosing four dots. See Figure 129.

VIII. Two-handled basket containing plant or flowers. The body of the basket showing basket work done with the diamond point. This design is copied from the Dutch pieces. See Figures 130 and 131.

IX. Vignettes of pavilions with flags flying alternating with a circle and a scroll design. The pavilion pillars are cut in with the diamond. See Figure 132.

X. A dove and flower or two love birds and a heart, enclosed in circle with sun burst radiations. See Figures 133 and 134.

XI. A beautiful floral design based on a conventionalization of the rose. See Figure 135.

XII. A design formed by the elliptical intersection of two wreaths inclosing four-petalled flowers. The wreath leaves are engraved; their center line is cut with the diamond. See Figure 136.

XIII. A design of pendant wreaths caught up with bow knots. Here again the center line of the wreaths are diamond-cut. See Figure 137.

XIV. Alternating palm leaves and trefoil designs with one straight and one wavy line as a border above and below. See Figure 138.

It now remains for us to consider the work done at the Stiegel factory in decorating glass with colored designs in vitrifiable enamels. And if pioneer honors in flint glassmaking, and in the fusing of varicolored glasses for esthetic purposes after the Venetian and English fashions, belong, in America, to Casper Wistar, to Stiegel is due the credit of being the first maker in this country to employ colored enamels for decorative glassmaking.

In enameling, as the term is used in ceramic and vitreous art, it is essential that the colored enamels used should fuse at a lower temperature than the body of the vessel on which they have been applied. Thus, when subjected to the heat of the annealing oven, they are capable of becoming completely fused, while the glass or glaze upon which they rest is not more than superficially softened. Enamel paints of this order have a base of silicate of lead, colored by various metallic oxides, and are applied with water or some other liquid as a medium.

Six opaque colors were employed at the Stiegel works; a white, a yellow, a blue, a nile green, a brick red and a black. These colors were applied without shading, and the black was sparingly used and seldom for outline purposes, but to enhance the effect of the designs.

Mr. Nathaniel W. Long, of Manheim, whose family is a very old one in the section, and who has himself been for years in touch with the oldest families of the region, told me early in my investigations that the tradition was widespread that the enameled pieces of Stiegel make all dated from the last eighteen months of the factory's existence. And this seems to be born out by the fact that enameled glass was not advertised by Stiegel until February, 1773. It was probably not made before some time in 1772.

From the nature of the employment of the various men at the time, as shown by the Stiegel accounts, and by the exceptional wages paid in certain instances, I infer that the men who did the enameling were Henry Nissle, Joseph Welch, Sebastian Witmer and Martin Yetters. And, as I have found it quite possible, through familiar handling and study of the great number of these pieces that I have seen, to distinguish four types of handiwork upon them, I have (since names make better tags than numbers) parcelled these styles out among the men in the order in which it seems possible that they may have belonged. With this explanation, and with the caution that two men have at times worked on a single piece, I will summarize the characteristics of these four styles of work.

I. (Henry Nissle?)   This work is distinguishable by the introduction of a red apple with yellow mottlings. Also by the parallel and equal-lengthed lines with which he formed the necks of birds with raised heads. He executed the steeple, dove, lovebirds, floral, and woman-in-boat designs, and floral and dove designs with inscriptions.

II. (Joseph Welch?)　Here was a most careful and conscientious workman. His designs are always well balanced. His black lines are finely pencilled. In drawing birds or animals he drew the eyes with a circular line above and a flattish elliptical one beneath. His designs, while they pull together into an effective whole, are usually composed of several separate designs, each a balanced whole in itself. He executed floral bouquets, dog, and dove designs, and floral decorations for the smaller pieces.

III. (Sebastian Witmer?)　A crude and rapid worker. The black lines vary greatly in thickness and are quickly and carelessly applied. He executed steeple, floral, fantastic bird, and cow designs. He used the heart and upright branch in his decorations. And he copied European floral designs on the Stiegel drug bottles.

IV. (Martin Yetters?)　Also a rapid worker, but daintier in his execution and more pedantic in his designs. In his floral work each leaf, bud and flower is painted separately. His black pencilling is lavishly used in the form of hair lines. He executed floral designs with love birds and flower wreaths with red tassels.

The following articles in white flint glass are known to have been decorated in enamel colors at the Stiegel factory:

Tumblers, plain and fluted:
 Half gill
 Gill
 Half pint
 Pint
Mugs:
 Gill
 Half pint
 Pint
 Quart
Cordial bottles with glass stoppers
Drug bottles, pewter capped with screw tops

And in blue flint glass

> Drug bottles, pewter capped with screw tops

"Carrofts enameled" were advertised for sale by Stiegel in 1773. The designs used were the following:

> Steeple
> Floral wreath with red tassels
> Conventionalized floral designs
> Dove
> Parrot
> Rooster
> Fantastic bird
> Dog
> Cow
> Woman in boat
> Phantom ship
> Floral designs with inscriptions
> Dove designs with inscriptions

In the Hunter Collection, the steeple, the dove and the fantastic bird designs are complete on the beer mugs, and examples of all the other designs listed are shown except the cow. The only specimen of this design I have ever seen is in the Pennyslvania Museum, at Philadelphia, the gift of John Story Jenks, and was painted by Sebastian Witmer. It is of course quite possible that other designs may turn up. Special designs with inscriptions were probably executed to order; one, in the Hunter Collection, a drug bottle with dove design by Henry Nissle, bears the following inscription in German, "Oh God! take this cross from me and that troublesome wife to you."

It appears that gilding, a decorative method much used in the Bristol factories, was also, though probably very sparingly and for a very short time, tried at the Stiegel factory. I have seen but the single specimen here described, which is a blue flint creamer, 5 inches in height (see Figure 158), with the inscription, "Make Welcome with the Cream," boldly pencilled on it in slightly decorative lettering by an unmistakably Teutonic hand. The gilding is remarkably well preserved, although a bit dark in places. The work is markedly different from the light lines, the floral ornaments, and the worn and tarnished gold, of the Bristol factories. In the "Cabinet Cyclopedia," published in 1832, the Rev. Dionysius Lardner says of the gilding methods employed in this sort of work, "Pure gold leaf was ground with honey or gum and was then known as 'shell gold.' It is made to adhere to the surface of the glass by the incipient fusion of the flux employed."

NOTES

1. This, I believe, is one of those errors which, by escaping capture during proof reading, bedevil author and publisher alike. For "straw" should read "stuck." It was the "stuck shank" Mr. Hunter was describing so graphically.

2. The usual method of obtaining the twisted ribbing was by twisting a vertically ribbed *molded* gather of glass as it was drawn out. The desired length for the stem was then cut from the "rib-twisted" rod and attached to the bottom of the wine-glass bowl.

3. It is extremely doubtful if the method of forming the so-called Venetian diamond pattern by pinching vertical ribs together was actually practiced at Manheim. By Stiegel's day, even in England where the resulting design was called "nipt diamond waies," the method had been largely superseded by molding. As a matter of fact the Venetian glass-blowers used molds for some of their diamond patterned glass. The presumably Stiegel diamond and more elaborated patterns like the diamond-daisy (daisy-in-square) were molded, and the molds unquestionably were metal part-size piece molds.

4. It is believed today that the method of engraving by diamond point was never used at Manheim. That engraving which Mr. Hunter mistook for diamond point was undoubtedly executed by a smaller size of copper wheel than used for the deeper parts of the design.

HMcK

CHAPTER VII

THE colorings of the bottle glass made at both the Elizabeth Furnace and the Manheim plants have already been described. Also the green glass made at these glass houses, and from which many articles of common, kitchen, household and professional use were made. Bottles were made in the following sizes: 4 gallon, gallon, half gallon, quart, pint, half pint and pocket bottles. Of the plain run of bottles made I have included none in the Hunter Collection except four specimens obtained from Mr. Long, of Manheim, who informed me that they had been in his family from the time of their purchase at the Stiegel store. They correspond, both as to glass and as to the character of their banded and collared lips, with the glass and the bottle tops found by me in excavating.

FIGURE 1. Coarse green glass full of bubbles. 11¾ inches high. Banded
lip.
2. Olive glass, showing bubbles. 14 inches high. Banded lip.
3. Nile-green glass showing bubbles. 10½ inches high. Sheared
lip with collar added.
4. Dark red-brown glass. 11 inches high. Sheared lip with
collar added.

Quart bottles were also made by Stiegel from a good quality of green glass, the bodies of which were pattern-molded with the medium or the narrow ribbing and subsequently twisted in the blowing. Most of these had circular bodies, but the bodies of some specimens are somewhat flattened on two sides.

FIGURE 5. Bottle. Light green glass. Twisted ribbed decoration. $7\frac{3}{4}$ inches high. Banded lip.

6. Bottle. Flattened sides. Light green glass. Twisted ribbed decoration. Sheared lip with collar added. $8\frac{3}{4}$ inches high.

Among the other articles for household and professional use made in green glass and open pot white glass of the same type, at the Stiegel factory, the following specimens are illustrated:

FIGURE 7. Jug stand. Green glass full of bubbles. $1\frac{5}{8}$ inches high, $5\frac{3}{8}$ inches in diameter.

8. Jug stand. Green glass full of bubbles. 2 inches high, $5\frac{1}{4}$ inches in diameter.

These are the pieces referred to in the description of my Elizabeth Furnace excavations.

FIGURE 9. Mustard Jar. Light green glass with turned-over lip. $2\frac{1}{2}$ inches high. These vessels are advertised in February, 1773, as made in flint and common glass.

10. Mug. Light green glass. Has crudely corrugated handle and a slightly contracted lip. $6\frac{7}{8}$ inches high.

11. Mug. Light green glass. Ribbed decoration. $4\frac{5}{8}$ inches high.

12. Chemical vessel with spout at side. Light green glass. Ribbed decoration slightly twisted. $7\frac{3}{4}$ inches high.

13. Bowl. Light green glass. Turned-over lip. Wide ribbed decoration extending to $\frac{3}{4}$ the height of piece. 3 inches high.

14. Molasses jug. Light green glass. Has flaring base, a tall body showing twisted ribbing, a slightly contracted neck and a spout. Plain handle. 7 inches high.

15. Sweetmeat jar. White open pot glass showing bubbles. Lip rimmed to accommodate cover. 7 inches high.

16. Pocket bottle. White open pot glass. Faintly marked with wide ribbing. $6\frac{1}{2}$ inches high.

The following articles in undecorated white flint glass[1] are illustrated:

FIGURE 17. Measure glass. White flint glass. Straight sides. Heavy bottom. These glasses, made to hold from two ounces to a quart each, were in great demand in the colonies. 5¾ inches high.

FIGURE 18. Flip glass with flaring foot. White flint glass. These glasses were made in sizes from 2 inches to 5⅜ inches high.

19. Carafe. White flint glass. 7¾ inches high.

20. Funnel. White flint glass. 4 inches high.

21. Toy. Child's decanter. White flint glass, with stopper. 3 inches high.

22. Toy. Figure of a cow on a hollow stem. White flint glass. 8½ inches high.

23. Lamp reflector. Globular, with short neck for cork. White flint glass. These reflectors were intended to be filled with water and hung before a lamp. The specimen here illustrated had come down in the family of Mr. Long. 6½ inches in diameter.

Blue flint glass was first advertised for sale by the Stiegel factory in March, 1770. Both the quality of this glass and its color are worthy of note. The glass itself is always of the finest, perfectly "cooked," with an exquisitely soft and brilliant surface. The blue is very rich and remarkably full of life. It varies in depth according to the thickness of the glass, but is always of the same tone in the pieces that I have seen. One fragment, excavated by me at Manheim and illustrated in color in Plate VIII, is of a decidedly paler cast, but is not flint glass. But I have never seen a finished piece made of this glass. The Stiegel pieces in blue flint invariably show, when the light is allowed to fall through their thicker portions, traces of purple color — an effect which, I am told by an expert in the present-day formulæ of the glassmaking business, Mr. Francis Storm, of New York City, is due to the presence of antimony. At the time when the Stiegel factory was just entering on its most successful period, — 1771, — there were, according to Evans, in his "History of Bristol," something like fifteen factories making glass in the neighborhood of Bristol, in England, and blue pieces were one of their specialties. But, where these Bristol pieces show the purple tints due to antimony, the color is very dull and dead compared to the Stiegel product. Indeed, the two, once seen and compared, are instantly distinguishable. The other Bristol blue glass has no antimony in its make-up and is, in addition, always full of small air bubbles and of specks of extraneous matter. The following Stiegel pieces in plain surfaced blue flint glass are illustrated:

FIGURE 24. Egg Glass. Blue flint. $3\frac{1}{2}$ inches high.

25. Mug. Blue flint glass. Straight sides and plain handle. 5 inches high.

26. Creamer. Blue flint. $4\frac{3}{4}$ inches high.

27. Sugar Bowl. Blue flint. Solid foot. Bell-shaped body. Low cover with knob handle showing faint traces of the wide ribbing. 6 inches high.

28. Sugar Bowl. Blue flint. Flat foot. Bell-shaped body, turban-shaped cover with spear-head handle. $6\frac{1}{2}$ inches high.

29. Sugar Bowl. Blue flint. Low foot. Bell-shaped body topped by a flaring, upturned rim. High conical cover with fancy knob handle. $6\frac{1}{2}$ inches high.

30. Vase. Blue flint. Wide, solid feet. Pear-shaped body. Wide neck with flaring lip welted at the edge. 8 inches high.

Plain pieces were also made in various colored flint glasses. Flasks, or pocket bottles, in very pale amber and in amethyst, are shown in the Hunter Collection. One of these is illustrated:

FIGURE 31. Pocket bottle. Amethyst flint glass. Showing striations of color. $7\frac{1}{4}$ inches high.

No single article of manufacture at Manheim showed a greater variety, in both form and quality, than the drinking glass. The straight-sided measures, made for convenient kitchen use and serving at once the purposes of a drinking glass and of a quart, pint, or half-pint measure, have already been referred to. The glasses commonly called flips, from the popular beverage that was often mixed in them, were also made in the greatest variety. We will have occasion to describe many of them among the engraved and molded pieces. The commoner kind of wine glasses made at the factory are well represented by the following selection, chosen from the Hunter Collection, and listed according to the names given to them by Albert Hartshorne in his "Old English Glasses" (1897). These are all in white flint glass.

FIGURE 32. Plain wine glass with flat foot. 4 inches high.
  33. Plain wine glass with welted foot. 4 inches high.
  34. Plain wine glass with welted foot and bubble stem. 8 inches high.
  35. Plain wine glass with flat foot and partly straightened sides. 4¼ inches high.
  36. Plain wine glass with welted foot and bell-shaped lip. 6 inches high.
  37. Straight-sided wine glass with welted foot and baluster stem. 4 inches high.
  38. Plain champagne glass with welted foot and partly straightened sides. 4 inches high.
  39. Plain sillabub glass with welted foot and straight sides. 4 inches high.
  40. "Measure." Flat foot with graceful, flaring body. 3¾ inches high.

The glasses of the type shown in No. 40 are called "measures" by Hartshorne, but they appear to have been made and used for drinking glasses. There is a wide difference of opinion as to the exact use to which the custom of the time put them. They are often called "whiskey glasses" in Pennsylvania, and Stiegel made them in various ribbed designs, as well as plain, and with a single knob of glass intervening between the bowl and the foot. They would seem to have gotten the name of measures from their close resemblance in shape to the modern graduate.

The more ornate wine glasses made by Stiegel are indicated by the following examples, chosen from the Hunter Collection:

FIGURE 41. Wine glass with flat foot, the bowl decorated with the narrow ribbing. $3\frac{3}{4}$ inches high.

42. Wine glass with welted foot, the bowl decorated with the narrow ribbing, twisted. 4 inches high.

43. Wine glass with flat foot and partly straightened sides, the stem and bowl (the latter for half its height) decorated with the narrow ribbing slightly whorled. $3\frac{3}{4}$ inches high.

44. Cordial glass with flat foot, baluster stem and bowl decorated with sunken panels. $3\frac{1}{4}$ inches high.

45. Straight-sided glass with plain foot, tall spiral "cotton" stem and the bowl ornamented with the engraved vine border (pattern No. VI). $6\frac{1}{2}$ inches high.

46. Champagne glass with flat foot, spiral "cotton" stem and plain bowl with partly straightened sides. 5 inches high.

47. High Champagne glass with plain foot, the short stem and the conical bowl ornamented with the medium ribbed pattern, sharply twisted. $4\frac{3}{4}$ inches high.

48. High Champagne glass with welted foot, short stem and the conical bowl decorated for $\frac{4}{5}$ of its height with the small ribbed pattern, sharply twisted. $5\frac{3}{4}$ inches high.

Although the Stiegel factory never made any pieces with fused bi-color designs in waved, palmated and other patterns, such as were made by the Venetians, and, afterward, at the Nailsea English factories and at Wistarberg, they did turn out quite a variety of pieces in which rims of one color were added to bodies of another, a few in which the interiors of vessels were flashed with opaque white, and a few upon the surface of which decorative lines in opaque white glass were imposed during the blowing.

The following specimens are typical of this class of the Stiegel workmanship:

FIGURE 49. Measure glass. White flint. The foot has been dipped in amethyst glass before being finished. $3\frac{3}{4}$ inches high.

50. Measure glass. White flint with amethyst flint rim added. 4 inches high.

FIGURE 51. Masonic shaped glass. White flint with blue flint rim added. Extra large bubble in stem. $4\frac{1}{4}$ inches high.

52. Masonic shaped glass. White flint with blue flint rim added. A group of small bubbles or "tears" in stem. Initials J. L. F. engraved on bowl. $4\frac{1}{4}$ inches high.

53. Creamer. White flint glass with blue flint rim added. 4 inches high.

54. Communion flagon in white transparent flint glass, the interior flashed with opaque white. $3\frac{7}{8}$ inches high.

55. Communion chalice in white transparent flint glass, the interior of the bowl flashed with opaque white. $5\frac{3}{8}$ inches high.

"Flashing" of this kind is done by making a very small gathering of the opaque white glass upon the blowpipe, allowing it to cool somewhat, and then gathering over this small bulb the usual amount of ordinary flint glass required to make the contemplated piece. When the double gathering is then blown, the opaque white glass forms a thin layer on the inside of the resulting bubble of glass.

FIGURE 56. Creamer. White flint glass ornamented with the broad ribbing and with a blue flint rim added. The handle is plain. $3\frac{1}{2}$ inches high.

57. Salt cellar. White flint glass with the body showing medium diamond pattern and a blue flint rim added. 3 inches high.

58. Creamer. Blue flint glass with opaque white rim added. $5\frac{1}{2}$ inches high.

59. Mug with cover. Blue flint glass. Slightly flared base. Straight sides. Plain handle. An opaque white rim has been added and an opaque white button has been added to the knob handle of the blue flint-glass cover. A beautiful piece of fine quality. $6\frac{1}{4}$ inches high.

60. Important Tall Vase. Blue flint glass. Flaring bell-shaped base and short spool stem, supporting a graceful body surmounted by a conical cover. An opaque white rim has been added to the base and an opaque white lip to the mouth of the vase. 13 inches high. An altogether remarkable specimen.

The ribbed and diamonded patterns, the obtaining of which we have already considered, were among the favorite decorations employed by the Bristol glassmakers, and it was for the purpose of competing with the Bristol wares, and as part of his campaign for supplying the colonies with home-made glass resembling that to which they were accustomed and partial, that Stiegel went so extensively into the making of the many pieces thus treated.

Practically all the good glass used in the colonies at this time was imported, and the weekly papers of Philadelphia, New York and Boston contain numerous advertisements of fresh consignments offered for sale at wholesale and retail, in box lots, by the dozen and by the piece. Of this body of glass, the pattern-molded Bristol wares probably formed a small but much sought after part; and Bristol glass, both of this character and of other kinds, is frequently found, handed down alongside of early American pieces, in the regions where the latter most abound. And in distinguishing the pieces of Stiegel origin from those of the Bristol manufacture (as in almost all similar distinguishments between articles of similar but different character), no amount of mere verbal instruction will take the place of the knowledge that comes with the familiar handling of many examples of both kinds. The following hints, therefore, are given as a guide to students, and not as constituting a royal road to connoisseurship.

We have already differentiated between the blue flint glass made by Stiegel and that made at the different Bristol factories. In the matter of the ribbed and diamonded pieces, two sharply distinguishable classes of these wares were made at Bristol; the one of noticeably heavy and thick character, the other of an exceptional, and at times almost paperlike, delicacy. The Stiegel pieces lie midway between the two. Again the bases or feet, of such pieces as creamers, bowls and wine glasses, tend, in Bristol specimens, to rest only on the rims with the undersides of them rising conically or dome-wise toward the stems. The Stiegel bases and wine-glass feet are much flatter. Moreover, on ribbed specimens, the Bristol ribbing generally runs all the way to the pontil mark, which is not the case with Stiegel specimens. And the Bristol pontil marks are particularly small, while the Stiegel pontils are uniformly rather large. Finally, the Stiegel glass itself is noticeably free from the small imperfections that fill the Bristol metal, and shows a surface softened and sheened by a larger admixture of lead. The following ribbed, fluted and diamonded pieces show the variety and the scope of the work done in these modes at the Stiegel works. It is well to note that, where Stiegel pieces of over $5\frac{3}{4}$ inches in height have handles, these are always hollow. See Figures 62 and 77.

FIGURE 61. Beer Mug. Amber flint glass. Showing wide ribbing. 6 inches high. See Plate I.

62. Pitcher. White flint glass. Showing wide ribbing. $6\frac{1}{2}$ inches high.

63. Salt Cellar. Blue flint glass. Showing wide ribbing. $3\frac{1}{4}$ inches high.

64. Salt Cellar. Blue flint glass. Showing wide ribbing. $2\frac{3}{4}$ inches high.

65. Salt Cellar. Amethyst flint glass. Showing wide ribbing. $2\frac{3}{8}$ inches high.

66. Child's flip glass. White flint. Showing medium ribbing. 2 inches high.

67. Flip glass. White flint. With lip welted. Showing medium ribbing. $5\frac{3}{4}$ inches high.

68. Salt Cellar. Blue flint glass. Showing medium ribbing. $2\frac{1}{2}$ inches high.

69. Salt Cellar. Blue flint glass. Showing medium ribbing. $2\frac{3}{4}$ inches high.

70. Creamer. Blue flint glass. Showing faint medium ribbing. 5 inches high.

FIGURE 71. Creamer. Blue flint glass. Showing medium ribbing. $4\frac{1}{4}$ inches high.

72. Creamer. Blue flint glass. Showing medium ribbing. $3\frac{3}{4}$ inches high.

73. Creamer. Blue flint glass. Showing medium ribbing. $5\frac{1}{4}$ inches high.

74. Creamer. White flint glass. Showing medium ribbing. 5 inches high.

75. Funnel. White flint glass. Showing narrow ribbing. $8\frac{3}{4}$ inches high.

76. Creamer. White flint glass. Showing narrow ribbing sharply twisted. 5 inches high.

77. Vinegar Cruet. White flint glass. Showing narrow ribbing twisted. 8 inches high.

The following pieces will show the fluted and sunken panel designs as applied to otherwise undecorated pieces. Examples of these molded decorations are also shown among the engraved and enameled specimens.

FIGURE 78. Flip glass. White flint. Showing narrow fluting. $5\frac{5}{8}$ inches high.

79. Measure glass. White flint. Showing wide fluting. $5\frac{3}{4}$ inches high.

80. Bowl-shaped vessel with spouts. White flint glass. Showing narrow sunken paneling on lower half of sides. 4 inches high.

81. Plate. White flint glass. Showing similar treatment. $1\frac{1}{4}$ inches high.

82. Flip glass. White flint. Showing sunken paneling on body. $5\frac{1}{4}$ inches high.

83. Rummer or Grog glass. White flint. Showing sunken panels on bowl. 5 inches high.

84. Rummer or Grog glass with cover. White flint. Showing sunken panels on bowl. Height, with cover, 8 inches.

85. Important Vase. Blue flint glass with downward flaring lip and sunken panels on side. $8\frac{1}{2}$ inches high. See frontispiece.

The last-named piece is the only one I have ever seen with the sunken panel decoration in anything except white flint glass. The design was used mostly for flips and rummers. The number of panels on these run from 12 to 30, and they are occasionally so arranged that they vary alternately in height. Usually, however, their tops are on a line. This sunken panel form of decoration is found also on many of the Dutch flip glasses of 18th-century make. But not only do the flip glasses themselves fall below the Stiegel grade in technical excellence, and differ from them considerably in the appearance of their bottoms, but the paneling is very crude. The tops of the individual panels lack the clean-cut rounded outline of the Stiegel ones, and the height of the panels is unequal with regard to one another.

The following specimens show the various aspects of the Venetian Diamond[2] decoration as used by the Stiegel factory:

FIGURE 86. Salt Cellar. Blue flint glass. Showing large diamond. 2¾ inches high.

87. Salt Cellar. Blue flint glass. Showing large diamond. 3 inches high. Mark the scalloped foot sometimes used on white and blue flint salts and blue flint creamers.

88. Creamer. Blue flint glass. Showing large diamond. 3¼ inches high.

89. Bowl. Amethyst flint glass. Showing large diamond. 3¼ inches high.

90. Sugar Bowl with Cover. Blue flint glass. Showing large diamond. 7½ inches high.

91. Toilet Bottle. Amethyst flint glass. Showing large diamond imperfectly pinched. 5¾ inches high. See Plate II.

92. Pocket Bottle. White flint glass. Showing medium diamond. 7 inches high.

93. "Measure." White flint glass. Showing medium diamond. 3¾ inches high.

94. Salt Shaker. White flint glass. Showing medium diamond. 4½ inches high.

95. Creamer. Blue flint glass. Showing medium diamond. 4½ inches high.

FIGURE 96. Sugar Bowl with Cover. Blue flint glass. Showing medium diamond. $7\frac{1}{4}$ inches high.

97. Double Flask. White flint glass. Showing medium diamond. The sides are ornamented with ribbon work done in molten glass. $8\frac{1}{2}$ inches high.

98. Salt Cellar. Blue-green flint glass. Showing medium diamond. 3 inches high. See Plate III.

99. High Bowl. Deep Amethyst flint glass. Showing medium diamond. $3\frac{3}{4}$ inches high. See Plate IV.

100. Salt Cellar. White flint glass. Showing medium diamond. $3\frac{1}{4}$ inches high.

101. Creamer. Blue flint glass. Showing small diamond. $4\frac{1}{4}$ inches high.

102. Creamer. Blue flint glass. Showing small diamond. $3\frac{3}{4}$ inches high.

103. Table Jug with Stopper. White flint glass. Showing small diamond. $4\frac{1}{2}$ inches high.

104. Foot to above Jug with stopper.

105. Toilet Bottle. Amethyst flint glass. Showing small diamond on part of bowl. $5\frac{3}{4}$ inches high.

106. Creamer. Emerald green flint glass. Showing small diamond. $3\frac{3}{4}$ inches high. See Plate III.

107. Plate. White flint glass. Showing small diamond. $4\frac{3}{8}$ inches in diameter. This piece came from the family of Mr. Nathaniel W. Long of Manheim.

The following specimens show the expanded " daisy in square" design, already discussed in the chapter on Materials and Methods, as well as the contact mold designs, there described as of possible Stiegel derivation:

FIGURE 108. Toilet Bottle. Amethyst flint glass. Showing the beautiful daisy and square design. 5 inches high.

109. Flip Glass. White flint. $7\frac{1}{2}$ inches high.

110. Sugar Bowl with Cover. White flint glass. $6\frac{1}{4}$ inches high.

111. Decanter. White flint glass. Showing ribbed design obtained by blowing in contact mold. $5\frac{1}{2}$ inches high.

112. Decanter. Blue flint glass. Showing ribbed design obtained by blowing in contact mold. 6 inches high.

113. Foot of the same piece, showing ribbed bottom.

Reference has already been made to the resemblances which some of the Dutch Flip Glasses bear to those made by Stiegel. This resemblance extends also to the fact that both were at times ornamented by engraved designs. Of course, in these cases, the differences in the glass and the superior workmanship of the Stiegel pieces still holds good as a means of identification. But the engraving is also different. It is neither so deep, nor, as is often the case in the foreign glasses, are the "ground glass" surfaces of the engraved portions ever polished afterwards on the Stiegel pieces. It is well to note that while Stiegel never placed engraved designs on any but flint-glass pieces, specimens are occasionally encountered in which, when observed in a good light and at the proper angle, a greenish tinge is discernible, due to an insufficient admixture of manganese. The following specimens show the range of this sort of decoration done at the Stiegel factory:

FIGURE 114. Flip Glass. White flint. Showing ribbed design and a Type I engraved border. $4\frac{1}{2}$ inches high.

115. Flip Glass. White flint. Showing sunken panels and a Type I engraved border. 6 inches high.

116. Flip Glass. White flint. Showing a Type I engraved border. $5\frac{3}{4}$ inches high.

117. Flip Glass. White flint. Showing sunken panels and a Type I engraved border. $5\frac{3}{4}$ inches high.

118. Jelly Glass with Handles. White flint. Sunken panels on under part of bowl and a Type I engraved border with wavy line above. $1\frac{7}{8}$ inches high.

119. Jelly Glass with Handles. The mate to the preceding, yet with differently spaced Type I border and without wavy line above. Diameter $3\frac{1}{4}$ inches.

This pair of Jelly Glasses came from an old house in the Island of St. Martin, in the West Indies. An old Stiegel stove was in the same house. Both facts are interesting in view of the trade we have seen that Stiegel carried on with the West Indian sugar planters.

FIGURE 120. Flip Glass. White flint. Showing sunken panels and a Type II engraved border. $2\frac{1}{8}$ inches high.

121. Miniature Flip Glass. White flint. Showing a Type III decoration engraved on bowl. $6\frac{1}{4}$ inches high.

122. Mug. White flint. Showing a Type III decoration. $6\frac{1}{2}$ inches high.

123. Cordial Bottle. White flint. Showing Type III of engraved decoration. $5\frac{1}{2}$ inches high.

124. Flip Glass with Cover. White Flint. Showing Type III of engraved decoration. $11\frac{1}{2}$ inches high.

125. Flip Glass. White flint. Showing sunken panels and a Type III engraved border. 6 inches high.

126. Flip Glass. White flint. Showing sunken panels and a Type IV engraved border. $5\frac{3}{4}$ inches high.

127. Flip Glass. White flint. Showing fluted treatment and a Type V engraved decoration. $5\frac{1}{4}$ inches high.

128. Flip Glass. White flint. Showing ribbed decoration and a Type VI engraved border. 5 inches high.

129. Flip Glass. White flint. Showing sunken panels of alternating length and a Type VII engraved border. $6\frac{1}{4}$ inches high.

130. Flip Glass with Cover. White flint. Showing a Type VIII engraved decoration. 10 inches high.

131. Tea Caddy with Glass Screw Top. White flint. Showing Type VIII engraved decoration. 7 inches high.

This type of caddy was made for the Boston market. One of those in the Hunter Collection came from Roxbury, and was purchased from Miss Caroline Everett, a niece of Edward Everett. The caddy had been in the family since 1773, and contains tea, said to be a relic of the Boston Tea Party.

FIGURE 132. Flip Glass. White flint. Showing a Type IX engraved border. $6\frac{1}{4}$ inches high.

133. Mug. White flint. Showing a Type X engraved decoration. $4\frac{3}{4}$ inches high.

FIGURE 134. Flip Glass. White flint. Showing a Type X engraved
decoration. 4¼ inches high.

135. Flip Glass with Cover. White flint. Showing a Type XI
engraved decoration. 11¼ inches high.

Miss Annie L. Boyer, of Harrisburg, Pennsylvania, who is a
great granddaughter of Stiegel's, informs me that her mother
told her this conventionalized rose design was first made for
the marriage of her grandmother, Elizabeth Stiegel, to William
Old.

FIGURE 136. Wine Glass. White flint. Baluster stem. Straight sides
showing a Type XII engraved border. 4 inches high.

137. Wine Glass. White flint. Showing a Type XIII engraved
border. 4 inches high.

138. Wine Glass. White flint. Showing a Type XIV engraved
border. 4 inches high.

There only remains for us to consider the Stiegel pieces
decorated with vitrifiable enamels, and to glance at the points
in which these pieces differ from similar pieces made abroad.
As we have already noted, the Stiegel workmen used six
opaque enamel colors, a white, a yellow that ranged from light
to chrome, a nile green that I have never seen used on any
other glass thus decorated, a cobalt blue used in a light and a
dark shade, a black, and, finally, a brick red that will remind
students of Japanese prints of the red lead color so successfully
employed by Horonobu and Koriusai in 1768 in representing
undecorated woodwork. These colors, as seen on the Stiegel
pieces, show a true vitrified surface, except in some instances
where the darker shades of red have not fused perfectly and lack
the proper glossy and brilliant finish. They have remarkable
purity of tone; were applied with considerable thickness; and, as
a consequence, the edges of the designs are cleaner cut than in
any similar pieces.

Switzerland was the home of a distinguished school of this

kind of painting on glass in enamel colors. In Swiss specimens the enameling is very carefully done, although on the whole the results lack the glossy surface of the Stiegel product. A pale buff color is used on these pieces for the faces of the figures introduced, and the designs are mostly Rabbit, Boy and Girl, and Milk Maid with a Yolk. The Swiss blue is very light and the Swiss red is dull and muddy. The Swiss green is entirely unlike the peculiar Nile green used on Stiegel pieces.

On French pieces of the kind, the designs are usually heraldic, or else consist of mythological and symbolic figures or portrait heads. The French colors are not remarkable for brilliancy, and one of them is the same pale buff noted in the Swiss faces.

The German pieces are more nearly akin to those of the Stiegel factory in design. But, taken collectively, the German enamel is bad in every way. The colors are muddy and dull. The yellow is a mustard yellow. The opaque blue is crude and unpleasant. A dull maroon is their usual substitute for red. And browns and drabs of undecided tints are frequently met with. Moreover the German technique ran commonly to the employment of a black outline. And, finally, the German enamels show frequent pin holes; a defect never found on the Stiegel pieces.

Black and white reproductions of these enameled pieces are far from satisfactory or illuminating. And readers of this book are referred to the three color plates in which both the fronts and sides of three representative beer mugs are shown as well as two typical enameled bottles. These illustrate the following designs:

FIGURE 139. Mug. White flint glass. Parrot design. $5\frac{5}{8}$ inches high. See Plate VI.

140. Mug. White flint glass. Rooster design. 5 inches high. See Plate V.

FIGURE 141. Mug. White flint glass. Steeple design. 5⅜ inches high. See Plate V.

142. Cordial Bottle with glass Stopper. White flint glass. Dove design. 4¾ inches high. See Plate VII.

143. Drug Bottle, Pewter Capped. Blue flint glass. Conventionalized floral design. 6 inches high. See Plate VII.

In addition to these Plates, from which an excellent idea of the colors used on Stiegel pieces may be had, the following reproductions in monochrome are given in order to illustrate the type of designs used and the workmanship of the four decorators whose technical characteristics have been summarized:

FIGURE 144. Mug. White flint glass. Steeple design. Henry Nissle. 7 inches high.

145. Tumbler. White flint. Fluted. Steeple design. Henry Nissle. 3¾ inches high.

146. Drug Bottle. Pewter Capped. White flint glass. Conventional floral design. Henry Nissle. 5¾ inches high.

147. Tumbler. White flint. Fantastic bird design. Henry Nissle. 4 inches high.

148. Mug. White flint glass. Woman in Boat design. Henry Nissle. 5⅛ inches high.

149. Mug. White flint glass. Dove design. Joseph Welch. 3½ inches high.

150. Drug Bottle, Pewter Capped. White flint glass. Dog design. Joseph Welch. 5¾ inches high.

The pieces decorated by "Joseph Welch" are extremely rare. The "Martin Yetters" pieces are also scarce.

FIGURE 151. Mug. White flint glass. Dove design. Martin Yetters. 6½ inches high.

152. Mug. White flint glass. Steeple design. Sebastian Witmer. 7 inches high.

153. Drug Bottle, Pewter Capped. White flint glass. Conventionalized floral design. Sebastian Witmer. 5¾ inches high.

FIGURE 154. Drug Bottle, Pewter Capped. White flint glass. Conventionalized floral design. Sebastian Witmer. $7\frac{1}{4}$ inches high.

155. Tumbler. White flint. Fantastic bird design. Sebastian Witmer. $3\frac{1}{4}$ inches high.

156. Tumbler. White flint. Fantastic bird design. Sebastian Witmer. 4 inches high.

157. Mug. White flint glass. Phantom ship design. Sebastian Witmer. $6\frac{3}{4}$ inches high.

Mention has been made of a piece of Stiegel glass bearing an inscription in gilding. The piece is as follows:

FIGURE 158. Creamer. Blue flint glass. Showing gilt inscription "Make Welcome with the Cream." 5 inches high.

159. Excavated "Cotton Stem" from Manheim Factory site.

It may interest collectors, in view of the rapidly rising prices which these pieces are commanding as their intrinsic beauty is more generally appreciated and their relation to early American handicraft realized, to know what Stiegel marketed them for at the time of their manufacture. From various entries in the Manheim account books I have compiled the following list of prices asked for the pieces named. The books do not state whether English money or Pennsylvania currency is intended:

```
Window Glass 8x10 panes . . . . . . . . . . .  8d. each
4 Gallon Bottles. . . . . . . . . . . . . . . . . . .  3s.   "
Gallon Bottles, special. . . . . . . . . . . . . .  3s.   "
    "        "      . . . . . . . . . . . . . . . . . . .24s. per doz.
Half Gallon Bottles. . . . . . . . . . . . . . . .  1s. 6d. each
Quart Bottles. . . . . . . . . . . . . . . . . . . . .  6s. per dozen
Pint Bottles. . . . . . . . . . . . . . . . . . . . . .  4s. 6d. per dozen
Pocket Bottles. . . . . . . . . . . . . . . . . . . .  6d. each or 5s. 6d. per doz.
Quart Mugs. . . . . . . . . . . . . . . . . . . . . .  1s. 6d. each
Bowls. . . . . . . . . . . . . . . . . . . . . . . . . . .  2s. each
Tumblers. . . . . . . . . . . . . . . . . . . . . . . .  9d. to 1s. each
Pint Tumblers. . . . . . . . . . . . . . . . . . . .10d. each
Half pint Tumblers. . . . . . . . . . . . . . . .  5d. each
Half gill Tumblers. . . . . . . . . . . . . . . . .  3d.   "
Best Wines. . . . . . . . . . . . . . . . . . . . . . .  1s. 8d. each
Flint Sugar Box and Cover. . . . . . . . . . .  4s. 6d.   "
Creamers. . . . . . . . . . . . . . . . . . . . . . . .  8d. to 1s. 3d. each
Pair Candle Sticks. . . . . . . . . . . . . . . . .  1s. 6d.
Ink Bottles. . . . . . . . . . . . . . . . . . . . . . .  3d. each
```

It was with the best of right that Stiegel called his Manheim plant the "American Flint Glass Factory." In no one of the glass-house sites that I have ever examined has the proportion of flint fragments found exceeded 10% of the total, except at Wistarberg, and even here it did not exceed 20% if it could be rated that high. But at Manheim the flint fragments found were about 30% of the whole.[3]

The specimens already described and illustrated give an excellent idea of the range and the character of the Stiegel output.

But for purposes of reference and check, and in order to place the facts definitely and succinctly before collectors and students, the following list has been compiled and is here published. It contains exact information as to the green, and various colors of flint glass, that I know Stiegel to have made, and a complete list of all the articles in each color and of each design that I have seen, or that I know from Stiegel's advertisements and account books that he made.

GREEN GLASS PLAIN

1. Bottle, banded lip
2. Bottle, sheared lip with collar
3. Chemical Vessel with spout at side
4. Jar
5. Jug stand
6. Mustard Jar
7. Mug
8. Pocket bottle
9. Tumbler

GREEN GLASS RIBBED

10. Bottle, banded lip
11. Bottle, sheared lip with collar
12. Bowl
13. Creamer
14. Ink Bottle
15. Molasses Jug
16. Pocket bottle
17. Salt cellar

The colors made in flint glass are:

Transparent white
Light amber
Amber
Emerald-green

Blue-green
Blue
Purple
Dark Amethyst

The pieces, transparent white, or colored; plain, or variously ornamented, are as follows:

WHITE TRANSPARENT, PLAIN

18. Bowl
19. Candle stick
20. Carafe
21. Champagne glass
22. Champagne glass with welted foot
23. Cordial glass
24. Cover for tumbler
25. Creamer
26. Creamer with scalloped foot
27. Creamer with 3 feet
28. Double flask
29. Electer glasses
30. Funnel
31. Flip
32. Jars
33. Jugs
34. Lamp reflector
35. Masonic-shaped glass
36. Measure with flaring lip
37. Measure tumbler
38. Mug
39. Mustard pot
40. Pocket bottle or flask
41. Pulse glasses
42. Rummer
43. Salt cellar
44. Salt cellar with scalloped foot
45. Salt cellar with 3 feet
46. Sillabub glasses with welted foot
47. Smelling bottle
48. Toys
49. Tubes for levels, barometers and thermometers
50. Vase
51. Wine glass
52. Wine glass with partly straight sides
53. Wine glass with welted foot
54. Wine glass with welted foot and bell-shaped lip
55. Wine glass with bubble stem

WHITE TRANSPARENT FLINT, RIBBED

56. Candle stick
57. Champagne glass
58. Champagne glass with welted foot
59. Creamer
60. Creamer with scalloped foot
61. Creamer with 3 feet
62. Cruet
63. Decanter, ½ Pint
64. Decanter stopper, 1 Pint
65. Flips
66. Funnel
67. Jug
68. Measure with flaring lip
69. Measure tumbler
70. Pocket bottle or flask
71. Pitcher
72. Salt cellar
73. Salt cellar with scalloped foot
74. Salt cellar with 3 feet
75. Tall salt cellars
76. Sillabub glass
77. Smelling bottle
78. Tumbler
79. Wine glass
80. Wine glass with partly straight sides
81. Wine glass with welted foot

WHITE TRANSPARENT FLINT, FLUTED

82. Flip
83. Plate
84. Tumbler

WHITE TRANSPARENT FLINT, SUNKEN PANEL

85. Bowl-shaped vessel with spouts
86. Cordial glass
87. Flip
88. Measure Glass
89. Rummer
90. Rummer with cover

WHITE TRANSPARENT FLINT, DIAMOND PATTERN

91. Double flask
92. Jug
93. Measure with flaring lip
94. Mustard bottle
95. Plate
96. Pocket bottle or flask
97. Salt cellar

WHITE TRANSPARENT FLINT, QUADRUPLE–DIAMOND DESIGN
98. Salt cellar

WHITE TRANSPARENT FLINT, CONTACT MOLD DESIGN AS IN FIGURE 109
99. Flip

WHITE TRANSPARENT FLINT, CONTACT MOLD DESIGN AS IN FIGURE 110
100. Sugar bowl

WHITE TRANSPARENT FLINT, CONTACT MOLD DESIGN AS IN FIGURE 111
101. Decanter, ½ Pint

ENGRAVED

WHITE TRANSPARENT FLINT, TYPE I

102. Flip
103. Flip, ribbed
104. Flip, sunken panel
105. Jelly glass with handles, sunken panel
106. Miniature flip, sunken panel
107. Tumbler

WHITE TRANSPARENT FLINT, TYPE II

108. Miniature flip, sunken panel
109. Tumbler

WHITE TRANSPARENT FLINT, TYPE III

110. Cordial bottle
111. Flip
112. Flip with cover
113. Flip, sunken panel
114. Mug
115. Tumbler

WHITE TRANSPARENT FLINT, TYPE IV

116. Flip, sunken panel

WHITE TRANSPARENT FLINT, TYPE V

117. Flip, fluted

WHITE TRANSPARENT FLINT, TYPE VI

118. Flip, ribbed
119. Flip, sunken panel

WHITE TRANSPARENT FLINT, TYPE VII

120. Flip, sunken panel

WHITE TRANSPARENT FLINT, TYPE VIII

121. Flip
122. Flip with cover
123. Tea caddy with glass screw top

WHITE TRANSPARENT FLINT, TYPE IX

124. Flip

WHITE TRANSPARENT FLINT, TYPE X
125. Flip
126. Mug

127. Tumbler

WHITE TRANSPARENT FLINT, TYPE XI
128. Flip
129. Flip with cover

130. Mug
131. Tumbler

WHITE TRANSPARENT FLINT, TYPE XII
132. Wine glass

WHITE TRANSPARENT FLINT, TYPE XIII
133. Wine glass

WHITE TRANSPARENT FLINT, TYPE XIV
134. Wine glass

"COTTON STEM" GLASSES
WHITE TRANSPARENT FLINT
135. Champagne glass

136. Wine glass

WHITE TRANSPARENT FLINT, TYPE VI
137. Straight-sided glass with tall spiral "cotton stem"

ENAMELED GLASS
WHITE TRANSPARENT FLINT, STEEPLE DESIGN
138. Mug, Gill
139. Mug, $\frac{1}{2}$ Pint
140. Mug, Pint

141. Mug, Quart
142. Tumbler, fluted. $\frac{1}{2}$ Pint

WHITE TRANSPARENT FLINT, FLORAL WREATH WITH RED TASSEL DESIGN
143. Tumbler, $\frac{1}{2}$ Pint

144. Tumbler, Pint

WHITE TRANSPARENT FLINT, CONVENTIONALIZED FLORAL DESIGN
145. Carafe
146. Drug bottle
147. Mug, Gill
148. Mug, $\frac{1}{2}$ Pint
149. Mug, Pint

150. Mug, Quart
151. Tumbler, $\frac{1}{2}$ Gill
152. Tumbler, Gill
153. Tumbler, $\frac{1}{2}$ Pint
154. Tumbler, Pint

BLUE FLINT
155. Drug bottle

WHITE TRANSPARENT FLINT, DOVE DESIGN
156. Cordial bottle
157. Drug bottle
158. Mug, Gill
159. Mug, $\frac{1}{2}$ Pint

160. Mug, Pint
161. Mug, Quart
162. Tumbler, $\frac{1}{2}$ Pint
163. Tumbler, Pint

WHITE TRANSPARENT FLINT, PARROT DESIGN

164. Tumbler, ½ Pint
165. Tumbler, Pint

166. Mug, Pint

WHITE TRANSPARENT FLINT, ROOSTER DESIGN

167. Mug, Pint
168. Tumbler, ½ Pint

169. Tumbler, Pint

WHITE TRANSPARENT FLINT, FANTASTIC BIRD DESIGN

170. Mug, Gill
171. Mug, ½ Pint
172. Mug, Pint
173. Mug, Quart

174. Tumbler, Gill
175. Tumbler, ½ Pint
176. Tumbler, Pint

WHITE TRANSPARENT FLINT, DOG DESIGN
177. Drug bottle

WHITE TRANSPARENT FLINT, COW DESIGN
178. Tumbler, ½ Pint

WHITE TRANSPARENT FLINT, WOMAN IN BOAT DESIGN
179. Mug, Pint

WHITE TRANSPARENT FLINT, PHANTOM SHIP DESIGN
180. Mug, Pint

WHITE TRANSPARENT FLINT, FLORAL DESIGN WITH INSCRIPTION

181. Drug bottle
182. Tumbler, ½ Gill
183. Tumbler, Gill

184. Tumbler, ½ Pint
185. Tumbler, Pint

WHITE TRANSPARENT FLINT, DOVE DESIGN WITH INSCRIPTION
186. Drug bottle

LIGHT AMBER FLINT, PLAIN

187. Carafe

188. Pocket bottle or flask

AMBER FLINT, RIBBED
189. Mug

DARK AMETHYST FLINT, DIAMOND PATTERN
190. Tall bowl

PURPLE FLINT, PLAIN

191. Pocket bottle or flask
192. Smelling bottle

193. Salt cellar

PURPLE FLINT, RIBBED

194. Bowl[1]
195. Salt cellar

196. Toilet bottle

[1] It is necessary here to note that I have never seen a purple cover to a bowl. I have seen a number of purple bowls with blue covers fitted to them, but never one with a cover that matched.

PURPLE FLINT, DIAMOND PATTERN

197. Bowl.   199. Salt cellar
198. Toilet bottle

PURPLE FLINT, DAISY IN SQUARE PATTERN
200. Toilet bottle

PURPLE FLINT, CONTACT MOLD DESIGN AS IN FIGURE 111
201. Decanter ½ Pint

EMERALD GREEN FLINT, DIAMOND PATTERN

202. Creamer

BLUE GREEN FLINT, DIAMOND PATTERN

203. Pocket bottle or flask   204. Salt cellar

BLUE FLINT, PLAIN

205. Bowl.   212. Salt cellar with scalloped foot
206. Creamer   213. Salt cellar with 3 feet
207. Creamer with scalloped foot   214. Tall salt cellar
208. Creamer with 3 feet   215. Sugar bowl
209. Egg glass   216. Smelling bottle
210. Mug   217. Vase
211. Salt cellar

BLUE FLINT, RIBBED

218. Creamer   223. Salt cellar
219. Creamer with scalloped foot   224. Salt cellar with scalloped foot
220. Creamer with 3 feet   225. Sugar bowl
221. Decanter, ½ Pint   226. Smelling bottles
222. Ink bottle

BLUE FLINT, FINE INCISED LINES
227. Salt cellar

BLUE FLINT, SUNKEN PANEL
228. Vase

BLUE FLINT, DIAMOND PATTERN

229. Creamer   231. Salt cellar
230. Sugar bowl

BLUE FLINT, CONTACT MOLD DESIGN AS IN FIGURE 112
232. Decanter, ½ Pint

BI–COLORED PIECES

WHITE TRANSPARENT FLINT WITH BLUE FLINT RIMS

233. Creamer   235. Salt cellar, diamond
234. Creamer, ribbed

BLUE FLINT WITH OPAQUE WHITE RIMS

236. Creamer   238. Vase
237. Mug with cover

WHITE TRANSPARENT FLINT WITH INTERIOR FLASHED IN OPAQUE WHITE

239. Communion chalice   240. Communion flagon

WHITE TRANSPARENT FLINT WITH OPAQUE WHITE VENETIAN DECORATION

241. Salt cellar with 3 feet

WHITE TRANSPARENT FLINT WITH PURPLE FLINT RIM

242. Measure tumbler

WHITE TRANSPARENT FLINT, WITH PURPLE FLINT FOOT

243. Measure tumbler

In addition to the above, window glass measuring $\frac{11}{128}$ to $\frac{5}{64}$ of an inch in thickness was made, also sheet glass and probably looking glass. Also bottles of the following sizes:

4 Gallon	Quart
Gallon	Pint
$\frac{1}{2}$ Gallon	$\frac{1}{2}$ Pint

having banded and collared lips, in "green glass" of the following shades:

Light green	Olive brown
Nile green	Light blue
Olive green	Dark red-brown
Olive	

NOTES

1. Throughout this chapter the note on page 133 should be kept in mind, and also that today all the types described and illustrated are called "Stiegel type." There are two exceptions to this general rule: the diamond-above-flute like Fig. 105, diamond-daisy like Fig. 108, and two similar designs are still called Stiegel since as yet they have been identified with no other glasshouse, American or foreign; and, the blown three mold glass like Figs. 109-113 is now known to be entirely 19th century (see also Note 1, page 184). Among the pieces purchased locally, but not identified for us as such, some unquestionably were Stiegel. Yet most of the pieces in the collection could equally well be specimens of the imported glass he was imitating. And several have features of a period later than Stiegel's. Supposed differences of color and techniques have dwindled or evaporated as larger numbers have been compared; though, of course, still further comparison may eventually establish a standard of differences. Until such time, however, the term "Stiegel type" should prevail.

2. See Note 3, page 170.

3. The patterns on these pieces were molded.

HMcK

GROUPED EXAMPLES OF
STIEGEL GLASS

3. Nile Green Glass Bottle
$10\frac{1}{2}''$ ($\frac{1}{4}$ size)

4. Dark Red-brown Glass Bottle
$11''$ ($\frac{1}{4}$ size)

1. Green Glass Bottle
$11\frac{3}{4}''$ ($\frac{1}{4}$ size)

2. Olive Glass Bottle
$14''$ ($\frac{1}{4}$ size)

5. Light Green Glass Bottle
7¾″ (⅓ size)

6. Light Green Glass Bottle
8¾″ (⅓ size)

7. Green Glass Jug Stand
1⅝″ (½ size)

8. Green Glass Jug Stand
2″ (½ size)

9. Light Green Glass Mustard Jar
2½″ (½ size)

10. Light Green Glass Mug
6⅞″ (½ size)

11. Light Green Glass Mug
4⅝″ (½ size)

13. Light Green Glass Bowl
3″ (½ size)

14. Light Green Glass Molasses Jug
7″ (½ size)

12. Light Green Glass Chemical Vessel
7¾″ (½ size)

18. White Flint Flip with Flaring Foot
5⅜″ (½ size)

17. White Flint Measure Glass
5¾″ (½ size)

15. White Glass Sweetmeat Jar
7″ (½ size)

16. White Glass Pocket Bottle
6½″ (½ size)

21. White Flint Child's Decanter
3″ (½ size)

20. White Flint Funnel
4″ (½ size)

19. White Flint Carafe
7¾″ (½ size)

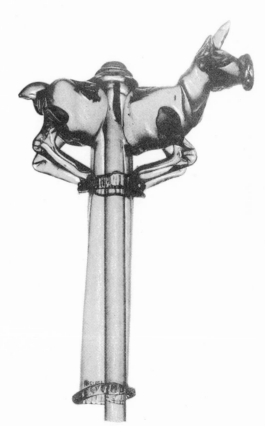

22. White Flint Toy Cow
8½″ (½ size)

24. Blue Flint Egg Glass
$3\frac{1}{2}''$ ($\frac{1}{2}$ size)

26. Blue Flint Creamer
$4\frac{3}{4}''$ ($\frac{1}{2}$ size)

25. Blue Flint Mug
$5''$ ($\frac{1}{2}$ size)

23. White Flint Lamp Reflector
$6\frac{1}{2}''$ ($\frac{1}{2}$ size)

31. Amethyst Flint Pocket Bottle
$7\frac{1}{4}''$ ($\frac{1}{2}$ size)

29. Blue Flint Sugar Bowl
$6\frac{1}{2}''$ ($\frac{1}{2}$ size)

27. Blue Flint Sugar Bowl
$6''$ ($\frac{1}{2}$ size)

28. Blue Flint Sugar Bowl
$6\frac{1}{2}''$ ($\frac{1}{2}$ size)

32. White Flint Wine
Glass 4¼″ (½ size)

33. White Flint Wine
Glass 4″ (½ size)

35. White Flint Wine
Glass 4″ (½ size)

30. Blue Flint Vase
8″ (½ size)

36. White Flint Wine Glass
6″ (½ size)

34. White Flint Wine Glass
8″ (½ size)

37. White Flint Wine Glass
4″ (½ size)

38. White Flint Champagne
Glass 4″ (½ size)

40. White Flint Measure
3¾″ (½ size)

43. White Flint Wine Glass
$3\frac{3}{4}''$ ($\frac{1}{2}$ size)

44. White Flint Cordial Glass
$3\frac{1}{4}''$ ($\frac{1}{2}$ size)

47. White Flint Champagne Glass
$4\frac{3}{4}''$ ($\frac{1}{2}$ size)

48. White Flint Champagne Glass
$5\frac{3}{4}''$ ($\frac{1}{2}$ size)

39. White Flint Sillabub
Glass $4''$ ($\frac{1}{2}$ size)

41. White Flint Wine
Glass $3\frac{3}{4}''$ ($\frac{1}{2}$ size)

42. White Flint Wine
Glass $4''$ ($\frac{1}{2}$ size)

46. White Flint "Cotton
Stem" Champagne
Glass 5" (½ size)

159. Excavated "Cotton
Stem" Manheim

45. White Flint Straight
Sided Glass
6½" (½ size)

49. White Flint and Amethyst Flint
Measure Glass 3¾" (½ size)

BI–COLORED

50. White Flint with Amethyst Flint Rim
4" (½ size)

56. White Flint with Blue Flint Rim
Creamer 3½″ (½ size)

57. White Flint with Blue Flint Rim Salt
Cellar 3″ (½ size)

54. White Flint Flashed with Opaque
White Communion Flagon
3⅞″ (½ size)

55. White Flint Flashed with Opaque
White Communion Chalice
5⅜″ (½ size)

51. White Flint with Blue
Flint Rim Masonic Shaped
Glass 4¼″ (½ size)

52. White Flint with Blue
Flint Rim Masonic Shaped
Glass 4¼″ (½ size)

53. White Flint with Blue
Flint Rim Creamer
4″ (½ size)

60. Blue Flint with Opaque White Rim Vase
13″ (½ size)

58. Blue Flint with Opaque White Rim
Creamer 5½″ (½ size)

63. Blue Flint Salt Cellar
3¼″ (½ size)

64. Blue Flint Salt Cellar
2¾″ (½ size)

62. White Flint Pitcher
6½″ (½ size)

59. Blue Flint with Opaque White Rim
Mug with Cover 6¼″ (½ size)

65. Amethyst Flint Salt Cellar
2⅜″ (½ size)

66. White Flint Child's Flip
2″ (½ size)

70. Blue Flint Cellar
5″ (½ size)

68. Blue Flint Salt Cellar
2½″ (½ size)

69. Blue Flint Salt Cellar
2¾″ (½ size)

67. White Flint Flip
5¾″ (½ size)

71. Blue Flint Creamer
$4\frac{1}{4}''$ ($\frac{1}{2}$ size)

72. Blue Flint Creamer
$3\frac{3}{4}''$ ($\frac{1}{2}$ size)

73. Blue Flint Creamer
$5\frac{1}{4}''$ ($\frac{1}{2}$ size)

74. White Flint Creamer
$5''$ ($\frac{1}{2}$ size)

76 White Flint Creamer
5″ (½ size)

75. White Flint Funnel
8¾″ (½ size)

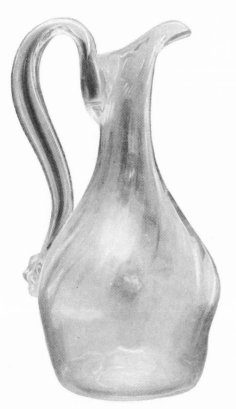

77. White Flint Vinegar Cruet
8″ (½ size)

81. White Flint Plate
1¼″ (½ size)

80. White Flint Bowl with Spouts
4″ (½ size)

82. White Flint Flip
5¼″ (½ size)

78. White Flint Flip
5⅝″ (½ size)

79. White Flint Measure Glass
5¾″ (½ size)

86. Blue Flint Salt Cellar
2¾″ (½ size)

88. Blue Flint Creamer
3¼″ (½ size)

87. Blue Flint Salt Cellar
3″ (½ size)

84. White Flint Rummer with Cover
8″ (½ size)

83. White Flint Rummer
5″ (½ size)

89. Amethyst Flint Bowl
3¼″ (½ size)

93. White Flint Measure
3¾″ (½ size)

90. Blue Flint Sugar Bowl
7½″ (½ size)

94. White Flint Salt Shaker
4½″ (½ size)

97. White Flint Double Flask
8½″ (½ size)

92. White Flint Pocket Bottle
7″ (½ size)

95. Blue Flint Creamer
4½″ (½ size)

103. White Flint Table Jug
4½″ (½ size)

105. Amethyst Flint Toilet Bottle
5¾″ (½ size)

104. White Flint Foot of above Table Jug
Diameter 2½″ (½ size)

96. Blue Flint Sugar Bowl
7¼″ (½ size)

107. White Flint Plate
Diameter 4⅜″ (½ size)

101. Blue Flint Creamer
4¼″ (½ size)

100. White Flint Salt Cellar 3¼″ (½ size)

102. Blue Flint Creamer
3¾″ (½ size)

108. Amethyst Flint Toilet Bottle
5″ (½ size)

109. White Flint Flip
7½″ (½ size)

113. Foot Blue Flint Decanter
Diameter 2⅜″ (½ size)

110. White Flint Sugar Bowl
6¼″ (½ size)

111. White Flint Decanter
5½″ (½ size)

112. Blue Flint Decanter
6″ (½ size)

114. White Flint Flip Type I.
4½″ (½ size)

115. White Flint Flip Type I
6″ (½ size)

116. White Flint Flip Type I.
5¾″ (½ size)

117. White Flint Flip Type I.
5¾″ (½ size)

118. White Flint Jelly Glass Type I.
1⅞″ (½ size)

119. White Flint Jelly Glass Type I.
1⅞″ (½ size)

120. White Flint Flip Type II.
2⅛″ (½ size)

122. White Flint Mug Type III.
6½″ (½ size)

123. White Flint Cordial Bottle Type III.
5½″ (½ size)

121. White Flint Flip Type III.
6¼″ (½ size)

124. White Flint Flip with Cover Type III.
11½″ (½ size)

125. White Flint Flip Type III.
6" (½ size)

126. White Flint Flip Type IV.
5¾" (½ size)

127. White Flint Flip Type V.
5¼" (½ size)

128. White Flint Flip Type VI.
5" (½ size)

130. White Flint Flip with Cover Type VIII.
10″ (½ size)

129. White Flint Flip Type VII.
6¼″ (½ size)

131. White Flint Tea Caddy Type VIII.
7″ (½ size)

133. White Flint Mug Type X.
4¾″ (½ size)

132. White Flint Flip Type IX.
6¼″ (½ size)

135. White Flint Flip with Cover Type XI.
11¼″ (½ size)

134. White Flint Flip Type X.
4¼″ (½ size)

136. White Flint Wine Glass Type XII.
4″ (½ size)

137. White Flint Wine Glass Type XIII.
4″ (½ size)

138. White Flint Wine Glass Type XIV.
4″ (½ size)

145. Steeple Design "Henry Nissel"
3¾″ (½ size)

147. Fantastic Bird Design "Henry
Nissel"   4″ (½ size)

146. Conventional Floral Design "Henry
Nissel"   5¾" (½ size)

149. Dove Design "Joseph Welch"
3½" (½ size)

148. Woman in Boat Design "Henry Nissel"   5⅛" (½ size)

144. Steeple Design "Henry Nissel"
7" (½ size)

150. Dog Design "Joseph Welch"
5¾″ (½ size)

153. Conventionalized Floral Design
"Sebastian Witmer"   5¾″ (½ size)

152. Steeple Design "Sebastian Witmer"
7″ (½ size)

151. Dove Design "Martin Yetters"
6½″ (½ size)

154. Conventionalized Floral Design
"Sebastian Witmer" 7¼″ (½ size)

155. Fantastic Bird Design "Sebastian
Witmer" 3¼″ (½ size)

156. Fantastic Bird Design "Sebastian
Witmer" 4″ (½ size)

157. Phantom Ship Design "Sebastian
Witmer" 6¾″ (½ size)

158. Blue Flint Creamer, Gilded
Inscription 5″ (½ size)

159. Excavated "Cotton
Stem" Manheim

APPENDIX

APPENDIX

SUMMARY OF DATES OF HENRY WILLIAM STIEGEL'S THREE GLASS HOUSES

ELIZABETH FURNACE GLASS HOUSE

September 18, 1763, to November 11, 1765.

MANHEIM GLASS HOUSES

November 11, 1765, to May 5, 1774.

MANHEIM FIRST FACTORY

October 6, 1764. Began work on building.
October 29, 1765. Glass Ovens finished and fire put in.
November 11, 1765. Glassmakers began work and glass made.
April 20, 1769. Glass House stopped manufacturing glass.
August 10, 1773. New roof put on Old Glass House.

MANHEIM SECOND FACTORY

Said to have been 90 feet high, dome-like in shape and walls built of red brick, $2\frac{1}{8} \times 4\frac{1}{8}$
  $\times 8\frac{1}{8}$, imported from England and brought from Lancaster, Pa., to Manheim, Pa., in
  Conestoga wagons.
1768. New Building begun.
1769 latter part. New Building completed and glass probably made.
December 18, 1770. Entry "This day fire was put in the furnace and glass making
  began."
1771 to 1772. Several additions added to New Building.
February 15, 1773. Last addition finished.
May 5, 1774. Glass House leased by Henry William Stiegel to Smith & Simund.

EMPLOYEES ELIZABETH FURNACE GLASS HOUSE

Daniel M. Daniel. Blower.
George Glass. Went to Manheim later and worked in the factory.
Martin Grenier. Expert Glassblower, went to Manheim and remained with Henry
  William Stiegel until the leasing of the Manheim factory May 5, 1774.
Michael Griesbach. Blower.
Mathias Hoffart.
Michael Miller.
Benjamin Misky. Expert Glassblower.
Christian Nassel. Expert Glassblower. Went with Henry William Stiegel to Manheim
  and remained until 1774.

Anthony Stiegel. Brother of Henry William Stiegel. Was paid £9.8.10 for supervising work in the Glass House.

Anton Walder.

EMPLOYEES MANHEIM GLASS HOUSES

Casper Adenstein. Shearer.

George Allen. Began work October 24, 1774. Smith & Simund lease.

George Allers. Cutter & Flowerer.

Peter Alloway.

Nicholas Anthony. Shearer.

Samuel Bamburner. Teazer.

Peter Bandenbach. Teazer.

Jacob Banman.

George Banman.

Hubard Baumgerdner.

John Beeker.

William Begs. Blower.

Casper Betz.

Martin Betz. Workman. Thrashed August 13, 1773, by Stiegel for making wrong delivery of glass in Lancaster.

Sharmand Betz. Window Glass.

George Bowman.

John Bowman.

Anthony Brerzer.

John Casey. Cutter & Flowerer.

Noah Casey.

Robert Clark. Window Glass.

Boha Ciese.

John Ciese.

George Custer. Workman.

Henry Custer.

Cyrus (Henry William Stiegel's Negro Slave). Shearer and Blower.

Jacob Daubeberger.

James Davidson. Assistant August 28, 1771.

John Duth.

John Dyer. Window Glass.

Michael Eberly. Attendant.

Jacob Eckardt.

Jacob Ehard.

Michael Everley. Attendant.

Edward Farrel. Cutter, Flowerer and Teazer.

Felix Farrel. Expert Blower. Fined for making glass for strangers.

Patrick Flanigan. Indentured June 5, 1772; 5 years at £15.

Henry Gipple.

George Glass. Left Glass House April 29, 1773, to work at Mill at £30.

Michael Godenpeck.

Conrath Grash.

Christian Gratinger. Blower.

William Green.

Martin Grenier. Expert Blower.
Michael Gudadel.
Albertus Hafner. Shearer. December 7, 1765, at £3 per month.
Jacob Halder. Blower.
Andrew Halter. Blower and Shearer.
Christian Hassel. Blower.
Hartman Heil.
Sebastian Henderle.
Henry Hernley.
Frans Hertsberger.
Frederick Hies.
Andrew Holder. Workman and Driver of ox-team.
Hannes Housam.
John Huber. Cooper.
Hartman Hull.
Lazarus Isaacs. Cutter & Flowerer. August 10, 1773.
Archibald Jackson. Indentured June 5, 1772; 4 years £15.
Culbert Jans.
Paul Kappenberger. October 10, 1766, left Stiegel's employ.
Joseph Kassel.
Sebastian Keller.
Michal Kentze.
H. S. King.
George Klopperdon. Teazer.
Martin Krame.
Nicholas Liberight.
Sam Logan. Experienced Workman. Salary £3.2.6. per month.
Joseph Long. Window Glass.
Abraham Longneck.
Daniel Longnecker.
Peter Longnecker. Window Glass.
Henry Luter.
Thomas Mandenbalk.
Philip Marslachung.
John Mayer. Blower.
John McCoy. Teazer.
Christopher Miller.
Henry Miller.
Jacob Miller. Cooper.
Jeremiah Miller.
George Munich.
Thomas Narday.
Christian Naselwas. Teazer.
Christian Nassel. Expert Blower.
Henry Nissle. Enameler. £5.10.6; later paid £5.11.4.
John Nowecker.
Theodore Nowman. Apprentice and Attendant.
John Godlep Nowman. Apprentice and Attendant.
George Ott. Shearer and Teazer.
Ulry Ott.
George Otto.

Frederick Plateberger.
John Plateberger.
John Rago.
William Rago. Expert Blower.
Christopher Reahm.
John Redelsberger. Window Glass.
William Reese.
Conrad Reinhard.
Christian Richter. Blower.
Uhr. Rupler.
Balzer Shaad. Blower and Cooper.
Peter Shantzem.
Henry Sharm.
Henry Sharman. Teazer.
Valentine Shefler. Tender. November 1, 1765.
Casper Sheibely.
J. Sholl.
Jacob Shultz.
Charles Smith.
J. Sowes. Apprentice and Attendant.
Ulry Spohn. Shearer.
Solomon Stenger. Blower. April, 1774.
Martin Thramer.
Balzer Thrames.
George Tishank.
Ludwig Truchenmiller.
Conrad Waltz. Blower, Shearer and Window Glass.
Frederick Weaver. Shearer. November 1, 1765.
Joseph Welch. Enameler.
Henry Werte.
John Williams. Indentured June 5, 1772; 7 years £15.
Thomas Williams. Expert Blower.
Thomas Williamson. Expert Blower. Given special order work.
John Wishard. Window Glass.
Sebastian Witmer. Enameler; £5.1.9.
Elias Wood.
Thomas Yardy.
Martin Yetters. Enameler.
Freder Yuoy.

133 men employed.

GLASS ENAMELERS, MANHEIM, PA.

Henry Nissle.
Joseph Welch.

Sebastian Witmer.
Martin Yetters.

GLASS CUTTERS AND FLOWERERS, MANHEIM, PA.

The following appear to have been the earlier Cutters and Flowerers.

George Allers.
John Casey.
Edward Farrel. Later became teazer at Works.
Probably others worked and had apprentices.
Lazarus Isaacs. August 10, 1773, to February 14, 1774.

PRICES PAID GLASS BLOWERS FOR WORK

At Elizabeth Furnace and at Manheim from September 18, 1763, to December 1, 1770, the great majority of the glass made, if not all of it, was paid for by the lot or piece.

WINDOW GLASS		BOTTLES	
8x10.	6/per dozen	Gallon size 3/ per dozen.	
7x9.	5/ per dozen	Quart size 1/ 6d. per dozen.	
6x8.	4/ per dozen.		
5x7.	2/ 6d. per dozen.		
4x6.	1/ 6d. per dozen.		

April 14, 1769, paid Martin Grenier the following prices.

Salts 2/ per dozen.
Cream Jugs 2d. each.
B. Salts 5/ per dozen.
Plates 4/ per dozen.

LIST OF STIEGEL GLASS AGENCIES AND DISTRIBUTORS

PHILADELPHIA, PA.

1769. Michael Hillegas in 2nd Street.
1769. Stiegel Store. Mulberry (Arch) Street near 4th Street.
1770. Brooks & Sharp at house of Nicholas Brooks in Front Street near Lombard.
1771. London Coffee House, South West Corner Front and Market Streets.
1771. Isaac Melchor, in 2nd Street.
1772. Charles Stedman, in 2nd Street.
1773. William Smith, Broker, in Front Street near London Coffee House. Also sold glass to John Thompson, Wendel Gilbrath, Peter Wikoff, Merchant in 2nd Street near Race, and Jacob Bartg, Tavern Keeper.

LANCASTER, PA.

Paul Zantzinger. Big distributor.
Also sold glass to Baker Lowman, Caleb Johnson, Hamilton & Moore, Lockards, Charles Wentz, Harris & McKuhn, Abraham Herr, John Barr, and Michael Diefenderfer.

YORK, PA.

1767. Thomas Usher.
1771. George Stake.
1773. Henry Klopper.
1774. Mr. Steeg.
Also sold glass to John Kean.

HANOVER, PA.

Richard McCalister.

CARLISLE, PA.

1766. George Steeg.
1771. Jacob Miller.
1772. Stephen Duncan.
1773. Joseph Wilkins.
1774. Michael Miller.

READING, PA.

1765. Mayer Josephson (Elizabeth Furnace Agency).
1767. Mr. Shlegel.
1767. Henry Hahn.
1771. Christopher Geygar.
Also sold glass to Fred Keyse.

EPHRATRA, PA.

Sold glass to Doctor Gideon.

MIDDLETOWN, PA.

George Fry.

ELIZABETHTOWN, PA.

1774. John Jamison.
1774. Abraham Holmes.

MANHEIM, PA.

1765. Manheim Glass Store.
Also sold glass to King of Prussia Tavern, John Kayl, Adam Diefenderfer, John Kays and John Schanck.

LEBANON, PA.

1771. Robert Patton.
1773. Philip Marshaller.

HEIDELBERG, PA.

B. Jacob.

BRICKERVILLE, PA.

1764. Elizabeth Furnace Store.

NEW YORK, N.Y.

Nov. 1771. Garrett Rapelje. Merchant opposite the Fly Market.
Jan. 1773. Henry W. Stiegel Ware House. Broad Street near the Exchange, opposite house of Mr. Waldron.
Feb. 1773. James & Arthur Jarvis, in the Fly Market between Burling and Beekman Slips.
Sept. 1774. Templeton & Steward, Auctioneers, sold unsold Stiegel glass at auction in New York City.
Glass was also sold to William Smith.

BALTIMORE, MD.

1771. John Little.
1773. Melchor Keener.

HAGERSTOWN, MD.

Mr. Harzo.
Also sold glass to Mr. Rohrer and Frederick Bohner.

FREDERICK, MD.

Conrad Geork.

BOSTON, MASS.

Mr. Cushing was the big distributor in Boston. This was probably Thomas Cushing, one of the founders of the American Academy of Arts and Sciences. In the New England Genealogical Society's Library, at 9 Ashburton Place, Boston, in John H. Dexter's Biographical Memoranda, the address of Thomas Cushing's shop is given as near the Bridge, Ann Street. Stiegel Glass was also sold by the following dealers:
Nov. 1771. James Perkins, two doors below the British Coffee House North side King Street.
Nov. 1772. Henry Perkins, Cornhill opposite the London Book Store.
July 1773. Elizabeth Perkins, two doors below the British Coffee House in King Street.

THE FOLLOWING ALSO PURCHASED STIEGEL GLASS

Mr. Bartram.
Jacob Billmeyer.
Samuel Boyer.
Cauffman & Fagan.
Peter Contar.
Y. Craford.
Christian Crofford.
Henry Custer.
George Eichelberger (had glass made from models).
John Fagan.
Anthony Fricker.
Robert Fulton.
Michael Gross.
M. Gudadel.
Hamilton & Moore.
J. Hopkinson.
Mathias Hough.
John Kleyn.
Lamberter & Shieley.
Daniel Levan.
Daniel May.
John Megomery.
Henry Miller. Special Order, August 31, 1773.

Benjamin Nathan.
Patton & Williams.
John Peter. Was one of the early purchasers.
Thomas Poultem.
Richard Ross.
Casper Singhaus.
John Spidler.
Richard Spingman.
John Spore.
Ephriham Steel.
Christian Tautz.
Francis Thomas.
Thomas Usher.
Jacob Vetter.
Christopher Wegman.
Paul Weixel.
Abner Wickersham.
Wishard & Edwards.
Ad. Witman.
Elias Wood. Stiegel's Nephew, Roxbury, Pa.
Isaac Young.

THE FOLLOWING MEN WERE PAID FOR WORK, LABOR AND SERVICES RENDERED IN BUILDING THE MANHEIM GLASS HOUSES

Nicholas Anthony. Workman.
William Appleton.
Martin Betz. Workman.
Frederick Bluch. Workman.
Henry Cordel.
William Crofoot. Carter.
Adam Dieffenderfer.
Michael Eberly.
George Ege.
John Eigenberger. Workman.
Martin Eigenberger. Workman.
Claudius Eleanor.
John Evans. Workman.
Andras Everman.
Conrath Fishborn.

Peter Fream.
George Frey.
Philip Frick.
Andras Gettinger.
Doctor Gideon from Ephratra.
Henry Glossmer. Workman.
Christian Gratwin. Workman.
Martin Grenier.
Andras Halder.
Jacob Halder.
Henry Hans.
Paul Hapenberger. Workman.
Prichard Hays.
Jerome Heinzelman.
Christian Hershey. Carting Material.

Mathias Hoffert.
Albertus Hofmier. Workman.
Frederick Holzorut.
Ulry Hornley.
Achartis Hosener.
Frederick Hummel.
Peter Hummer. Carting.
Paul Kappenberger.
Christian Kaufman. Workman.
John Eberhart Kreiss.
Adam Simon Kuhn.
Peter Kump. Stone Cutter.
George Lax.
John George Lay.
Charles Lentz. Mason.
Christian Lentz. Workman.
Frederick Leser.
Daniel Longnecker. Workman.
Henry Longnecker. Supplied lumber.
Ulry Longnecker. Workman.
Robert Markham. Workman.
Mathe Masbison. Workman.
Peter Mattler.
Hans Misky.
John Moore. Brick-layer.
Mathias Moslesson.
Christian Nassel.
John Paxton.

Christian Ream.
Michall Rib.
Peter Robley.
George Rudy. Carpenter.
George Sax. Carpenter.
John Ernest Schwartzel.
Balser Shaad.
Henry Sherer.
Michael Sherer. Carpenter.
Valentine Shifter. Workman.
John Shissley.
Carl Smith. Mason and carpenter.
Jacob Snyder.
Valentine Spingler. Workman.
Richard Spingman. Workman.
Ulry Spohn.
Anthony Stiegel.
Henry Thrister. Smith.
Martin Tresbaugh.
Christian Waltz.
Frederick Weaves. Workman.
Frederick Weber.
Pastian Wilmer.
John Wisherd.
John Wolf. Workman.
John Wriste.
Martin Yetter. Carpenter.

CHAIN OF TITLE, TOWN OF MANHEIM, LANCASTER COUNTY, PA. 1734–1775

September 30, 1734.

Patent issued by John Penn, Thomas Penn and Richard Penn to James Logan of Stenton province of Pennsylvania for 1400 Acres of Land (which included what is now the Town of Manheim) paying yearly unto the Proprietors at the Town of Lancaster yearly on March 1st, one English silver shilling for every 100 Acres. Recorded, Philadelphia in Patent Book A. Volume 8, page 48 &c.

James Logan in his lifetime sold 671 Acres leaving 729 Acres unsold of which he died seized.

Will of James Logan. Dated November 25, 1749 by which he devised 700 Acres (meaning and intending the unsold Manheim 729 Acres) to his daughter Sarah Logan who married Isaac Norris.

Sarah Norris, wife of Isaac Norris, daughter of James Logan, died; leaving daughter Mary Norris.

DEED. Lancaster.
Dated February 17, 1762.
Recorded Book H. page 66.

Isaac Norris of Fairhill, Township of Northern Liberties and Mary Norris his daughter spinster, now over 21 years of age

to

Charles Stedman and Alexander Stedman.

CONVEYS 729 acres including the Town of Manheim.

DEED. Lancaster.
Dated September 20, 1762.
Recorded October 4, 1764.
Liber L. page 4.
Consideration £1000 lawful money of Pennsylvania.

Charles Stedman, merchant of Philadelphia and Ann, his wife, and Alexander Stedman, Esquire of said City and Elizabeth his wife,

to

Henry William Stiegel.

CONVEYS ⅓ equal undivided interest in undivided tract of 729 Acres (Manheim).

DEED. Philadelphia.
Dated March 14, 1765.
Recorded January 26, 1768.
Liber I 4, page 107.
Consideration £370.

Charles Stedman of Philadelphia, Merchant and Ann his wife and Alexander Stedman of Philadelphia and Elizabeth his wife

to

Henry William Stiegel.

CONVEYS following 5 lots in Manheim. Shown on a certain Draught or Plan of the Town of Manheim and Lots adjacent lately drawn by Thomas Lincoln, Surveyor.

Lot 9 Containing about 10 Acres
 " 23   "   10 Acres
 " 26   "   10 Acres
 " 34   "   10 Acres
 " 35   "   about 3 Acres

PARTITION DEED. Lancaster.

Dated March 14, 1765.   Alexander Stedman of Philadelphia
Recorded September 5, 1766.   and Elizabeth his wife
Liber H. page 347.   to
                                   Henry William Stiegel.

CONVEYS the following Manheim lots.

Number 8.10 Acres; Number 24.10 Acres and 32.10 Acres.

PARTITION DEED. Lancaster.

Dated March 14, 1765.   Charles Stedman of the City of Phila-
Recorded November 22, 1783. delphia, Merchant and Ann his wife
Liber X. page 288.   and Alexander Stedman Esquire and
Consideration £370.   Elizabeth his wife
                                   to
                                   Henry William Stiegel.

CONVEYS the following Manheim Lots, 9–23–26–34 and 35.

MORTGAGE.   Charles and Alexander Stedman
Dated June 10, 1765.   to
Unrecorded.   Isaac Cox.

MORTGAGES for £2,700. Undivided ⅔ Manheim property. Mortgage mentioned in deed poll James Webb, Sheriff of Lancaster County to Isaac Cox. Dated August 4, 1769.

ADVERTISEMENT. Pennsylvania Gazette, March 24, 1768.

Charles and Alexander Stedman announce for sale ⅔ interest in Manheim property.

MORTGAGE. Lancaster.

Dated March 9, 1768.   Henry William Stiegel of Elizabeth
Recorded March 13, 1768.   Township. Iron Master and Elizabeth
Liber N. page 23.   his wife
                                   to
                                   Daniel Bennezet of the City of Phila-
                                   delphia.

MORTGAGES for £3000. Undivided ⅓ interest in Elizabeth Furnace and other lands in Elizabeth Township. 9 Tracts in Lebanon and Warwick Townships containing about 1200 Acres of land. Undivided ½ interest in Charming Forge, undivided ⅓ interest in Manheim property. Also H. W. Stiegel's Capital Messuage, Glass House and other buildings.

STIEGEL GENEALOGY

Barbara Stiegel
B. November 5, 1756.
Married Mr. Ashton of Virginia
Died without issue.

Elizabeth Stiegel
B. February 3, (?) 1758.
Married William Old, son of Jar
Old, Iron Master of Lancaster

HENRY WILLIAM STIEGEL.
B. May 13, 1729, Cologne, Germany.
D. January 10, 1785, Charming
Forge, Pa.
Married. November 7, 1752.
Elizabeth Huber, daughter Jacob
and Magdalena Huber.
B. March 27, 1734.
D. February 3, 1758.
Married. October 24, 1758.
Elizabeth Hölz (Wood) daughter
George Hölz (Wood)
B. about 1735.
D. 1782.

Jacob Stiegel.
B. About 1760.
D. September 1, 1783.
Married Rachel Holman.
Made his home with his sister
Barbara Ashton, Boiling Sprir
Va. Successful farmer, served
High Sheriff.

JOHN FREDERICK STIEGEL.
B. June 17, 1697.
D. June 22, 1741, in Europe.
Married.
Dorothea Elizabeth   (?)
B. May 11, 1704.
D. January 11, 1781, in America,
probably at Shaefferstown, Pa.

Catharine Elizabeth
B. November 25, 1730.
D. January 30, 1733.

Catharine Maria
B. April 4, 1733.
D. June 27, 1739.

Dorothea Elizabeth Stiegel
B. May 3, 1765.
D. November 26, 1768.
Her grandmother Dorothea Eliz
abeth Stiegel was her sponsor.

Maria Barbara Stiegel
B. April 28, 1766.

Matthew Frederick
B. September 12, 1735.
D. February 26, 1736.

John Henry Stiegel
B. December 7, 1767.
D. August 1, 1769.

Joanna Sophia
B. December 12, 1736.
D. June 6, 1741.

Maria Elizabeth Stiegel
B. January 23, 1770.
D. January 4, 1777.

Anthony.
B. September 2, 1739.
D. January 9, 1785, Schaeffers-
town, Pa.
Married.
Maria Elizabeth Glessner.
B. Allen Selbach, Germany.
D. January 29, 1770.
Married. January 8, 1771.
Christina Neip, daughter of John
and Agatha Neip.
B. January 1, 1751.
D. January 14, 1824.

Christina Stiegel.
B. October 27, 1771.
Married Thomas Achey.

Eva Stiegel.
B. September 29, 1773.
Married George Strichler.

Magdalena Stiegel.
B. March 8, 1775.
Married Michael Valentine.

John Stiegel.
B. January 24, 1777.

The above Stiegel Genealogy is copied from Anthony Stiegel's Elementary Book of True Christianity
the Ege Family with a few corrections by the author.

James Old.
B. October 16, 1773.
D. May 10, 1777.

William Old.
B. February 2, 1775.
Married Elizabeth Nagle, daughter of
    Captain Nagle.

Joseph Old.
Married Rebecca Ege, daughter
    of George and Elizabeth Ege of
    Charming Forge, Pa.
Died without issue.

Jacob Old.
B. December 25, 1777.
D. September 20, 1802, at St. Croix,
    West Indies.
Unmarried.

Jacob Stiegel, Jr.
Married Catharine Brecht, daugh-
    ter of Michael Brecht or Bright
    of Reading, Pa.

Louisa Old.
B. March 9, 1799.
Married Thomas Mills.
Had issue.

Caroline Old.
B. February 7, 1801.
D. June 5, 1889.
Married Henry Morris of
    Philadelphia.

Morgan Old.
B. August 26, 1803.
D. at Richmond, Ind.
Had issue.

Elizabeth Old.
B. 1805.
Married. Dr. Hamilton Witman
    of Reading, Pa.

Rebecca Old.
B. September 7, 1808.
D. May 21, 1896.
Married Dr. Louis Horning of
    Montgomery County, Pa.
Married Jerome K. Boyer of
    Harrisburg, Pa.
Had issue.

Rachel Stiegel.
B. June 1, 1807.
D. 1895.
Married David Dixon.
Had issue.

Louisa Stiegel.
B. October 4, 1810.
D. October 31, 1894.
Married M. B. Stover.
Had issue.

Elizabeth Stiegel.
B. 1812.
Married William A. Quick of
    Boiling Springs, Va.

Henry W. Stiegel.
D. in Mississippi.

David Bright Stiegel.
B. 1820.
D. 1866.
Married. Sarah Leibert of
    Madison County, Va.

Charles Bright Stiegel.
B. July 24, 1821.
Married Sarah Coffman.
Had issue.
Married Sarah Craig.
Had issue.

Sarah J. Stiegel.
B. October 5, 1827.
Married F. Koiner.
Had issue.

tofore referred to, and Rev. Thompson P. Ege's History and Genealogy of

Endorsement.

"In pursuance of a Power of Attorney to me directed from Daniel Benezet the within named mortgage. Dated the 29th day of January, 1770 and Recorded in Book P. page 55, I do hereby acknowledge Satisfaction on the within Mortgage as to the Manheim Estate therein contained in the name of the said Daniel Benezet and for him and in his name by Virtue of the Warrant aforesaid. Witness my Hand and Seal this 12 day of February, 1770. Edward Shippern. Recorder.

DEED POLL. Lancaster.
Dated August 4, 1769.
Recorded October 10, 1769.
Liber O. page 182.

James Webb the Younger Esquire High Sheriff of the County of Lancaster
to
Isaac Cox.

By virtue of a writ of *Levari facias* tested at Lancaster in the 9th year of his present majesty's reign.

CONVEYS undivided ⅔ of Charles and Alexander Stedman's interest in Manheim; reserving Henry W. Stiegel's ⅓ part as it appears that Charles and Alexander Stedman deeded ⅓ interest prior to making of the mortgage.

RELEASE OF MORTGAGE. Lancaster.
Dated January 29, 1770.
Recorded February 9, 1770.
Liber P. page 55.
Consideration 5/

Daniel Benezet of the City of Philadelphia. Merchant
to
Henry William Stiegel of Lancaster County Iron Master.

RELEASES Manheim property. Specifically mentioning King of Prussia Tavern and Glass House Lots granted to Henry William Stiegel by Anthony Stiegel.

DEED. Lancaster.
Dated February 1, 1770.
Recorded August 29, 1770.
Liber O. page 273.
Consideration £3000.

Isaac Cox of the City of Philadelphia, Merchant
to
Henry William Stiegel of the County of Lancaster, Iron Master.

CONVEYS Manheim property, described by lot numbers and by metes and bounds. Also ⅓ part of all the Annual Rent Charges in 259 town lots and 76 out lots and all the Estate of Charles and Alexander Stedman in said 729 Acres of Land.

MORTGAGE. Lancaster.
Dated February 2, 1770.
Recorded February 9, 1770.
Liber P. page 36.

Henry W. Stiegel of the County of Lancaster Iron Master and Elizabeth his wife

to

Isaac Cox of the City and County of Philadelphia, Merchant.

MORTGAGES for £2500. Stiegel's Manheim Mansion; all 18 yearly rent charges on both sides of High Street between Charlotte and Prussian Streets Nos. 1 to 18; all 105 yearly rent charges from Nos. 85 to 189; all 111 yearly rent charges from Nos. 250 to 359. 7 Lots Nos. 22–23–24–25–26–29–33. Containing 74 Acres and 33 Perches.

DEED OF MORTGAGE. Lancaster.
Dated February 2, 1770.
Recorded March 10, 1774.
Liber N. page 434.

Isaac Cox of Philadelphia, Merchant

to

Henry W. Stiegel.

In Consideration of £717.3. cancels a mortgage for £2500. recorded in the rolls office in Book P. page 36. and conveys Lots 1 to 18. Lots 8–10–11. Rent charges 258–264–265–266–267–273–274–275–284–285–287–293 294–299–302–303–304–325–338–241–247–248–249–250–351–352 and 353. Also Rent charges on Lots 2–4–6–19–20–21–22–23–37–39–45–47–63–66–68–69–70–83–98–99–100–101–102–104–105–106–107–108 and 109 and 3 larger of 10 Acre Lots 22–33–34 and part 35 and other large of 10 Acre Lot Number 5. in consideration £311.13. and authorizes and empowers Edward Shippin Esquire of Lancaster to discharge in the Recorders Office in Lancaster the above mentioned Lots. But Judgment entered upon Bond and Warrant of Attorney executed by Henry W. Stiegel shall stand and remain good and Lawful Security to and for the said Isaac Cox in respect to all and every the Estates in the aforesaid Deed of Mortgage.

MORTGAGE. Lancaster.
Dated February 2, 1770.
Recorded February 9, 1770.
Liber O., page 219.

Henry William Stiegel Iron Master and Elizabeth his wife

to

Isaac Cox of the City of Philadelphia Merchant.

MORTGAGES for £560. Glass House. Described as follows.
A certain Messuage or Tenement and Glass House with lots thereto

belonging, situated in the Town of Manheim in the County of Lancaster between Charlotte and Pitt Streets. Containing in Breadth on the said two Streets 342 feet and in Length or Debth from Street to Street 257 feet. Bounded Eastwardly with Charlotte Street Southwardly with Stiegel Street, Westwardly with Pitt Street and Northwardly with Martin Dorwards Lot. Numbers 79–80–81–82–83 and 84 which the said Henry William Stiegel purchased from sundry persons also lots 19–20–21 and 22. containing in breadth on Pitt Street 228 feet and in length or debth 257 feet. Bounded Eastwardly by Pitt Street; Southwardly by Stiegel Street; Westwardly by Jacob Rieffs line and Northwardly with out lot 23.

February 3, 1774.

John Ferree, High Sheriff of Lancaster County sells Manheim Estates to Isaac Cox for £2700.

August 23, 1774.

Stiegel in letter to John Dickinson (Historical Society of Pennsylvania) "that to August 2, 1774, there is due to Isaac Cox £2815 on Manheim Estates."

November 14, 1774.

Stiegel states in his handwriting (Historical Society of Pennsylvania) his losses were.

Manheim Estates Loss, £5562.7.8.
Manheim Improved Lots, £42.9.10.
Manheim Glass House Tools, £50.
Manheim House furniture, £342.19.0.
Manheim Store and Goods, £65.3.6.

DEED POLL. Lancaster.

Dated March 30, 1775.   John Ferree Esquire High Sheriff of
Recorded April 15, 1775.   the County of Lancaster
Liber Q. page 249.   to
Consideration £2,700.   Michael Diffenderfer.

CONVEYS All Manheim property of Henry W. Stiegel including the Glass House.

DEEDS AND RECORD REFERENCES. ELIZABETH FURNACE. LANCASTER COUNTY. PA.

BILL OF SALE. Philadelphia. Jacob Huber of Lancaster County Iron
Dated May 1, 1758. Master and Magdalina his wife
Recorded January 28, 1768. to
Liber I, 4, page 111 to 113. Charles Stedman, Alexander Stedman,
 Consideration £500. John Barr and Henry William Stiegel.

CONVEYS The Messuages, Buildings, Improvements, Ways, Waters, Water Courses belonging to Jacob Huber and Magdalina his wife now in actual possession of Charles Stedman, Alexander Stedman, John Barr and Henry William Stiegel.

Dated May 6, 1758. Jacob Huber and Magdalina his wife
DEED. Unrecorded. to
 Charles Stedman, Alexander Stedman
 John Barr and Henry William Stiegel.

CONVEYS ⅓ Elizabeth Furnace to Charles and Alexander Stedman, ⅓ Elizabeth Furnace to John Barr and ⅓ Elizabeth Furnace to Henry William Stiegel.

This deed is in the possession of the Historical Society of Pennsylvania.

Charles and Alexander Stedman evidently purchased John Barr's ⅓ undivided interest in Elizabeth Furnace as shown by the following mortgage.

MORTGAGE. Lancaster. Alexander Stedman Merchant of Phil-
Dated July 1, 1766. adelphia
Recorded September 30, 1766. to
Liber H. page 357. Daniel Wister Merchant of Philadel-
 phia.

MORTGAGES for £720, an equal and undivided ⅓ part of Elizabeth Furnace.

September 4, 1766.
Writ of Fieri Facias issued by Sheriff of Philadelphia against Alexander Stedman.

STATEMENT IN STIEGEL'S HANDWRITING OF MAY 12, 1767

May 12, 1767. Elizabeth Furnace Book. In possession of the Historical Society of Pennsylvania, and in Stiegel's own handwriting.

⅓ belonging to Henry Wm. Stiegel as Tenant in Common with Charles and Alexander Stedman.

	ACRES
2 Tracts of Land bought of Jacob Huber in Elizabeth Township Lancaster County with Furnace Buildings thereon erected containing	400
1 Tract. Bought of Jacob Gill joining the above unpatented about	150
1 Tract. Bought of Fred Jaesir joining the above unpatented	114½
1 Tract. Bought of Henry Mater joining the above unpatented	110
1 Tract. Bought of Jacob Gills joining the above unpatented	110
1 Tract. Bought of Jacob Seltser joining same unpatented	150
1 Tract. Bought of Jacob Huber joining above unpatented	150
1 Tract. Bought of Joseph Pugh in Township joining Mr. Reiser	380
1 Tract. Bought of Diemon Shitz in Township joining Mr. Gral unpatented	350
1 Tract. Bought of Joseph Hofman in Township joining Mr. Gral unpatented	250
1 Tract. Bought of Simon Dury in Township joining Mr. Gral unpatented	250
1 Tract. Bought of Stephen Jacob in Township joining Mr. Gral unpatented	270
1 Tract. Bought of Henry Barr in Township joining Mr. Gral unpatented	100
1 Tract. Bought of Jacob Ely joining Nicodemas unpatented	100
1 Tract. Bought of Alex. Shafer joining Uly, Riser &c. unpatented	150
1 Tract. Bought of Jacob Weisener joining Martin Weidman unpatented	150
1 Tract. Bought of George High joining the same unpatented	75
1 Tract of Woodlands. Surveyed by Warrants and ajdoining	1600
1 Tract of Woodlands Surveyed by sundry Warrants joining Ulery Riser, Harry Royets, Loderwick Weidman, Hoyle and others	1700

6559½

IN ELIZABETH TOWNSHIP

1 Tract of Land Lebanon with the Minehold and Buildings	134
Several Tracts not surveyed about	400
1 Tract in Heidelberg with improvements adjoining	140
1 Tract in Cocallico Township of Willing & Co. Michael Neave and patented about	$320\frac{1}{2}$
Sundry Tracts Surveyed by Warrants and bought of Gils & Cadwell in Cocallico Township about	1500
Sundry more Tracts Warrants Surveyed in Lebanon, Cocallico and Warwick about	1400
	10454

LIST OF LANDS BELONGING TO CHARMING FORGE $\frac{1}{2}$ THEREOF THE PROPERTY OF HENRY W. STIEGEL AS TENANT IN COMMON WITH CHARLES AND ALEXANDER STEDMAN

1 Tract of Patented Land in Tulpehocken Township with the Forge, Dam and Buildings thereon as patented	88
1 Tract joining the same bought of Selzer	50
2 Tracts Surveyed Warrants joining the same	50
1 Tract in Heidelberg joining John Palm patented	60
Several Tracts joining the same in the Hills	200
1 Tract Bought of Michael Miller one half joining ditto	200
4 Tracts of Land with Improvements bought of Berger, Rone, Smith & Jacob C. Beckad joining the Emerichs	700
Sundry Tracts. Surveyed Applications & Warrants near the Hills joining Wm. Kiefer, Geo. Emett, Jo Ulm, Morris Demble and others	1200
	2548

All the above Real Estate as also the personal Estate belonging to the said Works for the Manufacture of Pig Iron and Pots also the making of Barr Iron. Together with all the Tools, Utensils, Teams, Horses &c. to the said Company belonging to say $\frac{1}{3}$ part thereof at Elizabeth Furnace and $\frac{1}{2}$ part therein at Charming Forge the said Henry W. Stiegel proposes to sell at the low price for ready cash for £8000. Pennsylvania Currency upon the payment whereof he will Convey the whole Clear of all Incumbrances and deliver Possession as soon as the Blast of the Season is ended which shall be by the 1st. day of February Next.

Elizabeth Furnace. May 12. 1767.

HENRY WM. STIEGEL.

MORTGAGE. Lancaster.
Dated March 9, 1768.
Recorded March 13, 1768.
Liber N. page 23.

Henry William Stiegel of Elizabeth Township Iron Master and Elizabeth his wife

to

Daniel Bennezet of the City of Philadelphia.

MORTGAGES for £3000. Undivided ⅓ interest in Elizabeth Furnace and other lands in Elizabeth Township. 9 Tracts in Lebanon and Warwick Townships containing 1200 Acres of land. Undivided ½ interest in Charming Forge, undivided ⅓ interest in Manheim including Stiegel's Mansion, Glass House and other buildings.

On February 12, 1770, the Manheim property was released.

LEASE. Unrecorded.
Dated September 1768.
Consideration £ 300.

Charles Stedman of the City of Philadelphia, Merchant

to

Henry William Stiegel of the County of Lancaster, Iron Master.

LEASES for 1 year (April 1, 1768, to April 1, 1769). Undivided ⅓ part of Elizabeth Furnace, Mines, Lands &c. including Utensils, Implements and Stock. Also undivided ¼ part of Charming Forge including Utensils, Implements and Stock.

ENDORSEMENT on the above lease.

Recd. October 1st, 1768, the Sum of One hundred and fifty pounds being the first half years Rent by Bond Dated this Day.

CHAS. STEDMAN.

List of Moveable Stock at Elizabeth Furnace & Charming Forge Belonging to Alexn. Stedman & Henry Wm. Stiegel as per Inventory taken April 1, 1768.

AT FURNACE		AT FORGE	
Minehole	30. 8.	House Charge	18. 5.
Plantations	106. 0. 0.	Team Charge	253. .
Smith Shop	57. 8.10.	Smith Shop	120. 2.6.
House Charge	87. 0. 0.	Ship Stoves	12.
Furnace Charges	302.18. 6.	Saw Mill	12. 5.
Team Charge	744.10.	Plantations	76.15.
~~Cordwood~~	~~283. 6.~~	Forge Charge	123. 8.
~~Liquor~~	~~2. 6.~~	Castings	13. 6.6.
		~~Pig Metal~~	~~30.~~
£1,322.5.6	£1,608. 1. 4.	~~Coals~~	~~107. 9.~~
		~~Cordwood~~	~~28. 7.6.~~
			£794.18.6.

[IN STIEGEL'S HANDWRITING]

True & Exact Copies from the Books of Inventory at the said Furnace and Forge Books, October 1st, 1768.

Henry Wm Stiegel.

This lease is in my possession.

LEASE. Unrecorded. Alexander Stedman of the City of Philadelphia
Dated April 1, 1769.
Consideration. One Ton of good to
Merchantable Iron per month. Henry William Stiegel of Elizabeth Furnace in the County of Lancaster.

LEASES All Alexander Stedman's Right, Estate, Portion, Part, Share of Shares in Elizabeth Furnace and Charming Forge. Binding their Heirs, Executors, Administrators and Assigns in the Penal Sum of £100 lawful money.

This lease is in my possession.

August 13, 1774.

By Virtue of a Wit of *levari facias* John Ferree High Sheriff of Lancaster County offers to sell ⅓ part of Elizabeth Furnace and all Brickerville property being the estate of the said Henry William Steigle. Seized and taken in execution.

This Broadside is in the possession of the Historical Society of Pennsylvania.

August 23, 1774.

Letter H. W. Stiegel to John Dickinson. Dated Manheim. "This letter carried by Mrs Stiegel & enclose a copy of Jacob Huber's Last Will & the heirs would not sign the deed. Glad to hear what you have done about the Works" &c. &c.

This Letter is in the possession of the Historical Society of Pennsylvania.

September, 1774.

Sheriff John Ferree of Lancaster County sold to Daniel Bennezet Stiegel's undivided ⅓ interest in Elizabeth Furnace for £1450.

November 14, 1774.

The Historical Society of Pennsylvania has the following entry in Stiegel's handwriting, in the Elizabeth Furnace Account Books. "Elizabeth Furnace sold to Daniel Benezet for £1450. loss on sale £2250. On Mill sold to Daniel Benezet £550."

September, 1779.

The Historical Society of Pennsylvania has in handwriting of Henry Wm. Stiegel on back pages of Elizabeth Furnace Day Book for years 1771 and 1772, the following entry.

" Dr. Daniel Benezets account 1779.

Bonds and Mortgages £3000.

4 years interest on same £720.

" " Bill the day of Sale £540.

" " to September, 1779 interest £900."

LIST OF RECORDED DEEDS AND WARRANTS TO LAND ADJOINING ELIZABETH FURNACE

BILL OF SALE. Philadelphia.   Jost Hoffman of Heidelberg, Lancaster
Dated March 8, 1758.   County
Recorded January 29, 1768.
Liber I 4, page 115.   Henry William Stiegel and John Barr
Consideration £85.   of Elizabeth Township Iron Masters.
CONVEYS About 200 Acres of land in Elizabeth Township adjoining land of Jacob Blaser and Dillman Shitz.

QUIT CLAIM DEED. Philadelphia.   Alexander Shafer of Heidelberg Township Lancaster County
Dated December 21, 1758.
Recorded February 1, 1768.   to
Liber I 4, page 118.   Henry William Stiegel and Company of
Consideration £27.   Elizabeth Furnace. Iron Masters.
CONVEYS 100 Acres of land in Elizabeth Township adjoining land of Christian Zwallg.

BILL OF SALE. Philadelphia.   Stephen Jaky of Heidelberg Township
Dated May 17, 1758.   Yeoman
Recorded January 29, 1768.   to
Liber I 4, page 116.   Charles Stedman, Alexander Stedman,
Consideration £120.   Henry William Stiegel and John Barr
                         of Elizabeth Township Iron Masters.
CONVEYS The following described land "Have assigned and transferred and set over all my right, title and interest to the within mentioned Improvement, Tract of Land, houses, Buildings or whatsoever therein."

BILL OF SALE. Philadelphia.   Henry Barr and Mary Barbara his wife
Dated March 30, 1759.   Yeoman in the County of Lancaster
Recorded February 1, 1768.   to
Liber L 4, page 117.   Henry William Stiegel in Behalf of
Consideration £20.   himself and Company of Elizabeth in
                         the said County Iron Masters.
CONVEYS 50 Acres of Land adjoining land of Martin Shuders and Elizabeth Furnace Land.

April 10, 1758.

Patents for 325 Acres of Land in Elizabeth Township granted to Henry William Stiegel and John Barr. (Harrisburg, Pa.)

May 19, 1758.

Patents for 600 Acres of Land in Elizabeth Township applied for by Charles and Alexander Stedman and Henry William Stiegel. Not Issued until February 11, 1824, to Coleman (Harrisburg, Pa.).

BILL OF SALE. Philadelphia.   Jacob Seltzer of Lancaster County
Dated February 15, 1762.   Yeoman and Anna Maria his wife
Recorded January 29, 1768.   to

Liber I 4, page 114.   Charles and Alexander Stedman and
Consideration £380.   Henry William Stiegel.
CONVEYS 140 Acres in Elizabeth Township adjoining lands of Henry
Motes, Stephen Berringer and Henry Bels. Surveyed by Proprietary
Warrant dated September 5, 1749, to a certain Adam Househaller.

DEEDS AND RECORD REFERENCES TO CHARMING FORGE, BERKS COUNTY, PA.

The Historical Society of Pennsylvania has in its possession "Charming Forge Account Book 1763." The following entry is in Stiegel's handwriting.

Charming Forge North East border of Tulpehocken Township on Tulpehocken Creek several miles North of Wolmensdorf. Erected by George Nikoll a hammersmith and Michael Miller in 1749. (Passed through several hands before Henry William Stiegel and Michael Gross purchased.)

DEED. Philadelphia.   Michael Rice of Tulpehocken, Berks
Dated March 29, 1760.   County Iron Master and Anna Maria
Recorded January 21, 1768.   his wife and Gerhard Brenner of Maner
Liber I. 4, page 97.   Township in the County of Lancaster
Consideration £1450.   Iron Master and Lavisa his wife
                                               to
                                  Henry William Stiegel of Township of
                                  Elizabeth Iron Master and Michael
                                  Gross of the Borough of Lancaster
                                  Merchant.
CONVEYS Charming Forge 88 Acres. Patent granted to Michael Miller,
June 4, 1750.

DEED. Philadelphia.   Michael Rice and Anna Maria his wife
Dated March 29, 1760.   and Gerhard Brenner and Louisa his
Recorded January 23, 1768.   wife
Book I. Volume 4, page 101.   to
Consideration £50.   Henry Wm. Stiegel and Michael Gross.
CONVEYS ½ Moiety or undivided part in 61 Acres Charming Forge.

This deed is now in my possession.

DEED. Philadelphia.
Dated November 16, 1761.
Recorded January 27, 1768.
Liber I. 4, page 108.
Consideration £15.

Loderwick Stone, Innkeeper of Borough of Lancaster and Catharine his wife

to

Henry Wm. Stiegel of Township of Elizabeth Iron Master and Michael Gross Merchant of Borough of Lancaster.

CONVEYS ½ Moiety or undivided part in 61 Acres Charming Forge. Patent granted February 18, 1747. Recorded in Philadelphia in Patent Book A. Volume 13, page 344.

The deed Michael Gross to Henry Wm. Stiegel, is not recorded in Philadelphia, Lancaster or Reading.

The Historical Society of Pennsylvania has in its possession the Charming Forge Account Book dated 1763 in which is the following entry in Stiegel's handwriting.

"Purchased the 5th. day of February, 1763, ½ part by Charles and Alexander Stedman on February 12, 1763. An Inventory was taken of all the Estates and Lands now being in partnership between Henry William Stiegel for one undivided ½ part and Charles and Alexander Stedman for the other ½ part.

Containing 7 Tracts about 3100 Acres of Land as bought at prime Cost £4,519.10.0.

Charles and Alexander Stedman owe Henry William Stiegel for their balance ½ interest £1,028.4.6."

May 12, 1767.
Charming Forge Contained 2548 Acres of Land. VIDE.
Elizabeth Furnace Book of same date.

MORTGAGE. Lancaster.
Dated March 9, 1768.
Recorded March 13, 1768.
Liber N. page 23.

Henry William Stiegel of Elizabeth Township. Iron Master and Elizabeth his wife

to

Daniel Bennezet of the City of Philadelphia.

MORTGAGES for £3000. Undivided ½ interest in Charming Forge. Undivided ⅓ interest in Elizabeth Furnace and other lands in Elizabeth Township. 9 Tracts in Lebanon and Warwick Townships containing 1200

Acres of Land. Undivided $\frac{1}{3}$ interest in Manheim including Stiegel's Mansion, Glass House and other buildings.

On February 12, 1770 the Manheim property was released.

LEASE. Unrecorded
Dated September, 1768.

Charles Stedman of the City of Philadelphia. Merchant

to

Henry William Stiegel of the County of Lancaster. Iron Master.

LEASES for one year April 1, 1768, to April 1, 1769, for £300. Undivided $\frac{1}{3}$ interest in Elizabeth Furnace and undivided $\frac{1}{4}$ interest in Charming Forge including the Utensils, Implements and Stock.

This lease is now in my possession.

LEASE. Unrecorded.
Dated April 1, 1769.

Alexander Stedman of the City of Philadelphia

to

Henry William Stiegel of Elizabeth Furnace in the County of Lancaster.

LEASES. All Alexander Stedman's right, title and interest in Elizabeth Furnace and Charming Forge in consideration of the delivery in the City of Philadelphia of 1 ton of good merchantable Barr Iron on or before the last day of each month.

This lease is now in my possession.

AGREEMENT.
Dated January 24, 1770.

Alexander Stedman and Henry W. Stiegel.

That in consideration of Henry W. Stiegel paying 3 tons Barr Iron due on February 1, 1770, Henry William Stiegel shall retain so much of the stock as shall be sufficient for him to reimburse him in repairing the said Works during the continuance of the first lease.

This Agreement is now in my possession.

DEED POLL.
Dated February 15, 1771.
Unrecorded.
Consideration £1000.

Jacob Shoemaker High Sheriff of the County of Berks

to

Charles Stedman.

By virtue of a Writ of *Fieri Facias* issued by the Court of Common Pleas of the County of Berks for a debt of £2000. and costs £2.11.3. of William

Moore assignee of Margaret Abercrombie against Charles and Alexander Stedman take in execution one moiety or undivided ½ part of Charming Forge, and convey to Charles Stedman ¼ interest in Charming Forge.

This deed is now in my possession.

LEASE. Unrecorded.   Henry William Stiegel
Dated May 26, 1772.   to
Term 4 Years.   Paul Zantzinger.
LEASES ½ Charming Forge. Zantzinger having the privilege of cutting yearly 500 cords of wood. Term begins from the 1st day of May and can be terminated in any year by Zantzinger giving notice.

This lease is now in my possession.

June 2, 1773.
Pennsylvania Gazette Notice. Dated Reading, April 10, 1773. By virtue of a Writ Sheriff George Nagel will expose for sale at Charming Forge Tuesday June 8, 1773, the following ½ interest in forge for manufacture of iron bars, called Charming Forge &c. &c. &c.

The Historical Society of Pennsylvania has records showing that Sheriff George Nagel of Berks County, Pa., sold Henry William Stiegel's undivided ½ interest in Charming Forge 1291 Acres to Paul Zantzinger Merchant of Lancaster County for £1660.

Paul Zantzinger by deed dated February 9, 1774, conveyed his undivided ½ interest in Charming Forge to George Ege for £838.14.9. In 1783 George Ege Iron Master of York County, Pa., bought the Stedmans' undivided ½ interest in Charming Forge for £1563.13.6.

LIST OF RECORDED DEEDS TO PROPERTY IN HEIDELBERG TOWNSHIP

DEED. Lancaster.   Michael Miller of Cocallico in Lancaster County Yeoman
Dated May 5, 1760.
Recorded November 15, 1784.   to
Liber BB. page 21.   Michael Gross Merchant of Borough of
Consideration £100.   Lancaster and Henry Wm. Stiegel.
CONVEYS 300 Acres in Heidelberg Township Surveyed by Warrant from Proprietors of Pennsylvania to said Michael Miller adjoining lands of John Zimmerman and Ulrich Brunner.

DEED. Lancaster.
Dated September 10, 1760.
Recorded July 15, 1761.
Liber G. page 4.
Consideration £350.

Joseph Pugh of Borough of Lancaster
and Mary his wife

to

Henry William Stiegel of the Township
of Elizabeth, Iron Master, Charles
and Alexander Stedman of the City of
Philadelphia, Merchants and John
Barr of the Borough of Lancaster Innkeeper.

CONVEYS 80 Acres in Heidelberg Township adjoining land of George
Miller, Casper Bowman, Ulrich Reesers and Michael Neaff.

DEED. Philadelphia.
Dated December 1, 1762.
Recorded February 2, 1768.
Liber I. 4, page 120.
Consideration £90.

John Enders of Heidelberg Township

to

Henry William Stiegel of Elizabeth
Township.

CONVEYS 100 Acres in Heidelberg Township adjoining land of Michael
Neave and Michael Brecht. Surveyed by a Proprietary Warrant dated
April 15, 1755.

MISCELLANEOUS UNRECORDED DEEDS

DEED. Philadelphia.
Dated March 22, 1763.
Recorded February 2, 1768.
Liber I. 4, page 120.
Consideration £50.

J. Jacob Shmit of Bethel Township
Berks County

to

Charles and Alexander Stedman and
Henry William Stiegel.

CONVEYS 100 Acres of land in Bethel Township in the County of Berks
adjoining land of Balser Emrich. Originally granted to Agidius Meyer by
Proprietary Warrant dated April 12, 1750.

PHILADELPHIA STORE

DEED POLL. Philadelphia.
Dated March 15, 1765.
Recorded August 23, 1794.
Liber D. 47, page 15.
Consideration £450.

Henry Keppele of the City of Philadelphia Merchant and Catharinor his
wife

to

Henry William Stiegel of Elizabeth
Township Iron Master.

CONVEYS in the City of Philadelphia 2 lots, containing 49½ feet in breadth and 306 feet in length on the North side of Mulberry (Arch) Street the 4th Street from the Delaware. Bounded West and North by Henry Kelleles and other ground. East by Leonard Sheelers Massuage and ground and South by Mulberry Street.

Acknowledged by Mathew Clarkson, Mayor of the City of Philadelphia.

MANHEIM STATEMENT AND RECEIPT, CHARLES STEDMAN, MAY 1, 1770

LIST OF MANHEIM RENTS RECEIVED SINCE SETTLEMENT APRIL, 1769.

	Due.	Received.	Lots unsold & Owners gone off.	
Mich Becker	3. 6.	3. 6.		
Hans Moyer	4. 3.	4. 3.		
Benja Mishy	2. 9. 6	2. 9. 6		
Henry Custer	2. 9. 6	—	Daniel May	3. 6.
Christn Wertz	4.19.	—	Adam Thomas overcharged	8. 5.
Christ Wetterman	2. 9. 6	—	John Hambright	4. 2. 6
Adam Wiest	3. 6.	2. 9. 6	Henry Bousman	5.15. 6
John Camron	3. 6.	—	David Stout	2. 9. 6
Christon. Ream	4. 2. 6	4. 2. 6	Andrew Herauf	2. 9. 6
Peter Koch	3. 6.	3.	Martin Hoffman	2. 9. 6
Phillip Orrem	3. 6.	3. 6.	Christian Fox	2. 9. 6
Phillip Frick	1. 2. 6	1. 2. 6	Price & Hoofnagele	5.16. 0
Abrecht at Lancaster	16. 6.	—	Thos. Thornbury	4. 2. 6
Andrew Ereman	1.13.	1. 5. 8	Raelf & Hambright	23. 8. 5
Chl. Smith	1.13.	1.13.	Martin Durward	3. 6.
Jno. Reif	4.13. 1	—	Jacob Sherertz	3. 6.
Peter Butz	3. 6.	3. 6.	Peter Wolf	4. 2. 6
Pl. Capenberger	4. 2. 6.	4. 2. 6	Casper Keller	3. 6.
Casn. Singhaas	16. 6.	16. 6.	Widdow Bassler	6.12.
Widdow Kling	3.16.	3.16.		£85. 6. 5
Philn Sarius	16. 6.	16. 6.		
Matts. Eib.	1.13. 6.	—		
Widdow Seidestich	16. 6.	16. 6.		
Christn Steider	16. 6.	16. 6.		
Geo. Ross	3.17.	—		
Davd. Beler	3. 6.	—		
Bernd. Hubley	3. 6.	3. 6.		
Mil. Thompson	4.19.	—		
Philp Bush	5. 1. 2.	—		
	£83. 4. 1.			
	£27.14. 8¼	£46. 4. 2.		

"1770 May 1. Received of Henry Wm. Stiegel the Sum of Twenty Seven pounds 14s 8d in full for my part of the above ground rents on the Manheim Estate from the Beginning of the World to this Day Witness my Hand.

Charles Stedman"

This receipt and list of Manheim rents is now in my possession.

STATEMENT IN HENRY WILLIAM STIEGEL'S HANDWRITING OF ELIZABETH FURNACE AND MANHEIM ACCOUNTS WITH CHARLES AND ALEXANDER STEDMAN

Chs. & Alexnd Stedman Account with The Iron Works

Dr.			Cr.	
Ledger A.				
1759 Jan; 31. To Mesr. McCull Rue	150.	Same Year By Cash for		
		purchasers	411. 5.	
		By Dr. laid in stock	365.	
		By Merchandise	836.12. 3	
B.				
1760 Jan: 18. To 15 Ton pig Iron	120.	Same Year. By Sundry		
To Castings	9	Hauling paid	22. 2. 6	
To Mesr. McCull	600.	By Cash to purchase	300.	
		By merchandise	313.18. 3	
C.				
1761 July 23. To an oven per		Same Year		
Contract	114. 4. 8	By interest to Mrs. Day	130. 2. 9	
To Sundry pig iron		By Sundrys	188.10. 2	
Ware	103.11. 5	By Cash	200.	
1762 March 2. To Sundry Accts	38. 8. 1	Same Year		
		By Sundrys	42.12. 4	
		By Interest	212.15.	
1763 April To Sundrys	16.14.	Same Year		
D. To H. W. Stiegel for		By Sundrys	209. 4.	
Forge	1060.	By Cash	300.	
		By Dr. for pot Patterns	120.	
		By interest	306. 8.	
1764. July 12. To Sundry Accts	238. 7. 3	Same Year		
E.		By Cash	2300.	
		By Dr. for lands	400.	
		By Sundrys	21.13. 6	
1765. July 20. To Sundrys pd.		Same Year		
I. Yournull	197. 4. 5	By Interest	355.	
To bg'h Von Orisr		By Cash	250.	

Dr.		Cr.	
Iron ship and clear sale	1859. 4. 9	To Sundrys for palar-	
To Cash on Ac. Mr		bines	188.13.11
Clifton	95. 9.	By Ditto for Sundrys	193.16.
To Cash Pd. Michael		By Lands paid	195. 7. 9
Gross for their bond	832. 8		
To H. W. Stiegel	1028.14. 6		
1766. July 1. To Sundry Assts Forge	215. 4. 4	Same Year	
To Westindien Orders	418. 4. 4	By Cash	60.
To 100 Ton Pigs to		By Sundries	42.13. 7
Mr. McCull	830.		
1767. Jany. To 100 Ton Dr. to Mr.		Same Year	
Mc Cull	844.10.	By Cash H. W. Stiegel	190.
To Castings & Iron		By Sundrys	15.17.
Ware	262.19.10	By Willing &-Morris	244.13. 4
To 12¾ Ton of		By James Searls	88.10
Oxar Iron	335.15.	My Manheim Dels by	
To Interest to Gross Pd.	28. 2. 7	Books	331.13.11
To Interest woerch p.		By Hauling Pig Iron	22.10
Contra	57.18.12	By Ballance Due by	
To Sundry Accts	162.18.	Received out of the	
To Cash of Mr McCull	300.	Works Bonds & Interest	
To Henry W. Stiegel	326.16	Leaving their parts of	1568.11. 2
		the Estate amounts to	
		Bonds £450 given to them	
		by Mr. Hopron Nath.	
		Giles that year and Pd.	
		by H. W. S.	
	£10237.18.02		£10237.18.02

1768.

Dr.		Cr.	
Charles & Alexnr. Stedman acct with Manheim Estate.			
To H. W. Stiegel Pd for his part £1060		By Cash for the purchase	
1763. To Rent & Cash Discount		thereof	3000.
for their two parts	237.11. 7	By Clear profits to them	3045.15. 3
1764. To Ditto	184.12. 4		
1765. To Ditto	658. 2.10		
1766. To Ditto	1405. 8. 6		
To their parts Sold at			
Cash	2400.		
To H. W. Stiegel	100.		
	£6045.15. 3		£6045.15.3

Endorsement on back

ACCOUNTS TOTAL

Ch: & Allex Stedman HWS. the Iron Works and Manheim Estates taken from the Companys Ledgers Signed & Sealed every Year by each of the parties.

This statement is now in my possession.

STIEGEL STATEMENT

STIEGEL BIBLIOGRAPHY

1813. Pub. Edward Parker, No. 178 Market Street. W. Brown, Printer Church Alley. MEMOIRS OF THE LIFE OF DAVID RITTENHOUSE, LL.D., F.R.S., by William Barton, M.A., page 206.

1844. Pub. Gilbert Hills, Lancaster. HISTORY OF LANCASTER COUNTY, by I. Daniel Rupp, page 347.

1869. Pub. J. E. Barr & Co. AUTHENTIC HISTORY OF LANCASTER COUNTY, by J. I. Mombert, D.D., page 378.

1872. Pub. Elias Barr & Co. HISTORY OF LANCASTER COUNTY, by Alexander Harris, page 565.

1877. PENNSYLVANIA MAGAZINE OF HISTORY & BIOGRAPHY, vol. I, page 67.
Baron Stiegl by Rev. Joseph Dubbs, D.D.
Reprinted Cincinnati, Ohio, in German in DER DEUTSCHE PIONIER, *Baron Heinrich Wilhelm Stiegel*, vol. XII, No. 3, page 82, June, 1880.

1878. PENNSYLVANIA MAGAZINE OF HISTORY & BIOGRAPHY, vol. II, page 162. *Mary White—Mrs. Robert Morris*, by Charles Henry Hart.

1880. UNITED STATES CENSUS, Report on the Manufacture of Glass, by Joseph D. Weeks, page 80.

1883. Pub. Everts & Peck, Philadelphia. HISTORY OF DAUPHIN & LEBANON COUNTIES, by William Henry Egle.

1883. Pub. Everts & Peck, Philadelphia. HISTORY OF LANCASTER COUNTY, by Franklin Ellis & Samuel Evans, pages 303 & 607.

1886. PENNSYLVANIA MAGAZINE OF HISTORY & BIOGRAPHY, vol. X, page 127. *Notes of Travel of William Henry, John Heckewelder, John Rothrock and Christian Clewell to Gnodenettern on the Muskingum in the Early summer of 1797*, edited by John W. Jordan.

1886. Pub. Everts, Peck & Richards. HISTORY OF BERKS COUNTY IN PENNSYLVANIA, by Morton L. Montgomery.

1886. Pub. F. A. Battey Publishing Society, Chicago. HISTORY OF YORK COUNTY, PENNSYLVANIA, by John Gibson.

1892. Pub. Argus Publishing Company, Lancaster. *Israel Smith Clare* in BRIEF HISTORY OF LANCASTER COUNTY, edited by Anna Lyle.

1895. Pub. Lutheran Publication Society, Philadelphia. ANCIENT AND HISTORICAL LANDMARKS IN LEBANON VALLEY, by Rev. P. C. Croll, page 112.

1896. LANCASTER COUNTY HISTORICAL SOCIETY, vol. I, page 44. *Baron*

Henry William Stiegel, by J. H. Sieling, M.D., paper read September 4, 1896. Reprinted from the NEW ERA, 1896, page 24.

1897. Wyoming Historical Society & Geological Society. THE GERMAN LEAVEN IN THE PENNSYLVANIA LOAF, by M. M. Richards, Wilkes-Barre.

1897. Pub. Isaac Iba, Schaefferstown, Lebanon County. LIFE OF BARON HENRY WILLIAM STIEGEL, by Frank B. Brown & A. S. Brendle.

1898. LANCASTER COUNTY HISTORICAL SOCIETY, vol. III, page 68. *History of the Brickerville Congregation*, by Rev. F. J. F. Schantz, D.D., paper read December 2, 1898.

1899. THE PENNSYLVANIA-GERMAN SOCIETY, vol. IX, page 416. *The German Emigrant, his Influence from an Industrial Standpoint*, by Rev. Matthias Henry Richards, D.D.

1900. Pub. Patterson & White Co., Philadelphia. AMERICAN GLASS WARE, OLD AND NEW, by Edwin Atlee Barber, A.M., Ph.D., page 37.

1901. Pub. Dispatch Publishing Co., York, Pa. A BRIEF HISTORY OF SCHAEFFERSTOWN, by A. S. Brendle, Esq., A.M.

1901. LANCASTER COUNTY HISTORICAL SOCIETY, vol. VI, page 3. *The Red Rose*, by F. R. Dieffenderfer, paper read October, 1901.

1903. Pub. Lutheran Publication Society, Philadelphia. BARON STIEGEL, by Rev. M. H. Stine, Ph.D.

1903. Pub. J. H. Biers & Co. BIOGRAPHICAL ANNALS OF LANCASTER COUNTY, page 83.

1904. LANCASTER COUNTY HISTORICAL SOCIETY, vol. VIII, page 258. *Tour through the North East Section of Lancaster County*, by Hon. W. U. Hensel, paper read May, 1904.

1904. LEBANON COUNTY HISTORICAL SOCIETY, vol. III, No. 1. *Iron Industries of Lebanon County*, by H. C. Grittinger, paper read June 17, 1904.

1906. January Bulletin of the Pennsylvania Museum, Fourth Year, No. 13. SOME NEW DISCOVERIES IN EARLY AMERICAN GLASSWARE, by Edwin A. Barber.

1906. Pub. James T. White & Co. THE NATIONAL CYCLOPÆDIA OF AMERICAN BIOGRAPHY. *Baron Henry William Stiegel*, vol. XI, page 197.

1906. Pub. Kreibel, Lebanon, Pa. THE PENNSYLVANIA-GERMAN, vol. VII. *The Pennsylvania-German as Manufacturer and Merchant*, by Prof. Lewis Harley, Ph.D., Philadelphia.

1907. MITTEILUNGEN DES DEUTSCHEN, PIONIER-VEREIN VON PHILADEL-

PHIA, vol. v, Sept. 30, 1907. *Baron Heinrich Wilhelm Stiegel*, von C. F. Huch.

1908. PENNSYLVANIA-GERMAN SOCIETY, Lancaster, Pa., vol. XVII, page 472. *The Pennsylvania German in the Revolutionary War*, by Henry M. M. Richards.

1908. Pub. H. W. Kriebel, East Greenville, Pa. HENRY WILLIAM STEIGEL, translated and adapted from the German of C. F. Huch, Secretary of the Deutsche-Verein of Philadelphia, the sketch having appeared in the Mitteilungen published by the society, Pennsylvania-German, February, 1908, vol. IX, No. 2, page 71.

1909. Hudson-Fulton Celebration. CATALOGUE OF AN EXHIBITION HELD IN THE METROPOLITAN MUSEUM OF ART, New York City, article on *Glass*, by Edwin Atlee Barber.

1909. Pub. Houghton, Mifflin & Co., Boston & New York. THE GERMAN ELEMENT IN THE UNITED STATES, by Albert Bernhardt Faust, vol. I, page 140, vol. II, page 94.

1910. Pub. Conestoga Traction Company, Lancaster, Pa. SEEING LANCASTER COUNTY FROM A TROLLEY WINDOW, by Howard Wiegner Kriebel. Reprinted from THE PENNSYLVANIA-GERMAN.

1911. Pub. Star Printing Co., Harrisburg, Pa. HISTORY AND GENEALOGY OF THE EGE FAMILY, by Rev. Thompson P. Ege, D.D., of New York City.

1912. SOUVENIR BOOK MANHEIM OLD HOME WEEK (June 30 to July 5, 1912). Sketch of *Baron Henry Wilhelm Stiegel*, page 14.

1912. LEBANON COUNTY HISTORICAL SOCIETY, vol. VI, No. 9. *Henry William Stiegel*, by A. S. Brendle, paper read August 16, 1912.

1913. LANCASTER COUNTY HISTORICAL SOCIETY, vol. XVII, page 172. *Old Elizabeth*, some account of Baron Stiegel and his operations at Elizabeth, by Hon. W. U. Hensel.

1913. December Number of the BULLETIN OF THE METROPOLITAN MUSEUM OF ART. New York, vol. VIII, No. 12. *Baron Stiegel and American Glass*, by F. W. Hunter.

Reprinted in THE JEWELERS' CIRCULAR-WEEKLY, February 4, 1914.

INDEX